International Federation of Library Associations and Institutions
Fédération Internationale des Associations de Bibliothécaires et des Bibliothèques
Internationaler Verband der bibliothekarischen Vereine und Institutionen
Международная Федерация Библиотечных Ассоциаций и Учреждений

IFLA Publications 46

Newspaper Preservation and Access

Proceedings of the Symposium held in
London, August 12–15, 1987
Volume II

Edited for the Section on Serial Publications
and the Working Group on Newspapers

by Ian P. Gibb

K·G·Saur

München · New York · London · Paris 1988

IFLA Publications
edited by Willem R. H. Koops

Recommended catalog entry:
Newspaper. Preservation and Access:
Proceedings of the Symposium held in
London, August 12–15, 1987;
ed. by Ian P. Gibb.
Volume 2
München, New York, London, Paris: K. G. Saur, 1988
VI, 231–449 p., 21 cm. –
   (IFLA Publications; 46)
   ISBN 3-598-21776-5

CIP-Titelaufnahme der Deutschen Bibliothek

Newspaper, preservation and access: proceedings of the
symposium held in London, August 12–15, 1987 / ed. for the
Sect. on Serial Publ. and the Working Group on Newspapers by
Ian P. Gibb. – München ; London ; New York ; Paris : Saur.
NE: Gibb, Ian P. [Hrsg.]

Vol. 2(1988)
   (IFLA publications ; 46)
   ISBN 3-598-21776-5
NE: International Federation of Library Associations and Institutions:
   IFLA publications

© 1988 by International Federation of Library Associations
and Institutions, The Hague, The Netherlands
Alle Rechte vorbehalten / All Rights Strictly Reserved
K. G. Saur Verlag GmbH & Co. KG, München 1988
(A member of the international Butterworth Group, London)
Printed in the Federal Republic of Germany

Jede Art der Vervielfältigung ohne Erlaubnis des Verlags
ist unzulässig.

Druck / Printed by Strauss Offsetdruck GmbH, Hirschberg
Binden / Bound by Buchbinderei Schaumann, Darmstadt

ISBN 3598-21776-5
ISSN 0344-6891 (IFLA Publications)

CONTENTS

Volume 1

1. FOREWORD *Robert Harriman and Mary Sauer Price* 7
   EDITOR'S PREFACE *Ian P. Gibb* 9

2. KEYNOTE ADDRESS *Sir Denis Hamilton* 13

3. HISTORY AND BIBLIOGRAPHY OF THE PRESS 21
   The history and bibliography of the press *Hans Bohrmann* 23
   The history and bibliography of English newspapers *Michael Harris* .. 34
   The development of the press *Jeremy Black* 44

4. USES OF THE PRESS: current and research use of
   retrospective holdings 75
   The newspaper archivist *Dennis Griffiths* 77
   Newspapers as resources for social historians *Roy Porter* 84
   The use of retrospective newspaper resources in the libraries
     of the Federal Republic of Germany *Willi Höfig* 97
   The users of newspapers outside of libraries *Helmuth Bergmann* 112

5. THE GENERAL MANAGEMENT OF A NEWSPAPER
   COLLECTION *Else Delaunay* 119

6. MICROFILMING: WHAT YOU NEED TO KNOW 131
   Preservation by microfilming: some considerations on the planning
     of newspaper microfilming and its consequences for libraries
     and users *Johan Mannerheim* 133

7. WORKSHOPS
   i) Did not take place
   ii) Bibliographical aspects: cataloguing, retrospective bibliography,
       union lists, preservation and bibliographic control, and the problems of editions *Leaders: Robert Harriman, Hana Komorous* 182
   iii) The user's viewpoint *Leader: Jeremy Black* 197
   iv) Microfilm: hardware, storage, standards and the management
       of a microfilming programme
       Leaders: Johan Mannerheim, Terry Ilbury 201
   v) Indexing, press cuttings and on-line data-bases *Leader: Frank Dunn*. 208
   vi) Preservation strategies: policy, planning and budgeting
       Leader: Françoise Perraud 211
   vii) Conserving the original *Leader: Gerhard Banik* 216
   viii) New developments: the applications of computer technology, satellite transmission and optical disks *Leader: Bernard J. S. Williams* .. 227

Volume 2

8. NATIONAL APPROACHES TO NEWSPAPER PRESERVATION . . 231

   Brazil *Esther Bertoletti* 233
   Canada *Marianne Scott* 246
   China (People's Republic) *Ning Shufan* 254
   Denmark *Svend Larsen* 263
   Germany (Federal Republic) *Wilbert Ubbens* 267
   Greece *Panayotis Ph. Christopoulos* 280
   Hungary *Beatrix Kastaly* 285
   India *Ashin Das Gupta* 287
   Indonesia *Hardjo Prakoso* 305
   Iran *Mehrdad Niknam Vazifeh* 310
   Ireland *Donal O'Luanaigh* 314
   Japan *Akio Yasue* 315
   New Zealand *Penny Griffith* 316
   Nigeria *Gabriel Alegbeleye* 326
   Norway *Anne Grete Holm-Olsen* 338
   South Africa *P. R. Coates* 339
   UK *Eve Johansson* 342
      Scotland *Ann Matheson* 352
      Wales *Beti Jones* 354
   USA *Jeffrey Field* 356
   Yugoslavia *Dora Sečić* 367

   Summary by Chairman *Ian P. Gibb* 372

9. ELEMENTS OF A NEWSPAPER PRESERVATION
   POLICY WORLDWIDE 375

   The possibilities for co-operation *Hans Bohrmann* 377
   Microfilming co-operation world-wide *Mary Jane Starr* 382
   The international exchange of information *Hana Komorous* 391
   The needs of developing countries *Subhas C. Biswas* 406

10. SUMMARY AND CONCLUSION *Ian P. Gibb* 413

APPENDICES 419

1. The retention or disposal of newspapers after microfilming:
   draft policy statement 421
2. Survey on National newspaper collections of the world: answers to
   an IFLA Working Group on Newspapers Questionnaire 1981–83 424
3. Final list of Participants 442
4. List of Exhibitors 448

NATIONAL APPROACHES
TO NEWSPAPER PRESERVATION

THE NATIONAL PLAN FOR MICROFILMING BRAZILIAN PERIODICALS: A DECADE
OF ACTION

Esther Caldas BERTOLETTI

Co-ordinator of Restoration and Microreproduction,
Biblioteca Nacional, Rio de Janeiro, Brazil

1. INTRODUCTION

Brazil was discovered by the Portuguese in 1500 and today has about 135 million inhabitants spread over a continuous area covering more than 8.5 million square kilometres of the tropical region of South America. It is a country with an extremely young population (50% are under 20 years of age), with about 70% concentrated in the urban areas. Administratively, Brazil is a Federative Republic with 23 States, 3 Territories and more than 4,000 counties, split into five large regions: North, Northeast, Centre-West, South and Southeast; because of its size, it is definitely a country of geographical, economic, social and cultural contrasts.

In this broad and complex area the National Plan for Microfilming Brazilian periodicals, henceforth referred to simply as the Plan, has developed in spite of the difficulties faced by the Biblioteca Nacional (National Library), the failure to comply with the requirements of the legislation for legal deposit and the gaps in the study of the history of the press in Brazil.

The Biblioteca Nacional began its microfilming service in 1946, when the Microfilm Section, part of the Works and Publications Division, was formed. In the following years the laboratory was enlarged until 1982, when the present large, modern microfilm laboratory was built at the time of a thoroughgoing administrative reform and modernisation of the Biblioteca Nacional, which became part of the Fundação Nacional Pró-Memória (National Heritage Foundation), a body run by the Ministry of Culture. It was, nevertheless, thanks to a project financed by the Ford Foundation in the years 1975-77 that the Biblioteca Nacional was able to develop the framework of the Plan at a national level.

The former Reprography Service became the Centre for Microfilming and Reprography, incorporating the staff of the former section and of the National Plan for Microfilming Brazilian Periodicals. It took on the following tasks:

1. Execution of the Plan, within the established objectives;

2. Co-ordination and execution of the policy of preserving on microform the national newspaper collection and that of the Biblioteca Nacional;

3. Reproduction of texts and illustrations from the collection of the Biblioteca Nacional when requested by users, and of works which are out-of-print or difficult to conserve in order to complete the gaps in the collections of the Biblioteca Nacional.

The Plan's work goes beyond the collection of the Biblioteca Nacional, covering universities, archives, public libraries, institutes of history, research and documentation centres, publishers of newspapers and reviews... over 2,500 institutions are directly involved in this work. It has been the galvanising and dedicated effort of its technicians and researchers rather than the real and effective use of financial resources which has maintained the production rate of the Plan and guaranteed the success achieved so far.

2. THE BIBLIOTECA NACIONAL (National Library)

The Biblioteca Nacional of Rio de Janeiro is located in the centre of the former capital of the country and has remained there even after the transferral of the seat of government to Brasília during the administration of President Juscelina Kubitschek in 1960.

The Biblioteca Nacional (National Library) which is subordinate to the Fundação Nacional Pró-Memória, began with the collection of works brought by the Royal Family when the Court moved to Brazil in 1808-1809 following Napoleon's invasion of Portugal. Since 1810, the year the royal decree established the Library, the Biblioteca Nacional has in fact been increasing its very rich collections by means of Brazil's Legal Deposit System, and by purchase, exchange and gift arrangement.

The present building of the Biblioteca Nacional was inaugurated in October 1910. Its style exhibits neoclassical architectural elements and art nouveau decorative details.

The Biblioteca Nacional is the repository of Brazilian bibliographic production, the center for international exchange of publications and the agency in Brazil resonsible for assigning International Standard Book Numbers. The cataloguing of publications was automated beginning in 1982.

In December 1983 the restoration of the building including its architectural and decorative details was completed.

Built to hold 400 thousand volumes, the building of the Biblioteca Nacional now houses almost 5 million works and has been needing an extension for over twenty years. The lack of this new building means that the seventh largest library in the world (according to UNESCO classification) faces serious risks of deterioration in its valuable collection, putting at risk its own identity as the Biblioteca Nacional and preventing it from starting campaigns to fulfil its legal responsibilities.

It is worth emphasising also the role of the Biblioteca Nacional as a repository of knowledge. The growth of Brazilian universities running post-graduate, master's and doctoral courses has transformed the Library into an essential element in the search for Brazilian and foreign documents, both historical and contemporary, for these higher level students and researchers. Meanwhile, the absence of a network of public libraries with current, multi-disciplinary collections places on the Biblioteca Nacional the role of an institution open to the public and therefore accessible to students and readers of various educational levels, hastening the decay of its basic collections through intense handling and constant photocopying.

3. LEGAL DEPOSIT

The first law on legal deposit dates from 1822 and was improved during the second half of the 19th century. The text still in force dates from 1907.

For some years now the management of the Biblioteca Nacional has been concerned to update the legal text but, for reasons outside its control, this proposal has still not been approved by the National Congress. So the Biblioteca Nacional is prevented from taking action based on a strong text against publishers who fail to comply with legal deposit. There are countries like Portugal where the requirement amounts to the surprising and reassuring number of seven copies.

The ideal solution in my opinion, considering the continental size of Brazil, would be a federal law which required deposit at three levels: at county level (for works published in each city) and at state level (for works published within the borders of each of the federated states), the works should be deposited in public libraries at the appropriate level; and at the federal level (for all publications), they should be deposited in the Biblioteca Nacional. So if a work were lost or destroyed, there would be two others available to preserve the record. All these works would be identified as stemming from legal deposit and subject, naturally, to an effective conservation policy.

4. HISTORY OF THE PRESS IN BRAZIL

When Brazil was a Portuguese colony, the printing of books and newspapers was banned. The Royal Charter of 1747 expressly forbade any printing under pain of confiscation and exile. In Portugal there existed three types of censorship of printed material: the censorship of the Church Hierarchy, that of the Inquisition and the royal censorship (through the Lord Chancellor); these were in force from 1576.

In colonial Brazil works smuggled in from Europe began to circulate only at the end of the 18th century. In this way French and American ideas of freedom were brought into the colony and had a great influence on the Brazilian independence movements, particularly the so-called "Minas Conspiracy" in which, following its failure, the books of the conspirators figured as prosecution evidence.

The arrival of the Portuguese court in Brazil led to the installation of the Royal Printing Office which on 10 September 1808 published the first issue of the Gazeto do Rio de Janeiro, the official journal with four quarto pages. At the same time beginning on 1 June 1808, the Correio Brasiliense started publication in London in Portuguese and was then smuggled into the colony. Its publisher, Hipólito José da Costa, the doyen of Brazilian journalists, campaigned for the independence of Brazil through his pages, producing a doctrinal journal at monthly intervals free of Portuguese censorship. So 175 issues with 96 to 150 octavo pages were printed which, although published in London, only covered events in Britain which were related to Brazil or Portugal.

From 1808 onwards the periodical press sprang up and began to be seen in the provinces: in 1811 the Idade d'Ouro do Brasil appeared in Bahia; in 1821 the Aurora Pernambucana appeared in Pernambuco; in 1821 there also appeared in Rio de Janeiro the Diário do Rio de Janeiro, which was the first newspaper and which was published until 1878. In this same period there appeared the first newspapers of a political character such as the Reverbero Constitucional Fluminense in Rio de Janeiro and the revolutionary Typis Pernambucano of Frei Caneca. In reply there appeared conservative papers such as O Conciliador do Maranhão in 1821. Some of these papers were political, informative and conciliatory and have continued to appear up to the present, such as the Diáro de

Pernambuco, which first appeared in 1825, and the Jornal do Commercio of Rio de Janeiro which began in 1827. In 1831 over 54 periodical titles were appearing in Brazil, of which 16 were based in Rio de Janeiro.

From the Independence of Brazil in 1822 to the Proclamation of the Republic in 1889 there were numerous papers with republican ideas or which advocated the abolition of slavery, such as the A República, founded in 1870. There was also a great profusion of short-lived papers which supported movements such as the liberation of slaves. Also noteworthy was the publication of papers intended solely for women, such as the Jornal das Senhoras in Rio de Janeiro in 1852. After the Proclamation of the Republic there appeared the so-called "great newspapers", many of which still survive today, such as the O Estado de São Paulo in São Paulo, the Jornal do Brasil in Rio de Janeiro and the Correio do Povo in Rio Grande do Sul. In 1919, the country's press was consolidated with the foundation of the Associação Brasileira da Imprensa - ABI (Brazilian Press Association).

The first Brazilian newspaper chain, the Diarios Associados, which was formed in 1950, covered almost all the states and reached its peak with the advent of television news. Various newspapers followed this path and a good example is O Globo, founded in 1925 by Roberto Marinho, which gave rise to the Rede Globo radio, television and newspaper chain.

After the Second World War around 1950, the popular press expanded with some campaigning political papers such as Ultima Hora and Tribuna da Imprensa in Rio de Janeiro and the Folha de São Paulo in São Paulo. This was the period when great publishers like Bloch, Abril, EBAL, Rio Gráfica and Vecchi flourished. There was also a revival of illustrated and humorous reviews, the working class and trade union press and fashion magazines, which had been greatly in vogue at the turn of the century. The 1970s witnessed the appearance of the alternative or "dwarfish" press, with the publication of the first weekly opinion periodicals in tabloid format, which are badly underrepresented in the Biblioteca Nacional.

5. THE NATIONAL PLAN FOR MICROFILMING BRAZILIAN PERIODICALS

The Plan was officially created by the Ministry of Education and Culture, Department of Cultural Affairs, with the support and approval of the Federal Council of Culture, in Regulation DAC no. 31 of 11 December 1978, modified by Regulation no. 023 of 26 October 1982. Its objectives are to identify, locate, organise, preserve and record by systematic microfilming Brazil's newspaper collection located in the various areas of the country. It aims to complete the collections existing in the Biblioteca Nacional and to increase its holdings through micrographic copies.

The Biblioteca Nacional, the depository body responsible for the preservation of the manifold forms of storing knowledge, carries out the Plan through the Co-ordenadoria de Restauração e Microrreprodução (Co-ordinating Body for Restoration and Microreproduction) which runs the Centro de Microfilmagem e Reprografia (Centre for Microfilming and Reprography).

Since 1978 the Plan has received annual budgetary allocations for distribution by means of agreements to a specific number of institutions which amount to a third of the total number of bodies directly involved with the work. Besides finance, the Plan gives regular and occasional technical assistance which involves training and skill-building for operators and librarians, specific technical guidance and the production of procedural manuals, amongst other activities. The operational impetus of the Plan comes from the young multidisciplinary team of librarians, historians, assistants and microfilm operators.

The fact that the newspaper collections are scattered among hundreds of libraries, together with the continental size of Brazil, makes the tracing of collections much more difficult. In turn the process of microfilming depends on the availability of these collections which normally requires long negotiations with the bodies which own them. Because of this, the Biblioteca Nacional acts as a catalyst for the Plan, backing up the undertaking of projects at various organisational levels in the country with the wealth of its holdings and its socio-cultural position.

As a result of this effort and with the aim of reporting the progress already achieved by the Plan, four editions of the collective catalogue Periodicos Brasileiros em Microformas/Brazilian periodicals in microform have been published in 1976, 1979, 1981 and 1985. These documents are of vital importance for newspaper research and improve access to historical sources. It is interesting to note the extensive bibliography on the press in Brazil which includes information on the history, development and spread of Brazilian periodicals.

5.1. Collections of newspapers: where are they?

Although Brazil is five hundred years old, its history shows that its organisational structures are still forming and are in a state of constant flux. Libraries and state archives which were originally a single body are split up physically and administratively. Museums and public libraries appear and disappear. Institutional libraries and newspaper collections are founded but not installed... Besides this we also have to take account of the collections of the historical and geographical institutes, colleges, universities, literary societies, reading rooms, trade unions and religious bodies, in short, a multiplicity of institutions with varied aims and legal status, which hampers the flow of information and the numerical assessment of the collections.

The main difficulty which we encountered when we started work was precisely in tracing the titles which were held by institutions, given that the recording of titles which have appeared in the past - a basically historical project - is a task to be undertaken in the near future, probably using an automated system. In spite of all the obstacles, research was carried out in five hundred institutions scattered throughout the country and 15,000 titles were located in them. It is estimated that there are still 2,000 titles to be located in over 4,000 counties in the interior of the country which had a newspaper in the past even if they no longer have one now. As for the Biblioteca Nacional, at least 30% of the newspaper titles held there are of foreign origin. Amongst the Brazilian ones, we include newspapers, reviews, bulletins, annual reports, annals and all types of periodical publication.

At the same time as the research on the newspapers was going on, bibliographic research was also undertaken with the aim of outlining the history of journalism and the press in the country. As an initial result, 1500 references to monographs, articles and research in general were traced and published in the latest "Catálogo de Periódicos Brasileiros em Microformas", published by the Biblioteca Nacional in 1985. The research has been underpinning the process of locating new titles as well as helping to establish new access points to retrieve titles which were hitherto unknown because of the complete lack of information.

5.2. Incomplete collections of newspapers - difficulties in completing them.

The task of microfilming Brazilian newspapers includes the daily problem of completing collections. Even collections belonging to publishers are imcomplete. Trying to complete collections requires great patience, hopefulness and luck. We find that newspapers which have appeared for twenty years are incomplete and collections of papers which have appeared for one hundred and fifty years without interruption have fared no better. In order to film the two oldest daily papers in the country, the Diário de Pernambuco, dating from 1825, and the Jornal do Commercio of 1827, we had to gain access to six separate collections, which caused a real headache, and even then some issues could not be traced and the collections could not be completed. Often we have microfilmed incomplete collections and later traced the missing issues. At other times we have located scattered issues but problems in gaining access and the urgency of microfilming the issues already gathered together have prevented them from being microfilmed together, a task to be carried out at some other time.

The process of locating collections with the missing issues, more complete collections or better preserved ones is carried out by means of a collective newspaper catalogue which was compiled on the basis of a survey of the collections in the various cultural institutions of the country and which is being constantly updated.

As well as completing newspaper collections, we also complete collections of magazines, especially illustrated ones, often obtained on loan from private collectors.

The research needed to fill gaps covers collections spread throughout the country as well as the holdings of the Biblioteca Nacional. Of the 23 states of the Federation, 17 now have the means to microfilm documents and 10 carry out systematic microfilming "in loco" in parallel with the work done in the Biblioteca Nacional. The majority of the microfilming centres in the states, however, operate in a rather haphazard way as far as skilled manpower and the maintenance of equipment is concerned.

The average annual production in the last three years has been 1250 master reels - an average which reached 1800 reels in 1982-83. The operational capacity of the plan is 2500 reels per year or more but this would depend on the application of greater resources. The lack of resources to increase production, however, has meant that our main concern is to maintain a minimum rate of work, thus preventing any of the centres from coming to a standstill.

5.3. Collections of annual reports of Provincial Presidents (Empire period, 1822-1889), Governors (Republican period, 1889-1930) and Ministers (Empire and Republican periods): research and international assistance.

In 1976 a group of American researchers asked the Biblioteca Nacional to microfilm the annual reports of the Provincial Presidents and Ministers for the Empire period through the Center for Research Libraries - Latin American Microform Project (LAMP). After an initial check of the holdings of the Biblioteca Nacional, it was clear that the available collections were incomplete and in a precarious state of conservation. LAMP then financed a three-year project whose aim was to trace anywhere in Brazil copies which completed the Biblioteca Nacional collection or would replace those which had deteriorated. Over a hundred institutions were investigated and about 500 documents were listed, organised and microfilmed. Some of these were earlier even than 1835 when the issue of reports became compulsory as a form of government accountability.

After this first phase came the second phase of the project which covered the reports of the Fist Republic from 1889 to 1930 and for another three years we faced the same difficulties. The results were positive and produced 313 reels of microfilm.

Recently LAMP approved the third phase of the project: documentation from 1930 to 1960, a period of transition in Brazilian politics and which also saw many conflicts throughout the world.

All these reports form valuable sources of information on social, political, economic and cultural conditions in Brazil. Unforutunately the gaps in the collections which we were able to locate prevent us from producing a complete list of the documentation based on a national inventory. Our greatest difficulty lies, however, in the bureaucratic procedures which precede the process of lending these documents to the Biblioteca Nacional for microfilming. Today, thanks to the success of the first and second phase, the Biblioteca Nacional and the Center for Reasearch Libraries/LAMP in the United States hold complete collections of the reports and the majority of Brazilian states hold collections relating to their local area.

6. SYSTEMATIC MICROFILMING

After a detailed automated stock-taking, the Biblioteca Nacional realised how defective the collections deposited in its holdings were and how the physical deterioration of these collections increased as the use by researchers grew, particularly of the newspaper collections. Because of this it became urgent to adopt a more hard-wearing medium which would at the same time preserve the integrity of the original collections, which were old and valuable, and make them more complete. The decision to use systematic microfilming was a natural consequence after analysing the situation.

Obviously a job of such proportions would have very special characteristics considering our national quirks and the complexity of the tasks involving many disciplines. The constant flow of activities and the need for quality control imply a series of stages which, in turn, forms the methodology of systematic microfilming as developed in the Biblioteca Nacional through the Plan.

This methodology, which will be described below, was developed from the following criteria which defined the priorities:

a) historical importance, either national or local;

b) statistics on usage: titles and periods most in demand;

c) physical state of the volumes;

d) titles which were incomplete or missing altogether in the Biblioteca Nacional;

e) likelihood of early deterioration through excessive use.

Then it became possible to define the Plan's lines of action:

1. identify, research and locate Brazilian newspaper holdings in the Biblioteca Nacional and other institutions, state by state, through a detailed

checking of card catalogues, printed catalogues, scattered collections and specialised bibliographies;

2. analyse and compare the reference bibliography with the holdings which had been identified, researched and located, with the aim of recording the titles and dates of publication of periodicals from 1808 to the present, state by state;

3. indicate priority titles and periods, state by state, with the help of the State Cultural Councils and the institutions which hold the collections, following the criteria of priorities;

4. analyse the state of conservation of the available collections by titles and/or priority periods with the aim of listing gaps and defective copies, in order to fill them or replace them;

5. reproduce the collections on 35 mm unperforated silver-halide microfilm, with quality control according to international technical standards and criteria, with the aim of making Brazilian production compatible with international production and suitable for foreign researchers;

6. reproduce the newspaper collection of the Biblioteca Nacional, making it accessible to the reading public in the form of microfilms while preserving the original and facilitating the production of copies;

7. record and reconstitute the newspaper collection of each Brazilian state, where gaps and defective copies are estimated to measure between 20 and 70%;

8. provide access to the primary documentary sources for Brazilian history and, in a broader sense, democratise information by placing the newspaper documentaion required at the disposal of every researcher.

6.1. Methodology

The complexity of the Plan's tasks and of microfilming the holdings of the Biblioteca Nacional required constant quality control both of routine procedures and the final product. This control, whose methodology has now been confirmed in practice, set out a standard flow of activities which follwed the stages listed below:

1. <u>Tracing the collection</u>, which consists of:

a) checking for other complete copies which are available in various Brazilian and foreign institutions, describing their physical state;

b) examining the physical state of the basic collection, noting the degree of acidity, damage caused by the action of man, insects, microorganisms and rodents, torn pages and other general aspects;

c) comparing the copies traced with the aim of selecting originals which are compatible and complete.

2. <u>Preparing the collection</u>, which comprises:

a) disbinding the collection if needed to make the text on the inside margins of the pages legible;

b) removing paper clips, string, turned-down corners, wrinkles and furrows, aiming to make the surface to be microfilmed as smooth as possible;

c) putting the various parts of the collection into chronological sequence, taking account of the arrangement of years, volumes, issues offprints, etc.;

d) identifying page by page any marks, printing mistakes, illegibility of the text and any other imperfections, so that they can be filled or replaced if necessary;

(This phase in preparation gives rise to a series of procedures such as registering data which reflect the condition of the original; indicating problems encountered by inserting paper markers next to the pages concerned to guide the microfilm operators and having the entire procedure checked by a trained librarian).

e) working out the chronological arrangement of the collection on each reel of microfilm in a systematic, bibliographically-accessible way. The splitting-up of the reels is done after phases a, b, c and d of preparing each year of the periodical has been finished;

f) compiling bibliographical details which note the imperfections found in the originals microfilmed on the reel together with other important data.

3. <u>Microfilming</u> which follows international technical specifications and standards as well as basic procedures intended to produce a satisfactory result, such as the correct placing of the frame on the film, the degree of reduction to be used, etc. This stage consists of specific phases which range from identification procedures to the bibliographical description of the microfilm, namely:

a) making complete labels, which record all the information relevant to the identification and contents of the reel, such as administrative headings, data on the newspaper and the microfilm laboratory responsible for the filming - and partial labels which are subdivisions of the complete label, identifying the beginning of each day, month and year;

b) technical handling of the film, which includes processing, checking and duplicating. The process of checking, which is very detailed, goes hand in hand with the control over the density of the reel. Duplication consists of reproducing the master film in at least two copies - a second generation negative copy, to be used to duplicate other copies on microfilm and to obtain photocopies or for reader-printer machines - and a positive copy to be made available to users for reading;

c) archival storage of the films on their own plastic reels, wrapped with protective strips and stored in special acid-free cardboard boxes which in turn are marked with the details of the film and stored in specially-made steel cabinets. These cabinets are kept in a cooled environment, with constant control of temperature and humidity;

d) cataloguing and recording the microfilms using the "Anglo-American Cataloguing Rules", 2nd edition (AACR II), with the addition of data concerning the physical description of the microfilm, the number of reels corresponding to the periods filmed and the film size. The recording of the titles and reels follows an alpha-numeric code which indicates not only where the microfilmed originals came from but also the sequential order of the titles in the listing by place of publication and the location of reels in the microfilm archives.

Control is ensured through the use of standardised forms which record every piece of information about the periodical and the microfilm, such as the history of the title, an inventory of the copies microfilmed and a description of the entire technical process of microfiming in its various stages. This form of control allows incomplete microfilmed collections to be completed when missing issues are located at a later date.

The Biblioteca Nacional naturally lays down the policy guidelines and acts as the dynamic technical headquarters of the plan since all the master reels are sent to it after technical checking and analysis. These are used to produce a second generation negative or positive copy for the states where the documents originally came from; a second generation negative copy for the Plan/Biblioteca Nacional, for security purposes; and a positive copy available to researchers in the Biblioteca Nacional.

6.2. Preserving the originals

The greatest problem which we face today in the Biblioteca Nacional and the other main insitutions holding newspaper collections is the preservation of the originals.

How should we proceed after microfilming? How should we store them? What techniques in the restoration field can be set up in the short term but which will not be mere palliatives? What techniques may be available to transform the microfilm into a complete substitute for the original, of use to the researcher, bibliophile or the traditional reader? These and many other questions need replies in the form of definite technical guidelines, since they concern valuable items of the nation's historical heritage.

The Biblioteca Nacional has been developing a series of research projects on restoration procedures which can be applied to a small fraction of the holdings which need treatment or to specific problems which do not cover all those which need to be solved. We hope that the Symposium will allow us to pick up some techniques which can be transferred and modified to suit Brazilian conditions, helping us effectively to preserve our newspaper collections after microfilming.

6.3. Users of the system - institutional and business support

From the beginning of the systematic microfilming work, even before the formalisation of the Plan, the main users of the system have been researchers, historians and social scientists, particularly "Brazilianists" i.e. foreign specialists who first came to Brazil in the 1960s and took an interest in its history. From then on the Biblioteca Nacional and other insititutions holding newspaper collections woke up to the condition of their collections.

With the setting-up of the Plan and the notable increase in post-graduate courses throughout the country, demand grew significantly. A typical example of this growth is the State of Acre in the extreme north of the country where the Federal University and the Cultural Foundation of the State form potential users of the Plan based on their interest in exploring the history of their state by recording collections of local newspapers scattered throughout the country and liable to disappear. Another example worth mentioning is the State of Mato Grosso which was recently divided into two federated states - Mato Grosso and Mato Grosso do Sul - although the historical documentation was concentrated in only one of them. The viable alternative was to duplicate the collection through microfilming subsidised by the Plan.

Brazil's political instability and the changes which our society has gone through mean that a broad and ambitious undertaking like the National Plan for Microfilming Brazilian Periodicals has to face many obstacles from both a technical and cultural point of view. The obstacles are being overcome thanks to the enthusiasm which characterises the Plan's working teams and the positive results achieved in practice.

With regard to business support from the newspaper publishers, the plan has obtained significant collaboration in the last three years as a result of arduous efforts to increase management awareness. Besides this we have offered newspaper companies which are interested in preserving their collections or have been asked to do so a series of agreed benefits which include all the work of microfilming, the master film, a duplicating service and the archival storage for the camera or master film. This is in return for the use of originals in the publisher's collection, which are generally in a better state of conservation. At present there are about twenty current newspaper titles whose publishers have made agreements with the Plan. Of course this is only a small number compared with the number of papers which are in circulation but this is an obstacle which we are trying to overcome.

Another interesting example of institutional support for the Plan is the Istituto de Planejamento Econômico Aplicado/IPEA (Institute of Applied Economic Planning) of the Secretariat of Planning which is interested in economic history and has provided special resources for a project to systematically microfilm the relevant documentation. Interest is particularly centred on the Retrospecto Comercial do Jornal do Commercio, the Balanços Gerais da União, the Relatorios do Banco do Brasil and the newspaper collections of the Monitor Mercantil, O Auxiliar da Indústria Nacional and Willeman's Review, amongst other titles. The originals of these are incomplete and scattered among various insitutions.

6.4. Technical and administrative structure

An area of 380 square metres is occupied by the Centro de Microfilmagem e Reprografia (Centre for Microfilming and Reprography) which composes the technical and adminsitrative structure of the Plan. Here is installed all the necessary machinery and the relevant services are carried on.

A team of seven trained librarians is responsible for doing the research, identifying titles, locating originals, organising the collection to be microfilmed and the subsequent technical processing of the microfilmed holdings. Six university-educated technicians are responsible for the detailed preparation of the documentation to be microfilmed following the procedural manual of the Plan. In the microfilming and photographic laboratories a team of eleven technicians carry out the various stages of the system.

In terms of equipment, the Centre for Microfilming has four Kodak planetary cameras, three of model MRD-2 and one model MRC-4, with an average daily production of four negative reels. There are three processing machines, one PROSTAR-I, one KOSIBRA, both made by Kodak, and an old SMITH of German manufacture; the processing capacity of the three machines is estimated at 90 reels per day. We also have five inspection/viewing machines for visual quality control, three collators and two densitometers - one digital and the other manual. For the duplication service we have two EXTEK (pos/ddp) which allow us to duplicate approximately fifty reels per day although our requirements are one hundred reels per day.

The microfilm reading room is located on the second floor of the Biblioteca Nacional where there are nineteen reader machines available: ten DUKANE, five LEKTOR and four 3M models. It is open on Mondays to Fridays from 9 a.m. to 8.30 p.m. and on Saturdays from 12 to 6 p.m. Users of the reading room are received by two attendants who are trained in reference work and who act under the guidance of the librarians of the Centre for Microfilming. They can refer to a catalogue of all the works microfilmed, with special card catalogues for rare books, manuscripts, prints and drawings, music and general works. The newspapers, which comprise 90% of the holdings on microfilm, can be traced through two catalogues: a general alphabetical one and a geographical one.

Besides this reference service, the Biblioteca Nacional also has a counter where users can request various reproduction services using special forms. These include xerox-type photocopying, which is done immediately in 70% of the cases as long as it has been expressly authorised by the Section which holds the originals; paper copies from microfilm made on a reader-printer machine (IMTEC MS-2000 model); microfilm - in negative or positive copies and in complete reels or individual frames; and photographic enlargements in various sizes, glossy or matt. For the photographic enlargement services we have two enlargers (LEITZ and DURST) besides two REPROVIT-LEITZ machines which are used in special cases when it is particularly important to obtain a faithful reproduction of the original.

This technical and administrative service can also help users in other states and countries if they write by letter and pay the costs in advance.

7. CONCLUSION

We believe that the effort we have made to microfilm the main newspapers of each of the Brazilian states in order to preserve them, complete and make them more accessible will increase the awareness of those in government and positions of cultural influence. It will lead them to give strong support to a policy of preserving, restoring and microfilming Brazil's documentation, whether it be newspapers, reviews, bulletins, annals, annual reports, old books or recently published ones.

The message we have tried to put over through our philosophy of work and action is that once we have begun the process of recording newspaper documentation we should naturally go on to the work of recording all historical and cultural documentation. By taking on the great task of saving precious documentary collections, microfilming has appeared to be the best solution immediately to hand. It allows more time for the painstaking task of restoring the originals by protecting them from the action of time and handling.

We have now published 4 catalogues (1976, 1979, 1981 and 1985), we have located 15,000 titles in more than 250 cultural insititutions and we can rely on the increasing support of universities, archives, libraries and newspaper companies at a nations , state and county level. More than seventeen laboratories and around 200 reader machines scattered throughout Brazil are involved in the work of systematic microfilming. The role of information science , which was introduced into the Biblioteca Nacional in an effective and irreversible way during the modernising administration of Celia Zaher, will be consolidated through the present project for information science which is to be set up with the support of the Secretariat for Information Technology of the MINC. We maintain a permanent exchange with the Library of Congress and the Center for Research Libraries.

As you can see, I have described a situation of intense struggle and many difficulties to be overcome but also one of dynamic optimism, with some results already obtained, measurable short-, medium- and long-term goals and a sincere appeal for collaboration, without which we shall not be able to achieve all that we set out to do: to record the great national newspaper collections which are witnesses to our history, culture and way of life in Brazil.

BIBLIOGRAPHY

Bertoletti, Esther Caldas, 'O Plano Nacional de Microfilmagem de Periódicos Brasileiros.' Ciência e Cultura, São Paulo, vol. 32 no. 8, 1980 pp.1134-8. Separata.

Biblioteca Nacional(Brasil), 'Periodicos brasileiros em microformas; catálogo preliminar.' Rio de Janeiro, 1976. 31p.

_____; catálogo coletivo.' Rio de Janeiro, 1979. 50p. (coleção Rodolfo Garcia, 18- Serie B- Catálogos e bibliografias)

_____. Rio de Janeiro, 1981. 296p. (coleção Rodolfo Garcia, 18- Série B- Catálogos e bibliografias)

_____. Rio de Janeiro, 1985. 503p. (coleção Rodolfo Garcia, 18- Série B- Catálogos e bibliografias)

_____. Biblioteca Nacional. Rio de Janeiro, 1984. 27p., il.

_____. Relatório de Diretora da Biblioteca Nacional, 1978. Anais da Biblioteca Nacional, Rio de Janeiro, vol. 98, 1978 pp.333-4.

_____, 1982. Anais da Biblioteca Nacional, Rio de Janeiro, vol. 102, 1983 pp.235-258.

_____. Relatório da Diretora-Geral, 1985. Rio de Janeiro, 1986. 26p.

Brasil. Ministério da Educação e Cultura. Secretaria da Cultura. Plano Nacional de Microfilmagem de Periódicos Brasileiros. 'Manual preliminar de procedimentos adotados pelo Plano Nacional de Microfilmagem de Periódicos Brasileiros para preparo e microfilmagem de periódicos', Rio de Janeiro, 1981. ix, 58p., il.

THE CANADIAN APPROACH TO COLLECTION, PRESERVATION AND ACCESS

Marianne SCOTT

National Librarian, National Library of Canada, Ottawa

1. INTRODUCTION

Canada is a large country with a small population. Its twenty-six million inhabitants occupy six and one half million square kilometres of land in a rather sporadic pattern of densely-populated areas amidst vast open spaces. Canada is a federal state with a central government and twelve provincial and territorial governments. Given the geographic and demographic situation, Canadian newspapers play an important role in reflecting and recording the cultural, economic and social life of the country. Clearly, they are an important part of the Canadian published heritage; in fact, for those provinces with little monographic or serial publishing, newspapers are the published record of the jurisdiction.

2. NEWSPAPER PUBLISHING IN CANADA

Since the appearance of the Royal Gazette in Halifax in March 1752, over ten thousand newspapers have been published. Like the pattern of settlement, newspaper publishing began in the Atlantic region and moved in a westerly fashion to the Pacific coast. The publishing situation at present includes about one hundred urban dailies and several hundred weeklies and community newspapers. In addition, there are numerous labour, student, religious and other special interest papers. The ethnic press is especially vigorous in Canada, a country where multiculturalism is fostered.

Newspaper publishing represents the most dispersed publishing activity in Canada. Newspapers are produced in a large number of towns and cities throughout the country while the production of books and periodicals tends to be focussed in a few metropolitan centres.

In Canada, where the health of the publishing industry in general varies, newspaper publishing is one component that thrives. Canada's newspaper publishers generate more than twelve hundred distinct bibliographic items every week. The trend in daily newspapers, moreover, is to a greater number of editions tailored to meet the needs of specific markets.

While the books produced in the few urban centres receive nationwide distribution, the newspapers originating in many locales rarely leave the immediate vicinity. The distribution mechanisms reflect the publishing pattern. With the exception of subscription by mail, newspapers do not travel over great distances from the point of production to the point of sale to the point of consumption. Indeed, the three most frequent methods of distribution are unlike those of any other form of publication in Canada. Newspapers may be acquired through local stores, boxes on the street, and home delivery. One notable exception is the Globe and Mail. Referring to itself as Canada's national newspaper, the Globe is headquartered in Toronto and is published there as well as being transmitted via satellite for publication in five other Canadian centres. Since 1977, the Globe has been available on-line as Info-Globe, the electronic edition of the paper.

3. THE DECENTRALIZED PROGRAM FOR CANADIAN NEWSPAPERS

The National Library, created in 1953, is a federal government department with responsibility to gather, preserve and make known Canada's published heritage. It is assisted in this endeavour by the legal deposit regulations of its Act of 1969, whereby two copies of all publications offered for public distribution or sale in Canada must be deposited with the Library [1]. While the Library could collect Canadian newspapers using this mechanism, it elected not to do so because of the enormous resource requirements in terms of personnel and physical facilities. Instead, in 1979 the National Librarian presented a blueprint for the future which recommended a decentralized approach to the preservation of Canadian newspapers in support of Canadian studies [2]. The detailed planning of this approach fell to the National Library Advisory Board's Resource Network Committee. The Committee, with its representation of various types of libraries from across the country, proposed a voluntary and co-operative model that would build on existing activity and would enable and encourage participation of all the provinces and territories. The resulting Decentralized Program for Canadian Newspapers [3], approved by the National Library Advisory Board in late 1982, rests on a framework of shared responsibilities between the federal and provincial levels.

At the federal level, the National Library of Canada assumes responsibility for the overall planning and co-ordination, for the promulgation of standards, for the provision of limited financial assistance to the provinces, for publicity and public relations, for the provision of national and internatioal lending, location and reference services, and for maintaining a comprehensive collection of the ethnic press in Canada. The National Library also agrees to acquire a positive service copy of each newspaper that is microfilmed by provincial projects for its own collection.

At the provincial level, there are two crucial responsibilities: bibliographic control and planning. Under the Program, bibliographic control is defined as the identification and description of all newspapers published in the province past and present. A plan describes in some detail the mechanisms for collecting, preserving and making available the province's newspapers. It rests with the provinces to decide which of the two responsibilities to undertake first.

Response to the National Library's Decentralized Program has been positive, although the nature of the response has varied according to the provincial or territorial situation. The first provinces to respond, British Columbia, Nova Scotia and Ontario, established ad hoc committees or task groups. In several jurisdictions, a single institution took the initiative in responding to the Library's Program. Examples are the Yukon Archives in the Yukon Territory, the Public Archives of Prince Edward Island in P.E.I. and the Bibliothèque nationale du Québec, in the province of Québec. Elsewhere, existing co-operative bodies came forward to spearhead provincial efforts, for example, the Council of Head Librarians of New Brunswick, the Manitoba Library Association and the Library Association of Alberta.

In several cases, bibliographic control was viewed as a necessary first step and one that had to be completed prior to any planning. Other provinces,

where there was existing bibliographic groundwork, took the opposite view. In
their opinion, the formulation of a provincial plan included the elaboration
of bibliographic control. In one case, where the amount of newspaper publishing is well-defined and rather limited, both functions (bibliographic control
and planning) were accomplished simultaneously. The National Library has
provided financial assistance in the form of contracts to groups and individuals in the provinces and territories to complete these fundamental responsibilities.

4. COLLECTIONS OF CANADIAN NEWSPAPERS

The National Library has, as described above, under the terms of its Act of
1969, a legal deposit regulation, although newspapers have not been subject to
deposit. Rather, the Library has built a strong collection of Canadian newspapers through subscription and gift. The collection now comprises almost
70,000 reels of microfilm and 18,000 bound volumes of early Canadian papers.
These bound originals were transferred from the National Archives of Canada
and the Library of Parliament in 1967 and formed the nucleus of the Library's
collection. While the collection is large and growing it is by no means comprehensive. In fact, the comprehensive collections have been built by the
provinces and territories and comprise the newspaper publishing record of
their respective jurisdictions. The set of provincial and territorial collections collectively comprise the nation's heritage of print journalism. The
pattern is one of complementarity rather than duplication as there are few
overlaps among collections.

At the provincial level, two collecting patterns predominate: one major repository, or a co-operative arrangement among several institutions. These collections have been built and maintained through provincial legal deposit
regulations, purchase, and gift. Unfortunately, there are some Canadian newspapers for which there are no extant holdings, but these titles are in the
minority.

5. THE PRESERVATION OF CANADIAN NEWSPAPERS

As a provincial level responsibility, the preservation of newspapers is an
issue addressed by each province in the formulation of its plan. In Canada,
microfilming is the generally-accepted medium of preservation at the present
time. Almost all provinces have microfilming programmes but they are in varying states of vigour. The National Library does no filming on its own but
does make its originals available for filming to both public and private
sector interests in exchange for a positive service copy. At the present
time, when newspaper microfilming is done by commercial firms or service
bureaux, industry standards are followed. Archival quality filming is more
likely to be found among the library and archives communities. Currently,
substandard filming is not a problem although some refilming needs to be done
because of lax practices in the past. As stated above, the National Library
acquires a positive service copy of all Canadian newspapers that are microfilmed by the provinces. This arrangement provides a guaranteed sale to the
province as well as increasing the Library's own stock of Canadian titles.

Newspaper publishers in Canada are becoming increasingly conscious of the
commercial value of their files in light of researchers' demands for access to
their back runs. This heightened awareness, coupled with threat of loss from
fire and theft, have led them to view microfilming in a positive light. For
many years the large urban dailies have worked with the commercial micro-

publishers in having their papers committed to film. More recently, in the
province of Ontario, the Ontario Community Newspapers Association established
its own microfilming programme. The members' papers are microfilmed and
offered for sale in microfiche format. In Alberta, newspaper publishers have
been very receptive to the provincial Legislative Library's programme to
microfilm the weekly newspapers, often lending their entire backfiles which
are returned to them newly-bound after filming.

The economic issue is an important one in the microfilming of Canadian newspapers. While the filming of the large dailies on an ongoing basis is a profitable endeavour for both the publishers and the commercial filming companies,
the weekly papers and back files pose a different set of circumstances as the
number of potential sales is much smaller. It is libraries and archives that
face the major challenge of filming retrospective files (for which the market
for sales is limited), of refilming incomplete and poor quality files, and of
filming the small community newspapers as they are produced currently. In
some provinces, government agencies support the microfilming of newspapers
either directly through a central agency or indirectly in terms of grants and
subsidies.

There are other aspects of the microfilming of Canadian newspapers that must
be considered. Copyright is a concern that must be dealt with by those who
would commit newspapers to film.

The creation of a master negative and an intermediate negative and the safe
and secure storage of both are yet other issues. Once a newspaper has been
microfilmed, information on the holder and the location of the microform
master must be gathered, recorded and made available. This information, if
readily available, enables users to locate and acquire copies, enables those
who would film to avoid unnecessary duplication and provides a basis for preservation planning on a provincial and national scale.

Not all agree that microfilming newspapers is the complete answer to the preservation question. The question arises whether to discard or retain the newsprint copy of the newspaper after the microfilm copy is received. The debate
centres on the costs of storage and handling versus the needs of research and
reprography. Consequently, the retention of original issues after a microfilm
copy is available is not a consistent practice among Canadian libraries. Some
institutions maintain collections of originals in newsprint form; others do
not. There are, however, among those institutions which do retain originals,
some very good preservation practices. The Bibliothèque Nationale du Québec,
for example, stores its newspapers in folders within specially-designed boxes
on shelving constructed for newspaper storage in environmentally stable conditions. Unfortunately, the costs of such treatment are high and therefore, by
necessity, less rigorous practices are often followed elsewhere to attempt to
protect and prolong the life of Canadian newspapers.

While, at present, microfilm is the accepted preservation medium; in the
future, newer technologies may be utilized for the purpose of preserving the
intellectual content of the newspaper. Optical disk is one possibility that
is often mentioned and the Globe and Mail has published one year of its paper
on CDROM as a trial project. The high density storage and indexing capacities
would seem to make optical disk an attractive choice from the perspective of
both the storage and the retrieval functions.

6. THE USE OF CANADIAN NEWSPAPERS IN RESEARCH

Canadian newspapers have two distinct groups of users. The first group is the reader of today's paper. Canada's newspaper publishers meet the needs of this constituency, assisted by the carrier, the newsstand and the corner store. The second group of users comprises researchers, those individuals who seek information in back issues. Generally speaking, librarians and archivists attempt to meet the needs of this group. They provide services based on their collections of the Canadian press. The strong provincial and territorial collections are complemented by collections in academic and public libraries which typically concentrate on the regional or local newspapers. Most libraries lend their microfilm copies on interlibrary loan although this practice is less common among the archives. Almost all institutions, however, allow on-site access to their newspaper files.

Beyond physical access, there is the issue of intellectual access. The recently-published "Checklist of Indexes to Canadian Newspapers" [4] gives an excellent indication of the number of indexes available. When the survey was completed in 1984, more than 350 were identified. The publication of the "Checklist" may bring even more indexing work to light. Indexing is a pressing concern if the information contained in Canadian weeklies and dailies is to be readily accessible to users.

7. ACHIEVEMENTS TO DATE

After several years of operation, the Decentralized Program for Canadian Newspapers is nearing one of its primary goals: the identification and description of every newspaper published in Canada since 1752. Bibliographic control has been exercised in a number of formats from an on-line union catalogue of British Columbia newspapers to a checklist of Yukon newspapers prepared on word-processing equipment. By 1988, all provinces and territories will have completed the identification of newspapers published in their respective jurisdictions. Financial support for this bibliographic work has emanated from the National Library of Canada, the Social Sciences and Humanities Research Council (another federal agency) and scores of provincial and local government agencies, library and archival associations, and heritage foundations.

The National Library, for its part, is working towards an on-line union list of all Canadian newspapers which will bring together the information in the twelve provincial and territorial lists. In 1977, the Library published a "Union List of Canadian Newspapers". Although it has been kept up-to-date in manuscript form, an on-line inventory and accompanying microfiche product are sorely needed to reflect all the additional titles and holdings information identified in the provincial listings, to provide researchers with one comprehensive source of information on newspapers, and to support the Library's national and international location service.

Another goal of the Decentralized Program is the development of plans for each jurisdiction which detail the mechanisms for and approaches to collection, preservation and accessibility. Three provinces (British Columbia, Manitoba and Nova Scotia) have completed this process [6]. Each has delineated a different approach to making newspapers available which reflects the particular provincial situation. For those provinces where planning remains, the task is not a particularly onerous one for in most cases there are existing mechanisms to ensure the continuing custodianship of newspapers. These must be documented however in order to be shared, understood and accepted.

The newspaper Program's voluntary and decentralized approach enables the institutions that are already well-positioned to get on with the issue of preservation. It encourages the provinces and territories to build on their traditional collection strengths in formulating plans to ensure that the province's papers are collected, preserved and made available and it enables each province and territory to plan for its jurisdiction in a manner that reflects and takes advantage of the particular situation.

In 1985, the National Library invited representatives of each province and territory to a National Newspaper Symposium in Ottawa [7]. The participants exchanged information on their respective projects, in addition to discussing common concerns such as bibliographic standards, retention of originals and a comprehensive finding aid. The National Library has responded to each concern.

In January 1987, the Working Group on Technical Services, established the previous year under the chairmanship of Hana Komorous, delivered its report "Guidelines for the Minimum Bibliographic and Holdings Information for Newspapers" [8]. The report specifies the minimum data elements and defines the minimum content designation for newspaper records in machine-readable form. Adherence to the standard will assure consistency and compatibility of newspaper records created by the provinces and will facilitate merging of these records into the nationwide union list. The report has been circulated to all provinces and territories.

The National Library also set up the Working Group on Original Issues to develop guidelines for the storage, handling and consultation of Canadian newspapers in original newsprint form. The report which will incorporate existing standards will be submitted to the Library in 1987.

A second national meeting was convened by the Canadian Library Association's Serials Interest Group in June 1987. The National Library lent its sponsorship and support in the form of staff participation. The agenda focussed on accomplishments to date in collecting and preserving Canadian newspapers and highlighted specific collections and provincial approaches. Bibliographic control was another focus with demonstrations of both the United States Newspaper Program records on OCLC and the on-line Union Catalog of British Columbia Newspapers. The meeting confirmed and reinforced the significant progress achieved to date.

8. FUTURE PLANS

The Canadian approach to the preservation of print journalism takes advantage of social, historical and political factors. Through co-operation, political will, financial assistance and hard work, a great deal has been accomplished in the last few years. These recent accomplishments are based on sound practices that have gone before. With the experience of the past and the incentives of the present, the Program is poised to tackle the challenge of the future - the provision of greater intellectual access to the thousands of Canadian newspapers. A recent survey published by the National Library identified three hundred and fifty indexes to Canadian newspapers ranging from clipping files limited to biographical information to the "Canadian News Index" (an index of seven English-language dailies), and "l'Index de l'actualité vue à travers la presse écrite" (an index of three French-language dailies) [9].

Several papers are available in full text data bases, most notably the Globe and Mail which has been on-line as InfoGlobe since the late seventies. Despite these tools, a great deal of work remains to be done to render accessible to users the contents of Canadian newspapers.

As an incentive to future endeavours, the Manitoba Newspaper Project is preparing a manual for indexing Canadian newspapers. The National Library, in addition to financially supporting the preparation of the manual, will reproduce and distribute it to ensure that it is widely available to individuals and organizations embarking on newspaper indexng projects.

With the comprehensive identification and description of all Canadian newspapers, and accelerated preservation microfilming, the challenge of bringing together researchers and information in newspapers is closer at hand, and the ultimate goal of preserving Canadian newspapers in support of Canadian studies will be closer to realization.

REFERENCES

1   Canada. Laws, statutes, etc., "National Library Act, 1968-69, ch. N-11." in: Revised Statutes of Canada, 1970. Ottawa, Queen's Printer, 1970.

2   National Library of Canada, 'The future of the National Library of Canada = L'Avenir de la Bibliothèque Nationale du Canada'. Ottawa, 1979.

3   National Library of Canada. National Library Advisory Board. Resource Network Committe, 'Decentralized plan for Canadian newspapers preservation and access = Plan decentralise pour la conservation et la consultation des journaux canadiens'. Ottawa, 1982.

4   Burrows, Sandra and Gaudet, Franceen. 'Checklist of Indexes to Canadian newspapers held by Canadian Libraries = List contrôle des index de journaux canadiens'. Ottawa, National Library of Canada, 1987.

5   National Library of Canada. Newspaper Section, 'Union list of Canadian newspapers held by Canadian Libraries = List collective des journaux canadiens disponible dans les bibliothèques canadiennes'. Ottawa, 1977.

6   Murphy, Lynn, 'Nova Scotia Newspaper Plan'. Halifax, Nova Scotia, 1987.

   British Columbia Library Association. BCLA Newspapers Committee, 'Plan for the British Columbia Newspaper Project'. Victoria, BC, 1984.

   Manitoba Library Association, 'Plan for the Manitoba Newspaper Project'. Winnipeg, Man., 1987.

7   National Library of Canada, 'National Newspapers Colloquium, November 12 & 13, 1985: Report = Collôque national sur les journaux les 12 & 13 novembre 1985: compte rendu'. Ottawa, 1986.

8 National Library of Canada. Decentralized Program for Canadian Newspapers. Working Group on Technical Services. 'Guidelines for the minimum bibliographic and holdings description of newspapers = Lignes directrices relatives a une description minimale des notices bibliographiques et des fonds des journaux'. Ottawa, January 1987.

9 Canadian news index. Toronto, Micromedia, 1977 –

   L'Index de l'actualite vue a travers la presse ecrite. Quebec, Quebec: Microfor – C.E.J., 1972 –   .

THE PUBLICATION AND STORAGE OF THE CHINESE NEWSPAPERS

Professor Ning SHUFAN

Department of Journalism, Fudan University, Shanghai, P R China

1. HISTORICAL SURVEY OF THE PUBLICATION OF THE CHINESE NEWSPAPERS

Chinese newspapers have had a long history. Some scholars both in China and abroad have asserted that Chinese newspapers came into being during the Han Dynasty (206 BC-220 AD), but they have no reliable materials to prove their assertion. The fact, however, that there were newspapers during the Tang Dynasty (618-907 AD) has gradually gained public recognition in recent years. The newspapers then mainly carried imperial edicts, memorials to the throne and the state and situations of the government and had not any news or commentaries as they are today. The publication of the newspapers were strictly controlled by the government, and all the materials that they collected came from some special department set up by the government. The newspaper editors could not collect materials for themselves, to say nothing of freedom in writing news reports. For those newspapers, Chinese scholars usually refer to them as ancient papers in order to be distinguished from their modern counterparts. Titles of ancient papers were various: initially there were such papers as Official Report of the Department for the Presentation of Memorials, Boa Zhang, Chao Bao, etc.. Beginning from the Song Dynasty (960-1279 AD), there appeared Ti Pao, and Jing Pao that had a fixed title came into being at the end of the Ming Dynasty and the beginning of the Qing Dynasty and gradually replaced some other newspapers and became the dominating one at the time. However, the title Ti Pao was used for long and is now used as a name for all the ancient newspapers in China. From the Tang Dynasty to the end of the Qing Dynasty (1911 AD), the publication of the Chinese ancient newpspapers already existed for about 1200 years. The issuance during the Tang Dynasty was very small, it became large in Song Dynasty, and during the Yuan Dynasty (1273-1368 AD), it was again small. It grew larger during the Ming Dynasty (1368-1644 AD) and was popular during the Qing Dynasty. Beginning from the Qing Dynasty, Jing Pao was issued by certain newspaper offices run by common people and hence became a sort of commodity for public sale. Because of this, its issuance grew rapidly. Up to the reign of Emperor Guang Xu, major newspapers in various cities all printed Jing Pao and sent them together with their own newspapers, thus making Jing Pao the most popular newspaper at the time. Apart from this, there appeared certain local papers such as Yuan Meng Chao in various provinces.

It is upon entering the 19th century that China began to have its modern newspapers, all of which were founded and run by foreigners before the 1870's. Papers in foreign languages appeared first. A Abelaha Da Chine in Portuguese was the first newspaper in a foreign language in China. It was founded at Xiameng in 1822. To 1911, there were about 40 newspapers written in Portuguese, most of which were circulated at Xiameng, Hong Kong and Shanghai. The most influential and widely published were English newspapers, the first being founded in 1827 by some British publishers under the title Canton Register. According to inexact statistics, up to the end of the Qing Dynasty, there had been approximately 80 English newspapers, half of which were in Shanghai, then Hong Kong and Canton. There were two such newspapers in Fu Zhou, Han Kou, Tienjing and Xiameng and there was one in Yantai. Most of those English newspapers were published by British publishers, and some by American ones. Of those English papers, the important ones were <u>North China Daily News</u>, <u>Celestial Empire</u>, <u>Shanghai Mercury</u> and <u>China Press</u> in Shanghai, <u>China Mail</u>, <u>Daily Press</u>, <u>Hong Kong Telegraph</u> in Hong Kong, <u>Chinese Times</u> and <u>Peking and Tienstsin Times</u> in Tienjing. Beginning from the 1880s, there appeared French and German newspapers in Shanghai, of which <u>L'chode Chine</u> and <u>Der Ostasiatische Lloyed</u> were two typical ones. Beginning from the 1890s Japanese newspapers appeared and the Russian ones, but there were very few of the above newspapers in foreign languages.

Before the Opium War, no modern Chinese newspapers had been published. <u>Dong Xi Yang Kao Mei Yue Ton Ji Zhuan</u>, founded in Canton in 1833, had certain basic characteristics of modern papers, but being a monthly, it still could not be called a newspaper. The first Chinese modern newspaper published in China was <u>Xiang Gang Chuan Tou Huo Jia Zhi</u> founded by Hong Kong Zhai Ci newspaper office in 1857. Afterwards the Chinese newspapers run by foreigners began spreading from Hong Kong through Shanghai to the coastal areas, the port cities along the coast and various big cities in North and Northeast China as well as to the island of Taiwan. Up to the end of the Qing Dynasty, there had been at least 70 such newspapers. At first, British people had the largest share of the newspapers in China but after the Sino-Japanese War of 1894-95, the Japanese surpassed the British in publishing all of a sudden more than 20 newspapers. American, French, German and Russian people had also a few Chinese newspapers in China, of which the well-known ones were <u>Shanghai Xing Bao</u>, <u>Sheng Bao</u>, <u>Zi Ling Hu Bao</u>, <u>Zhong Wuai Xing Bao</u>, and <u>Hua Zi Ri Bao</u> by the British, <u>Xing Wen Bao</u> by the Americans, <u>Tong Wen Hu Bao</u>, <u>Shang Jing Shi Bao</u> and <u>Shun Tien Shi Bao</u> by the Japanese, and <u>Zhi Bao</u> by the Germans, etc. There were also some Chinese newspapers abroad run by foreigners.

The newspapers published by the Chinese themselves began to emerge during the 1870s. The earliest one was <u>Zhao Wen Xin Bao</u> published at Hankou in 1873. Afterwards, others began to appear at Hong Kong, Canton, Shanghai and some other coastal cities. Before the Sino-Japanese War of 1894-95, there were more than 10 such newspapers, the most well-known being <u>Xun Huan Ri Bao</u> by Wang Tao. It was during the Constitutional Reform and Modernization of 1898 and the preparation for the Revolution of 1911 [1] that the Chinese people began publishing their own newspapers at fast speed. The newspapers then were circulating in every province except a few minority areas such as Qinghai and Ningxia provinces. To avoid the possible suppression from the Qing government, a lot of such newspapers were published abroad. There have been no accurate statistics of the number of the newspapers at the time, but, there is no doubt that it surpasses the total number of the newspapers run by the foreigners in China several times. Of the above mentioned Chinese newspapers, the most numerous were political ones run mainly by bourgeois revolutionaries and the, Qing government. There were a lot of commercial newspapers, too. Besides, there were many literary newspapers purely for the purpose of entertainment. The newspapers that had great social influence were <u>Zhong Wai Ji Wen</u>, <u>Guo Wen Bao</u>, <u>Xiang Bao</u>, <u>Zhong Wai Ri Bao</u>, <u>Shi Bao</u>, <u>Shi Shi Xing Bao</u>, <u>Su Bao</u>, <u>Zhong Guo Ri Bao</u>, <u>Sheng Zhou Ri Bao</u>, <u>Ming Li Bao</u>, <u>Da Jiang Bao</u>, etc. Abroad there were <u>Tang Shan Xing Bao</u>, <u>Zhong Xing Ri Bao</u>, <u>Na Yang Zhong Hui Bao</u> etc..

After the founding of the Republic of China, Chinese newspapers entered a new phase of rapid development. Soon after the Wuchang Uprising, newspapers mushroomed across the nation, the total amounting to almost 300. The most numerous were political newspapers run by various parties and they came and went rapidly without much influence. Afterwards during the struggle against the Northern Warlords headed by Yuan Shikai, Chinese newspapers again flourished, of which the well-known ones were Ming Guo Ri Bao and Zhong Hua Xing Bao in Shanghai and Cheng Bao and Jing Bao in Peking. During the May 4th Movement, Chinese newspapers entered a new phase of rapid development. The number of all the newspapers across the country up to 1921 amounted to well over 800. Since then the Chinese Communist Party began its own publication of newspapers. At first, however, it mainly published certain journals dealing with current political affairs. Before 1928, its only party newspaper was Re Xue Ri Bao, but the newspapers jointly published by Chinese Communist Party and KMT were all over the country, of which the famous ones were Ming Guo Ri Bao in Canton, Ming Gou Ri Bao in Wuhan and Ming Guo Ri Bao in Peking, etc.. Besides, other newspapers developed quickly too, the influential ones being new Da Gong Bao and Shi Jie Ri Bao etc. During the decade before the Anti-Japanese War, newspapers of every sort developed quickly. Newspapers run by KMT developed most rapidly. The KMT established not only the newspapers attached to its central organs, but also newspapers affiliated to its party organizations at province, city and town levels, thus creating a party newspaper network. Besides, there were also newspapers by various cliques of the party and by the armed forces at various levels. Among the newspapers mentioned above the representative ones were Zhong Yang Ri Bao, Hua Bei Ri Bao, Wu Han Ri Bao, Zhong Hua Ri Bao, Sao Dang Bao etc. The newspapers run by the Chinese Communist Party began developing rapidly at this time, too. Inside the KMT governed areas, for example, there appeared party newspapers at various levels and a lot of factory newsletters, all of which were illegal then. After 1931, those publications became more and more difficult, and up to 1935, there were only few existing. Hong Qi Ri Bao, the newspaper of CCP's Central Committee, was published in Shanghai and Shanghai Bao was also a popular newspaper then. Inside various base areas set up by Chinese Communist Party, there were newspapers, which were mostly party newspapers or army newspapers in addition to a few other newspapers. Except a few newspapers with typeset printing, most ones were mimeographed small newspapers, of which the important ones were Hong Se Zhong Hua. Hong Xing Bao, with Deng Xiaoping as its chief editor. Most of these newspapers stopped in 1935, except Hong Xing Bao, which continued during the Long March [2]. At the same time, private newspapers developed quickly, too, with the birth of some influential newspapers such as Li Bao in Shanghai, Shi Bao in Peking and Xing Ming Bao in Nanking. During the Anti-Japanese War, there appeared a major change in the publication of newspapers. Along with the continued fall of the territory, a lot of newspapers had to stop its publication. The centre of the publication of newspapers, as a result, had to move first to the central, then to the southwest and northwest areas of the country. Chong Qing became the city where there were most KMT newspapers. Influential newspapers were more than a dozen there. Chengdu, Kunming, Xian and Guilin became important places for the publication of newspapers, too, where KMT government consolidated its newspaper by creating some local editions to its major newspapers, thus expanding Zhong Yang Ri Bao into 11 editions, Guo Ming Ri Bao into 13 editions and Sao Dang Bao into 3 editions, all of which penetrated deeply into various major cities in the rear of the war. There was a good increase in local newspapers as well. In Guangsu Province, for example, the original 7 newspapers were expanded into 15. And newspaper men were quite active then. There appeared such well-known newspapers as Jiu Wang Ri Bao and Weng Hui Bao, CCP founded Xing Hua Ri Bao in KMT governed areas. Inside the base areas set up by CCP, newspapers flourished,too. The major newspapers there were CCP's Xing Zhong Hua Bao, Jie Fang Ri Bao and the newspapers of the base areas such as Bian Qu Qun Zhong Bao, Jing Cha Ji Ri Bao, Kang Zhan Ri Bao, Xing Hua Ri Bao, Northern China Edition, Da Zhong Ri Bao and the New Fourth Route Army's [3] Kang Di

Bao. Besides, there were well-known mimeographed newspaper Fuo Xiao Bao and popular newspaper Yan Fu Da Zhong Bao. Some anti-Japanese personnel and patriotic overseas Chinese abroad and at Hong Kong published some anti-Japanese newspapers such as Nan Yang Shang Bao, Xing Dao Ri Bao, Hua Sheng Bao, Guang Ming Bao, etc. Within the fallen areas, there appeared a great many enemy or Japanese newspapers. According to the statistics of 1943, there were about 150 newspapers (in Chinese, excluding the ones in Northeast and Taiwan), the major ones being Zhong Hua Ri Bao, Xing Sheng Bao, Guo Ming Ri Bao and Xing Ming Bao etc. After the Anti-Japanese War, the formerly stopped newspapers were mostly restored in KMT controlled areas and there appeared a number of new newspapers. In 1947, there were as many as 1503 newspapers in KMT controlled areas according to the statistics of the KMT Internal Affairs Department. Shanghai once again became the centre of the publication of the newspaper across the nation. There were 85 newspapers published in Shanghai in 1947. KMT increased its publication of newspapers in Shanghai, too. Compared with the newspapers before the Anti-Japanese War, there appeared Zheng Yan Bao, He Ping Ri Bao, Shanghai edition, Dong Nan Ri Bao and Qian Xian Ri Bao. KMT also took charge of Sheng Bao and Xing Weng Bao, the two newspaper with long history. China Youth Party published Zhong Hua Shi Bao in Shanghai as well. But soon afterwards, KMT newspapers published on the mainland either stopped or were moved elsewhere. To the end of 1949, almost all of them stopped with only Xi Kang Ming Guo Ri Bao circulating until 1951. Chinese Communist Party once published Jie Fang Bao in Peking but after several months it had to stop. Along with the pushing forward of the People's Liberation Army across the nation, CCP newspapers developed by leaps and bounds. At first in the north-east part of China and then in the whole country there appeared a great many city newspapers, for example, Dong Bei Ri Bao of Shi Jia Zhuang Ri Bao. In August 1949, People' Daily officially became the newspaper of the Central Committee of the Chinese Communist Party. Except Xingjiang, Tibet, Shichuan, Yuannan, Guizhou, Guangxi, Guangdong, in all the provinces, municipalities and autonomous, there were newspapers for the party at various levels. In those places, some of the formerly private newspapers continued their publication, too, e.g. Da Gong Bao. Weng Hui Bao. Xing Wen Ri Bao, formerly Xing Wen Bao and Xing Ming Wan Bao.etc.

Between 1911 to 1949, there were many foreign newspapers published by foreigners in China. Those papers were mainly Japanese newspapers, then English, Russian, French and German ones. There are no statistics for the actual figures of their publication. In addition, Chinese people also published some English newspapers, such as China Republican and China Press.

2. STORAGE OF MODERN CHINESE NEWSPAPERS

Before the founding of the People's Republic of China, there was no accurate figure as to the total number of the newspapers in China. According to general estimation, however, it should be about 10,000, excluding foreign and ancient newspapers. This figure is fairly admirable. But, during the entire process of the publication of the modern Chinese newspapers, political situation changes frequently, war and turmoil occurred often, causing great damage to the storage of newspapers. However, the vast territory of China and the numerous units of storage have provided on the other hand a favorable condition for the storage of newspapers. According to the recent statistics from the information given by 131 units of storage across the nation, we have stored more than 7000 different Chinese newspapers published before the birth of PRC. The actual numbers should surpass this figure. In other words, the figure for the publication of the newspapers and the figure for the storage of them are not much different. The resources for newspapers in China are therefore still fairly rich.

Originally, the units of storage of newspapers in China were rather unsystematic and irregularly spread out. After readjustment and construction for a long time, we have now set up a big storage system in the country.

The chief organizations for the storage of newspapers are the libraries in the capital, various provinces, municipalities and localities. Shanghai Library has the largest holdings of newspapers in China. It has now stored 3,600 different newspapers published before the founding of the PRC, especially the ones before 1919. These newspapers are not only fairly complete, but also quite a few of them are really rare or even the only copies of the papers found in China. What is of the same importance is the fact that these rare newspapers are well kept in their entirety. The library now keeps the most complete volumes of Sheng Bao. Xing Wen Bao, Zi Ling Hu Bao, and Tong Wen Hu Bao. It also stores Shanghai Xing Bao. the first Chinese newspaper in Shanghai that was founded in 1861, with its entire volumes except the first 44 volumes, hence making the newspaper the only precious collection in the country. Because the Chinese newspapers published during the 1860s could hardly be found either at home and abroad, the above collection has an extremely high historical value. Besides, it keeps in their entirety the earliest newspapers run by the Chinese themselves in Shanghai - Hui Bao, Hui Bao, Yi Bao and Xing Bao, all of which were founded during 1870s and could hardly be seen elsewhere. As to the influential newspapers such as Shi Bao, Zhong Wai Ri Bao and Ming Guo Ri Bao, Shanghai edition, the library also has had a fairly complete collection of them, with only very few numbers missing. In this respect, Shanghai Library surpasses all the other libraries in the country. Besides, the library has in store a rich collection of newspapers published during the early years of the Republic of China, the newspapers circulated in the concessions of Shanghai when the City was occupied by the Japanese invaders during the Anti-Japanese War, and also Shanghai Bao, Bai Hua Ri Bao, Hong Qi Ri Bao etc. that were secretly published by CCP in Shanghai and are extremely precious now. It also stores a very rich amount of foreign newspapers published before 1949. All together, there are 92 different newspapers, including the complete collection of North China Herald in English, North China Daily News (lacking the first half of the year 1864), and Der Ostasiatische in German. The English newspapers that were founded during 1860-70s and the French newspapers founded during 1890s in Shanghai that Shanghai Library owns now have a lot of value, too. The most valuable, however, are the complete collection of all the numbers of the first year of The China Mail, which was founded in Hong Kong in 1842.

Peking Library ranks the second in the storage of newspapers in China. It altogether stores 1800 different newspapers published before the founding of PRC. It is known for its fairly complete collection of the newspapers published and circulated within the area governed by the Northern Warlords. Also, it has the richest storage of the newspapers published within Peking area. Such newspapers as Ya Xi Ya Ri Bao, Xing Ji Yuan Bao, Ming Shi Bao, published by Yuan Shikai [4] and his followers, which can rarely be seen in other libraries of the country, are kept in the Peking Library. Besides, it holds a fairly complete set of Zhong Hua Xing Bao and Cheng Bao in Peking, Guo Ming Gong Bao, Jing Bao edited by Shao Piaoping, She Hui Ri Bao, edited by Ling Baishui, all of which are very important newspapers at the time. As for Jing Hua Ri Bao, Shi Jie Ri Bao, Shun Tian Ri Bao and Chong Qun Qiang Bao that the library keeps, they are also very valuable. The library also keeps some important newspapers published elsewhere in the country. For example, it has fairly complete collection of Guo Wun Bao published in Tienjing, which is really valuable in China and also Da Gong Bao, Tienjing edition, which is

rare. Besides, Peking Library has stored a lot of the important newspaper
Sheng Zhou Ri Bao published in Shanghai and ironically cannot be found now in
various libraries in Shanghai. In addition, it surpasses Shanghai Library in
its storage of a fairly complete collection of Zhong Wai Ri Bao. Furthermore,
the library has in store more than 100 different newspapers published in the
areas controlled by CCP before 1949. These are the newspapers mainly published and circulated in northern and central areas of China.

Nanjing Library is also one of the libraries that keeps a lot of newspapers
published before 1949. It has about 1,000 different newspapers then, especially the ones published after the May 4 Movement in 1919. Of all the newspapers it keeps now, there are fairly complete collections of the newspapers
published by KMT government. It has Zhong Yang Ri Bao published in 15 city
editions, Ming Guo Ri Bao published in 20 city editions, Guo Ming Ri Bao published in 7 different city editions and He Ping Ri Bao published in 9 different city editions etc.. The library has also kept about 150 different newspapers published in the areas controlled by CCP since 1940, especially the
ones in the central area of China. Besides, it has a rich storage of the
enemy newspapers published south of the Yangste River. Of the newspapers
before May 4 Movement that the library stores, the most valuable is Zhi Bao
published by Tienjing Shi Bao Guan.

Some other provincial and municipal libraries that have large collections of
newspapers are Zhongshan Library in Canton, Hubei Provincial Library, Sichuan
Provincial Library, Beipei Library in Chongqing, Hunan Provincial Library,
Luda Municipal Library, etc., each having its own features and local color.
For example, Zhongshan Library in Canton has a rich storage of the newspapers
published in Canton and Hong Kong areas, e.g., Ling Nan Ri Bao, Wei Xing Ri
Bao, Ren Quan Bao, An Ya Bao and Ming Guo Ri Bao (Canton edition),etc., which
cannot normally be found in other libraries. Hubei Provincial Library keeps
the well known Han Bao published in Wuhan area, Da Han Bao, Zhong Hua Ming Gua
Gong Bao which were founded and published during the first uprising in
Wuchang, and many valuable newspapers published during the first co-operation
between CCP and KMT. Sichuan Provincial Library stores the earliest newspapers such as Chengdu Ri Bao, Xi Chu Xing Weng, Sichuan Qun Bao, Chu Bao,
etc.. As for the Beipei Library in Chongqing, it is known for its richest
storage of the newspapers published in the area during Anti-Japanese War.
Hunan Provincial Library has fairly large amount of the newspapers published
in Hunan and Hubei Provinces, especially the rare newspaper Zi Ling Han Bao
founded in 1893. Ludan Municipal Library is characteristic of its fairly
large amount of Japanese newspapers published in the northeast areas; altogether there are more than 100. As for the Chinese newspapers, it surpasses
other libraries in storing a lot of the newspapers published during the early
years of the Republic of China. And the other provincial and municipal libraries have their own features and their own rare collections. Shanxi Provincial Library, for instance, has Jie Fang Ri Bao (Xian Edition) published
during the well-known Xian Incident [5] and Fujian Provincial Library stores
the entire collection of People's Daily published during the Fujuan Incident,
which occurred in November 1933, and which has a high historical value.

Another important source of storage of the newspapers is the libraries in all
the institutes of higher learning (mainly humanities departments), research
institutes of social sciences at country, provincial or municipal levels, and
cultural publishing units. In certain institutes of higher learning, especially the ones with a long history such as Peking University, Fudan University, Nanjing University, Zhongshan University, Wuhan University and Sichuan
University, etc., the newspaper holdings are very rich. In China People's
University, which does not have a long history, the storage is fairly good,

too. Fudan University keeps almost more than 900 different newspapers published before the founding of PRC, most of which are kept in the reference rooms of its department of journalism. The University may be at the top of all the universities of the country in its rich storage of newspapers and among its large collections of newspapers, many are really precious ones, e.g. Ming Li Bao, Zi Ling Hu Bao, Shi Wu Ri Bao, Zhong Wai Ri Bao (lacking the late issues), Li Bao, Mei Ri Yi Bao, Dao Bao, Jing Bao, etc.. Besides, it also keeps the earliest literary newspapers for the purpose of entertainment in Qing Dynasty such as Xiao Ling Bao, You Xi Bao, Shi Jie Fan Hua Bao, etc. Some of the newspapers the library keeps are not systematic, but still have a very high historical value, for example, Guo Wen Bao published after 1911 Revolution, Ya Xi Ya Ri Bao, (Shanghai edition, with its founding issue) published by Yuan Shikai in Shanghai, Ming Hu Ri Bao and Ming Yu Ri Bao published by Yu Youren, Ming Quan Bao published by Dai Jitao, women's newspaper Lao Dong Yu Fu Nu run by Canton Communist group, the first newspaper for workers such as Lao Dong Zhou Kan and Gong Ren Zhou Kan published by CCP, etc. The Di Bao kept by the reference rooms of the journalism department of China People's University, which was published during the reign of Emperor Qian Long of the Qing Dynasty, is the earliest ancient newspaper that we have today. The department also keeps a rich variety of other newspapers as well. As for the research institutes, the department of the recent Chinese history of the Chinese Academy of Social Sciences has the richest storage of newspapers. Among the cultural publishing units, the library attached to Shanghai Dictionary Publishing House (formerly the library of Zhong Hua Publishing House) has the richest storage of newspapers. At the same time, newspaper publishing houses at central, provincial and municipal levels have also kept a large amount of newspapers. Because a lot of these come from the party newspapers of CCP in the area, the newspapers that these publishing houses store are mostly the newspapers published in the base areas during the Anti-Japanese War or in the liberated areas during the Liberation War. The reference room of the People's Daily for example, stores many party newspapers of CCP published in the northern China area such as Xing Hua Ri Bao (North China edition). The reference room of Da Zhong Ri Bao keeps not only the complete set of Da Zhong Ri Bao but also a lot of party newspapers of CCP circulating in Shandong Province.

Besides these, museums, memorial halls and archives halls for the revolution at central, provincial and municipal levels are another important source of storing newspapers. The main characteristic of the storage of these places is that they mainly store CCP party newspapers, newspapers led or published by the CCP and other revolutionary newspapers. After 1956, these newspapers were sent to Peking in great number, hence, making the Central Museum of Revolution, Central Archival Hall and some other central institutes places with extremely rich holdings of CCP party newspapers and other revolutionary ones. They are unsurpassed by other places for their storage of newspapers. However, the museums, memorial halls and archival halls of revolution in various provinces and municipalities still keep the CCP party newspapers and other revolutionary newspapers in the locality. Anhui Museum of Revolution, for instance, stores the first newspaper Anhui Chuan published by the revolutionaries af the Anhui Provinces after the first Wuchang Uprising and a newspaper published soon afterwards - Jun Bao. Besides, it keeps a lot of newspapers published in the base areas of Jiangsu and Anhui provinces during the Anti-Japanese War, among which there are the well-known Kang Di Bao (and northern Jiangsu edition) and Fou Xiao Bao published by New Fourth Army and the small-sized newspaper Huang Shan Bao (including the special issues) published by CCP-led guerilla at the southern Anhui Province during 1947-1949. Canton Museum of Revolution, for another instance, stores the patriotic newspaper Shu Bao published at the end of the Qing Dynasty, Shi Jie Gaong Yi Bao edited by Zheng Guangong and the newspapers edited and published by CCP in

Canton and Hong Kong areas. The memorial hall for Nanchang Uprising in Jiangxi Province has in store Nanchang Ming Guo Ri Bao, which carried the pronouncements and documents of the Nanchang Uprising. Some other units among the masses keep certain valuable newspapers of their own. Shanghai General Trade Union, for example, has Shanghai Zhong Gong Hui Ri Kan published during May 30th Movement of 1925 and Shanghai Zhong Gong Hui Wu Ri Kan issued during the armed uprising of Shanghai workers, all of which can hardly be seen in other places and therefore have a very high historical value.

Besides, there could have been some other newspapers kept among the people. The news that some valuable newspapers have been found is often heard. But, it is hard to estimate how many we do have in this way.

So far as we know, there are still a lot of very valuable newspapers that have not been found in China. The foreign newspapers published in Canton before the Opium War, various foreign newspapers circulated in China after the Opium War, the earliest Chinese newspaper Hong Kong Chuan Tou Huo Jia Bao and Xun Huan Ri Bao in Hong Kong, etc., are examples. It should be pointed out that quite a few such newspapers have been found abroad, but still there are considerable numbers of newspapers that have not been seen anywhere. So far as Chinese newspapers are concerned, the undiscovered ones include: Jing Shi Bian Lu founded in Hong Kong in 1864, Zhong Wai Xing Bao and Hua Zi Ri Bao (only one issue found so far) published in their early years in Hong Kong, the first newspaper published by the Chinese themselves in China Zhao Wen Ri Bao, the earliest newspaper published in Canton by the Chinese Guang Bao, and Shangh Wu Bao and Da Jiang Bao that are known for their advocacy of anti-Qing revolution. On the other hand, we keep some precious newspapers, but they are quite incomplete. Take Xun Huan Ri Bao edited by Wang Tao for example. From its founding issue in January 1874 to 1879, we have only a few dozens of its issues since No.82. Of the first newspaper attached to Xing Zhong Hui Zhong Guo Ri Bao, we now lack its issues during its beginning years of publication. As for the well-known Guo Ming Ri Ri Bao, only a little more than ten issues can be seen. And we have only a couple of issues from Shi Bao published in Tienjing and Wei Xing Ri Bao issued in Hong Kong. The storage of newspapers became better after May 4 Movement. But, because of the large amount of the newspapers, some valuable newspapers still could not be preserved due to the bad printing condition and paper quality. For example, the earliest workers' newspapers Ji Qi Gong Ren and You Shi Hua Bao, Jing Han Lu Ri Kan edited by Xiang Ying for the Great Strike along Peking-Hankou Railway, KMT Nanchang Branch newspaper Guan Che Ri Bao during the first revolutionary war period and Hong Qi Bao founded by Yun Daiying for the preparation of Canton Uprising, etc., can nowhere be found today. There are more cases of incomplete collections. As for the ancient newspapers, what we have now in greatest quantity are Jing Bao, (including Gong Meng Chao and Yu Zhe Hui Chun etc.) published during the reign of Emperor Guang Xu. The newspapers before Guang Xu are seldom seen. The earliest ancient newspaper that can be seen is probably Di Bao published during the reign of Emperor Qian Long.

It is a tough problem how to preserve well the newspapers that we have already stored. There are many problems, the chief one confronting us now being the prevention of newspapers from turning yellow and brittle and therefore becoming broken. In recent years, because there are more and more readers for newspapers, the damage of newspapers becomes more and more serious. On the other hand, although some newspapers are not used often, they still become "crumbling". The phenomenon occurred not only to the Xing Wen Bao published at the end of the Qing Dynasty, but also to Dao Bao, published durign the the Anti-Japanese War. They all turned yellow and became brittle. Things became better in some large libraries where stack condition was improved and certain measures were taken such as moist-proof or light-proof measures. But many libraries try to prevent newspapers from damage by stopping or limiting their circulation. Shanghai Library, for instance, has in store more than 3600 different newspapers, but right now only about 100 are in normal circulation. This creates a lot of problems for the readers. To solve the problem, therefore, photocopy is introduced in some places. Owing to the limitation of certain conditions, photocopy of newspapers does not progress quickly. Up to now, we have photocopied about 30 different newspapers, including <u>Jie Fang Ri Bao</u> (Yanan edition), <u>Xing Hua Ri Bao</u> Yanan edition), <u>Peoples Daily</u> (Shanxi-Hebei-Shandong-Hubei edition), <u>Dong Bei Ri Bao</u>, <u>Ming Guo Ri Bao</u>, (Shanghai edition), <u>Ming Guo Ri Bao</u>, (Canton edition), <u>Da Gon Bao, Sheng Jing Bao</u> and the fairly comprehensive <u>Sheng Bao</u>. The work of photocopying is still continuing at present. In order to save as early as possible the heritage of newspapers and to solve the contradiction between the storage of newspapers and the reference needs of the readers, the Ministry of Culture in 1984 asked libraries across the country to form a centre for reproduction of newspapers, whose duty is to make microfilm copies of a group of important newspapers. To 1986, we have done 277 different newspapers and it needs another two years before we finish the job. On the other hand, because of the price for the microfilm of the newspapers (more than 100 yuan RMB per roll), they do not sell well. Besides, the reading machines in China now are not of very good quality and are not convenient for use. All this adds to the failure of microfilming to fulfil the due role it should have played.

It is still a serious task for us how to preserve well the newspapers. The facilities and the management in many libraries in China have been improved a lot, but to deal with those yellow and brittle newspapers, those newspaper of very poor paper quality, especially the ones printed on earthen papers during the Anti-Japanese War or those papers containing a lot of acid, we still feel our technical inefficiency. The situation becomes worse for the libraries in the grass-root units. Because of these problemsd, China is much in need of some advanced technology and experience from our foreign friends. We also very much hope to establish relations with various countries for the exchange of information regarding newspaper reproduction and microfilm materials.

REFERENCES

1   The Chinese bourgeois democratic revolution led by Dr. Sun Yat-sen which overthrew the Qing Dynasty.

2   A major strategic retreat of the Red Army led by CCP from 1934-35.

3   A branch of CCP-led armed forces during the Anti-Japanese War.

4   Yuan Shikai was originally one of the Northern Warlords and later stole political power from Dr Sun Yat-sen after 1911 Revolution.

5   An incident in 1935, when two of Chiang Kai-chek's generals, during his visit to Xian, imprisoned him and forced him to agree to stop the civil war and to resist the Japanese invasion.

NEWSPAPER PRESERVATION AND ACCESS IN DENMARK: A BRIEF SURVEY

Svend LARSEN

Vicedirector (Act.), State and University Library, Aarhus, Denmark

1. INTRODUCTION

The National Newspaper Collection (Statens Avissamling) is the main collection of newspapers in Denmark. The collection was established by an act of the Danish Parliament in 1916. It is part of the State and University Library in Aarhus (Statsbiblioteket). The State and University Library, which was founded in 1902 as the first academic library outside the capital, is the second legal deposit library in Denmark (next to the Royal Library). The State and University Library has a number of national functions, inter alia in the field of mass media. Recently, it has been commissioned to build up new national archives for Danish radio and TV records.

The National Newspaper Collection has the most complete collection of Danish newspapers. All Danish newspapers are received in pursuance of legal deposit act. The collection is complete from c.1820 and comprises approx. 78,000 bound volumes. Scarcely half of the collection is available on microfilm. The most complete collection of the earliest Danish newspapers (late 17th century - early 19th century) is to be found in The Royal Library and The University Library of Copenhagen.

In The National Newspaper Collection there are also foreign newspapers to a small extent, but the following survey will only deal with Danish newspapers.

2. MICROFILMING

Since 1976 microfilming of all current Danish Newspapers has been effected. The filming takes place in co-operation between the State and University Library and a private company, Minerva Mikrofilm. The State and University Library films 60 newspapers and 16 local editions, while Minerva films 15 newspapers and 3 local editions. In the State and University Library approx. 280,000 exposures (negatives) are made yearly. On an average, 4.8 copies (positives) are made from each negative. The newspaper films are sold to public and academic libraries, newspapers, and local archives. In the State and University Library the sales profit covers the filming costs.

In filming the ISO standards are used. Technical control of the films is according to a simplified version of the standards. This control is now under consideration.

Silver films are used. As relatively few distribution copies are made of the films produced in the State and University Library, it is considered unnecessary to produce both archival film and master. The archival films are stored under stable climatic conditions in basement store. After filming the newspapers have been bound up to now. But as the originals are only used in a few exceptional cases, the binding has now been stopped (primarily for reasons of economy). After filming the newspapers are wrapped in strong, acid-free paper and stored flat.

The current microfilming project was started on the initiative of the Newspaper Committee of the Danish academic libraries. This committee was reorganized in 1986 and now belongs under the newly established Office of the National Librarian.

The Newspaper Committee is a consultative body. In addition to representatives for the Office of the National Librarian and the legal deposit libraries there are representatives for users from the public and academic libraries buying the newspaper films.

At present, the Newspaper Committee is working on a project for <u>retrospective</u> filming of Danish newspapers before 1976, when the current filming started. Earlier newspapers have been microfilmed to a certain extent, usually on a commercial basis. Thus some of the major metropolitan newspapers have been microfilmed to a great extent. But only <u>approximately half</u> of the Danish newspapers are available in microfilm. In Denmark, just like in other countries, newspapers are the type of material most liable to vanish. This applies particularly to the newspapers from the period, c. 1880-1920, when the paper quality was specially bad.

In Danish libraries it is the generally accepted view that microfilming is the most effective method for <u>preservation</u> of the contents of the newspapers for posterity. Simultaneously, microfilming permits an improved <u>access</u> to this material, which is used very much. As far as newspapers are concerned, the use of other methods of preservation (e.g. deacidification) has not been considered.

Both regard for preservation and improved access requires initiation of <u>systematic</u> microfilming of <u>all</u> Danish newspapers. There is no financial basis for starting up a large microfilming programme, but plans of starting up on a small scale are now being worked out. (The preliminary object of planning is equipment and staff for 250,00 exposures a year). With financial support from the Ministry of Cultural Affairs filming of the newspapers most in danger of vanishing could presumably start in 1988. It is planned to place the retrospective filming in the State and University Library, which houses the National Newspaper Collection, and which has experience from the current filming.

Most of the early newspapers have been bound, and in order to obtain good results of the filming, cutting of the volumes is necessary. This process makes rather heavy demands for manpower, as machines can only be used on a limited scale. The original newspapers will be preserved, as the loose newspaper pages will be wrapped in strong, acid-free paper. For newspapers on microfilm it is already now the rule that the original papers are only used in quite special cases.

As is the case in filming the current newspapers, the films will be sold, and the profit will probably contribute to financing a continued retrospective filming.

3. USE AND ACCESS

Newspapers are very much used, both in academic research and by the public in general. In Denmark, access to the newspapers is rather easy. This is due to the fact that comparatively many Danish newspapers are microfilmed, including some national newspapers. Furthermore, many public libraries have collections of local papers within their own area.

Last, but not least, in this connection there is reason to mention the special collection of press cuttings in the State and University Library. It was started in 1940 and includes feature articles, signed articles and book, film, music and theatrical reviews from a number of Danish newspapers. In the beginning, the cuttings were registered in a special index, which was published monthly. Since 1979 this index is integrated in the Danish periodical index, which registers articles in Danish newspapers and periodicals. This index is accessible in monthly booklets, the review part however is only in microfiche. In the near future, the index will be accessible online. The cuttings are collected and registered by the Danish Library Bureau, an independent institution giving bibliographical and technical assistance to Danish public libraries on a commercial basis. The collection of press cuttings is run by the State and University Library in the capacity of Danish centre for interlibrary loans. Borrowers apply direct or through their public library. Loans from the collection are effected in the form of free photocopies of the cuttings (in 1986 69,000 copies).

4. BIBLIOGRAPHICAL CONTROL

In Denmark preservation, at first in the form of binding, later in the form of microfilming, has been given a higher priority than bibliographical description of the newspapers.

In The National Newspaper Collection there is a preliminary index of the collection with specification of stock, and the Newspaper Collection also publishes a current list of Danish newspapers on microfilm ('Newspapers on Microfilm in Aarhus State and University Library', ed. K. Munck, 12th ed. 1986). There are several indexes of the contents of newspapers. In addition to the index of the press cuttings collection mentioned earlier there is the Danish News Yearbook (Avisårbogen, 1924 ff), which is a chronological summary of the events of the year in Denmark and abroad collected from articles in Danish newspapers (with index by name and subject). Furthermore, card indexes have been made of several national newspapers in certain periods (e.g. Berlingske Tidende 1864-1918 and Politiken 1884-1924; transfer of these indexes to microfiche is being considered).

However, a comprehensive bibliography of Danish newspapers has been wanted for a long time. It is therefore gratifying to learn that a major handbook of Danish newspapers is being prepared at present. The project is supported by State Research Councils and Danish daily papers. The handbook will contain detailed information on all newspapers in Denmark (incl. Norway until 1814, the West Indies until 1917, Iceland until 1919, etc.). In addition to bibliographic description and stock information it will contain information on editors, ownership, politics, economy etc.. The handbook is prepared by researchers attached to The Institute of Economic History, University of Copenhagen (Prof. Dr. Niels Thomsen and Jette Sollinge). The first volume is being printed.

5. SUMMARY

It is not fair to say that Danish newspapes have been treated as "stepchildren" in Danish libraries.

A national newspaper collection was established at a comparatively early stage. Large parts of the contents of Danish newspapers since 1940 are currently registered and lent through a special press cuttings collection in the State and University Library.

For more than a decade cuurent filming of Danish newspapers has taken place. Almost half of the Danish newspapers are estimated to be on microfilm. For reasons of preservation starting up a systematic filming of the newspapers not yet filmed, is urgently required. A minor project for retrospective filming will presumably start in 1988.

A long-desired comprehensive bibliography of Danish newspapers is in preparation.

NATIONAL APPROACHES TO NEWSPAPER PRESERVATION: THE FEDERAL REPUBLIC OF GERMANY

Wilbert H UBBENS

Official responsible for Communication, Theatre literature, Newspapers, Staats- und Universitätsbibliothek, Bremen

1. COLLECTION DEVELOPMENT

Newspaper collections in German libraries and archives - as in most countries - are based on two fundamentally different principles of collection development: they have been developed either on the strength of an interest in the contents of newspapers or on the basis of formal legal requirements. By interest in newspaper contents we may understand a broad spectrum of interest in political-historical information, current daily news, cultural/educational interest and regional/local information, leading to acquisition by donation or by a take-over of existing collections. Collections of this type in general research libraries mostly comprise the representative newspapers of the Federal Republic of Germany and some foreign 'prestige papers' as well as some regional and local papers from the library's locality. In addition some copies of papers are kept for display in reading rooms but are not destined for permanent preservation. In public libraries the current collections are mostly, for financial reasons, not very comprehensive.

These rather rudimentary collections stand in contrast to the collection and preservation of newspapers in accordance with the legal deposit regulations for the Länder of the Federal Republic and for the Federation itself. Most Länder, in accordance with para 12 of their press laws, provide for the deposit of printed publications by publishers/printers to certain libraries, albeit in different ways. The scale of provision runs from mere obligation to offer for commercial purchase (e.g. Berlin) to free deposit of several copies in different libraries (e.g. Schleswig-Holstein). The legal deposit legislation which has grown historically from the printing privilege of princes is the only basis for the collection of newspapers appearing in the Federal Republic, a collection which is only in principle comprehensive and complete. Only total and continuous collection in the regional copyright libraries can ensure the passing on to posterity of our daily press.

The growing collection of deposit copies in the Deutsche Bibliothek in Frankfurt is based on a legal ruling which provides expressly for selection among the newspapers. At the moment the Deutsche Bibliothek collects over 300 newspapers from the Federal Republic, albeit only on microfilm, while the regional copyright libraries have in principle to preserve the original paper copies (cf. Appendix 1).

The practical management of newspaper collections in copyright libraries varies according to the legal mandate and the consequent regulations, so, for example, not all editions of a newspaper may always be fully collected, but sometimes only their variant (local) parts. It has never been easy to recognize these variant parts with certainty and place them together, now the development of printing technology in recent years has removed a clearcut distinction between main and local editions. To ensure complete coverage all editions of newspapers have therefore to be collected in their entirety; this also applies to the successive editions of one day (e.g. as long-distance, postal edition or local edition with a later copy-deadline). Library practice is not, however, consistent on this very point; in the main only one edition is collected, either the postal or courier edition, although the variation between editions is evident and known.

The emphasis on the duty of copyright libraries to acquire a complete set of the newspapers appearing in the area for which they are responsible and to preseve them in the original is all the more understandable and urgent because there cannot be any expectation of this being done anywhere else: the Deutsche Bibliothek collects newspapers selectively and only on microfilm; local and state archives have duties other than the collection of newspapers, although complete runs of newspapers are kept there; publishers' archives are moving away from the preservation of their own newspapers long-term, linked as they are to the economic fate of the publishing house. Local public libraries often collect local papers, but no longer collect and preserve extra editions not concerning their town. The continuous collection of the regional press would be expected in those regional libraries which were, from the regional point of view, formerly copyright libraries of historical, now non-existent, Länder and provinces. However, these are the very libraries which are now suffering from insufficient financial and accommodation provision, with the result that, unfortunately, complete collections will not longer be developed there.

There are no supra-regional libraries and special libraries in the Federal Republic which could maintain complete collections. Collections in such libraries have to be limited to a selection of newspapers because of the complex multiplicity of historic newspapers and their generally fragmentary nature. Their stock is representative, perhaps, but not complete. As examples one can name the library of the Institute for Newspaper Research in Dortmund (ca 39,000 rolls of film, 1700m of bound volumes) and the State and University Library of Bremen (ca 15,000 film rolls, 1300m of bound volumes, a total of ca 950 titles) which have built up comprehensive collections of historic German newspapers, mostly on microfilm. Complementary to the comprehensive historic and current holdings of the large copyright libraries, these libraries satisfy a large part of inter-library loan requests for German newspapers.

Studies on the use of newspapers in libraries, which could provide information on the extent to which newspaper stock should be kept in libraries, are not available in the Federal Republic. Therefore, the recommendations for collection development from the Newspaper Committee of the Deutsches Bibliotheksinstitut are based on systematic consideration of supra-regional provision and conservation. In its recommendations the Committee proceeds from the premise that the paper originals of newspapers are kept in copyright libraries. The more positively and unequivocally this is regulated and executed, the easier it is for the Committee to recommend that all other libraries should as a rule collect and preserve newspapers only on microfilm. Paper copies are so space-consuming in storage and so delicate in their preservation of information that their replacement by microfilm cannot be opposed. If there are no legitimate reasons for the preservation of paper copies then libraries should store them on microfilm instead.

A graded system of preservation can be considered: microfilms of newspapers with national distribution should be available in each inter-library loan region in several copies; newspapers with non-local distribution should be available in each inter-library loan region in only one copy; newspapers with local distribution, including extra editions, should be available on microfilm only in the relevant inter-library loan region. The accessibility of microfilms for inter-library loan is introduced as a criterion here, which in the Federal Republic rests on the principle of regional responsibility for the provision of literature. The reality of newspaper collections is far from the recommendations outlined here; these should however be guidelines for the acquisition of microfilms in libraries and replace the present casualness and shortcomings.

The emphasis placed on the principle of managing the collection of newspapers outside copyright libraries as a collection of microfilms should not lead us to discard or destroy the paper copies which have been replaced by microfilms without further ado. Before such a step is taken there must be a careful review of whether and where the relevant newspapers are available and whether a paper copy is preserved in the relevant copyright library. The principle of only keeping a paper copy commits us to a careful examination and consideration of other interests and other collections. Microfilm editions of historic newspapers can only be treated as replacements for paper originals if they are the same edition and are at least as complete as the paper copy destined for relegation. In spite of the recognition of the historically nurtured character of newspaper collections, fragmentary collections of paper copies should be offered to other libraries with more complete collections of the relevant newspaper.

On 11 July 1986 the Research Council presented its recommendations for the storage needs of research libraries in which it recommended, on the grounds of the space needs of library storage, the concentration of 'non-essential' material in a few libraries with archival responsibility which will be set up. This concerns firstly collections of periodicals and newspapers. For newspapers it recommends the deposit of the originals in a 'regionally responsible' archival library after microfilming and also the fulfilment of inter-library loan requests by microfilm copies kept there. Furthermore, the Research Council recommends that no duplicate collections should be kept in the archival library. Given that the provision of historic newspaper collections is exceedingly bad as a result of the war and earlier restrictive collection policies, no collection of a historic newspaper title corresponds with another of the same title and only in the rarest cases do they cover anything approaching a complete set of the editions of their period. Experiences in retrospective microfilming of newspapers as collected by the libraries co-operating in the microfilm archive of the German language press since 1965 illustrate this only too clearly. Because of the possible careless or incorrect declaration of collections as duplicates, newspaper collections in the so-called archival libaries or already in the holding libraries could be liable to destruction on the basis of these recommendations. Newspapers are too valuable and rare a posession to be exposed to this danger. Their microfilming serves to increase stock and to protect the paper originals, it is no grounds for the destruction of the originals.

In addition and without regard for the interest in the permanent preservation of newspapers, paper copies which act as users' copies should be kept for current information in library reading rooms and are not to be stored. Likewise with the copyright libraries which must make available for use microfilms of their newspapers which are preserved in the original, provided that reader interest is above the minimum.

The guidelines outlined for the development of collections of German newspapers in libraries apply also analogously to foreign newspapers. The interest of libraries is directed mostly only at the acquisition of a few so-called prestige papers; more comprehensive regionally oriented stocks are only to be found in a few large (specialist) libraries. A formal commitment to collect the foreign press in as far as it is not already collected elsewhere is undertaken by the Staatsbibliothek Preussischer Kulturbesitz. With financial help from the Deutsche Forschungsgemeinschaft some 800 foreign papers are acquired currently on microfilm in the main. As this capacity is not sufficient to build up a comprehensive collection, the remaining libraries are requested to co-ordinate the acquisition of foreign newspapers with the Staatsbibliothek Preussischer Kulturbesitz. A list of foreign newspaper desiderata, requests for which could not be met via inter-library loan, is maintained there. Analysis of this list can reveal not only individual gaps but also structural defects in collection development. Foreign newspapers as a rule should be preserved on microfilm; paper copies are only to be kept for current information in the library's reading room.

2. CATALOGUES

The historically based decentralised collection of newspapers is accompanied by bibliographic attempts to describe holdings and to bring them together in local and supra-regional catalogues. Incomplete library catalogues and the ravages of World War 2 have rendered all previous efforts to build up national catalogues for selected collections fruitless. A first step towards inter-regional co-operation, a questionnaire by the then German University of Strasbourg about newspaper holdings, was lost as a result of World War 1. A short survey of 'Newspaper collections and locations in Germany' by Walther Heide and a first 'Location catalogue of important newspaper collections in German libraries' by Hans Traub from the years 1928 to 1933 is now unusable due to the destruction and political change of World War 2. The attempt by the librarian Hans Jessen to compile a 'Union catalogue of the German press' in the fifties at the Staatsbibliothek Bremen came to nothing due to lack of resources and support. The upshot of this enterprise was two reference tools which are still today the most sought after for German newspapers: the card index of locations for the German press, maintained by the Staats- und Universitätsbibliothek Bremen, and the locations index 'German newspaper holdings in libraries and archives' by Gert Hagelweide published in 1974. Hagelweide has during many years' work at the Staatsbibliothek Bremen brought together holdings information for 2018 newspaper publishers in 579 libraries. The Bremen location catalogue lists ca 58,000 titles but can, however, not give locations and larger holdings for all titles, so that information for loan purposes must be put at about 20,000 titles.

New initiatives are moving away from special newspaper catalogues to general periodicals listings, such as those arising from inter-regional co-operation among a growing number of libraries. The serials database of the Deutsches Bibliotheksinstitut lists the newspaper holdings of 60 libraries which cover more than 200 lending libraries (as of 1985). The catalogue is published annually on microfiche and is also available on-line. This is an indispensable listing based on voluntary contributions from the co-operating libraries. However, as library catalogues often list newspapers inadequately or incorrectly, many holdings have not been entered on the serials database. The real situation concerning information about newspapers must still be described as follows: there are indeed supra-regional catalogues, they are, however, incomplete and based on insufficient information. The fact that the inadequate state of library catalogues is recognised and accepted as a responsibility is evident from the continued efforts to build up local newspaper catalogues fresh from the autopsy.

3. USE

The reading of individual numbers of newspapers from current display can be regarded as an unproblematical instance of newspaper usage in libaries. All that is needed is to ensure that genuinely usable copies are available for use, that there are sufficient copies and titles and that copying machines are assigned directly to the newspaper reading room, so that attempts to misappropriate newspapers are kept to the minimum.

As regards the use of archival bound newspapers one can proceed from the assumption that newspaper volumes are not lent to users but are only available in the reading room. Reading rooms for newspaper use, i.e. with large enough reading tables and sufficient room to put the volumes down, will not be provided in all libraries. In general, one can assume that newspaper volumes will not be copied directly (because of handling problems and damage to the paper by intensive light and heat). But already the inadequate supply of photographic workshops where the copies can be produced from intermediate negatives increases the probability of a softening of the ban on direct copying. Libraries which keep paper originals must ensure that, in the interests of preservation of their stock, there is no copying from bound volumes: reproductions should only be produced photographically from an interim negative. If material and personnel resources do not allow this, then photographic commissions should be done outside. Libraries must provide readers and readerprinters for the use of microfilms. With the provision of such equipment users can make the desired copies from the microfilms themselves.

Newspaper usage is characterised by the reader's desire to wish to look through complete runs for particular subject matter. There will be borderline cases where, in the interests of readers, consideration must be given to whether perusal of microfilm is reasonable, whether the numerous volumes required are to be transported to the reading room or whether the reader can be allowed access to the newspaper stacks. Information about newspaper contents by means of printed indexes or on-line databases helps to limit such extensive use of newspaper holdings to the few cases in which the use of the originals is unavoidable for systematic shcolarly research such as quantitative content analysis in the social sciences. Only when use of the original is to be kept to the minimum by the availabiity of all possible aids will the reader have to be told to travel to more distant libraries and library depositories.

In all other cases the inter-library loan service of the library should be able to help the reader get hold of requested newspaper articles which cannot be found in the library. Inter-library loan regulations envisage the supply of the newspaper article to the reader in photocopy. Requests for complete volumes are not as a rule fulfilled because of the unwieldiness of the volumes and the danger of damage to them. On the other hand microfilms available for use in libraries can be lent as complete rolls to be read in the reading room of the requesting library. Microfilms are only subject to loan restrictions if they are original silver film and not (diazo) copy film commercially produced or produced for one's own use. These can only be lent if the production of a further copy (paper copy) for the requester is not possible or feasible because of the extent of the order.

Long distance loan requests are passed to the nearest holding library subject to the regional principle. If the newspaper requested or part requested is not listed in printed or other accessible catalogues, the requests are sent to the appropriate specialist central catalogue: in the case of German newspapers this is the locations catalogue of the German press at the Staats- und Universitätsbibliothek Bremen, in the case of foreign newspapers to the locations index of foreign newspapers and serials at the Staatsbibliothek Preussischer Kulturbesitz Berlin. The special central catalogue in Bremen can be consulted for newspapers from libraries in the German Democratic Republic. The special central catalogues are responsible for forwarding loan forms. It should be possible for them to identify incorrect requests which cannot therefore be met and return them to the requester. They also exercise editorial functions by completing and correcting inexact requests (e.g. changes of title among others). They are also the starting point for international library loans.

4. EXPLOITATION

Exploitation of the subject content of newspapers does not as a rule take place in libraries, if one ignores some efforts by public libraries to develop regional or current reference tools with the help of newspaper cuttings. Analysis and indexing are the domain of private and public archives which have set up thematic collections of cuttings.

The "Handbook of press archives" by Hans Bohrmann and Marianne Englert gives detailed information about this in its description of 266 such archives and their collections. Editorial archives exploit their papers traditionally by means of cuttings collections which can only be used on the spot. Until now only the economic section of the Frankfurter Allgemeine Zeitung, the Handelsblatt and the Wirtschaftswoche, important newspaper sources for economics and commerce, are available via on-line databases. Economics is also the basis of the most comprehensive publically accessible newspaper cuttings collections, those of the HWWA-Institute for Economic Research in Hamburg and the Institute for World Economics in Kiel, with over 14 million and 9 million cuttings available respectively. Both institutions have been operating with somewhat different missions since 1908 and 1920 respectively in the field of economics and foreign economics and are available wihout restrictions, while the next largest collection, comprising c.12 million press cuttings, that of the Press and Information Office of the Federal government in Bonn, serves first and foremost the government machine.

Published bibliographies of newspaper contents and indexes of individual papers do not meet the immediate standard of an active press documentation but do have the advantage of information which is independent of place. There are no printed indexes of individual daily papers, except for the economic section of the Frankfurter Allgemeine Zeitung and the Handelsblatt; the weekly magazines Der Spiegel and Stern publish their own indexes, the Spiegel since 1947 and Stern since 1983. But there is a tradition of overlapping national newspaper indexes (for the years 1909 to 1944 and since 1974). The "Newspaper index" of Willi Gorzny covers almost 20 frequently archived daily and weekly papers without subject restrictions and meets a frequently expressed user need in indexing book reviews. The willingness to co-operate on the part of publishers' archives and the Institute for Newspaper Research in Dortmund makes it possible for interested persons to order copies of the indexed newspaper article from them. Gorzny has limited his bibliographic work to a relatively small number of press organs, whereas the "Half monthly index to articles in German newspapers" covers up to 100 papers from 1909 to 1944. In this small number one can see not so much an expression of the necessary regard for the expenditure of a commercial enterprise as a reflection of the change in the press landscape of the Empire and Weimar Republic to the present day. Gorzny only takes account of original contributions (contributions by the editorial staff) which are to be found in fewer and fewer papers on account of the increase in agency output and the contributions of journalists working for several papers. On average 6-7 articles are analysed per issue; the intention is less a complete exploitation of the newspaper than coverage of a broad subject scenario by a few newspaper articles. This selection criterion is demonstrated by the large number of subject key words (e.g. names) with only a few articles assigned which hardly permits a comparison of the treatment of the subject in different papers. It is doubtful to what extent this selection criterion corresponds to the prevailing search requirements of users, as with a numerically small selection of indexed newspapers, an indication of the reporting profile of these papers would still be possible and desirable. The "Newspaper index" inclines towards those archival publications which amalgamate agency and press reports to offer information about historic events or persons, institutions etc.. A second criticism of the "Newspaper index" lies in the delay of the provision of reports which can no longer correspond to current interests. A forthcoming financial grant renews our hope for a more up-to-date compilation.

5. CONSERVATION OF STOCK

Because of the rare and fragmentary nature of our inheritance of historic newspapers, the result of a lack of interest by libraries in the collecting of newspapers and of World War 2 damage, the practical interests of those libraries which are interested in newspaper conservation have been directed from an early stage away from their own efforts at restoration towards stock improvement by microfilming. As the remaining stock has to be protected from too intensive use it is not only a case of preserving the paper copies by conservation methods but of switching use away from them to microfilm and increasing the number of newspaper copies in libraries by the spread of microfilm copies. In 1965 some libraries and archives with more comprehensive newspaper collections joined forces in a 'Microfilm Archive of the German Language Press' to support the filming of historic papers and to co-ordinate the distribution of microfilms. A considerable number of papers have been filmed by the member libraries and the Microfilm Archive, and have been listed in a union catalogue in 1982 and offered for sale. The associated relations with industry have contributed to the elaboration of standards for the microfilming of newspapers. The standard of the German Institute for Standardisation DIN Norm 19057 'Microfilm technology. Filming of newspapers. Reproduction on 35 mm film' was passed first in 1976 and there is now a 1984 edition; it corresponds essentially to ISO-Standard 4087 'Microfilming of newspapers on 35 mm microfilm ...'. 35 mm microfilm is preferred to microfiche for the filming of large format papers because of its fewer storage problems and the lower reduction factor.

These self-help efforts by libraries have received central support: in 1978 the Deutsche Forschungsgemeinschaft (German Research Association) initiated a programme of assistance for the filming of unique historic newspapers whereby they financed relevant projects in libraries. In 1986 this programme was revived, expanded from unique issues to newspapers of general historical value and increased considerably from the financial point of view. Up until now over 50 projects of varying size have been supported with more than 2.2 million DM: it will be continued over several years. In this programme special attention has been paid to the important role of inter-library lending of microfilms by producing two copies of the film.

Care is taken to ensure that only these copies go into use while the original (master) films are stored and excluded from use. The Federal government has supported independently, within its programme of the preservation of cultural assets, the filming of newspapers in public archives in the interests of safeguarding them.

International efforts to develop techniques for the preservation of mechanical wood pulp papers have also been echoed in the Federal Republic and different research projects have been initiated. Discussion on the application of particular procedures to the mass restoration of newspapers is not yet complete. Well known deacidification processes do not seem to be very suitale for various reasons; an essential barrier would have to be the decentralised independence of the Länder in cultural matters with the consequent difficulties in financing supra-regional projects. Up until now the crucial initiative for further development and practical testing under library conditions appears to be lacking. Attempts by the Newspaper Committee of the Deutsches Bibliotheksinstitut to bring discussion before the library public at the Librarians' Conference in 1985 are too weak to give the necessary impulse. Perhaps the formation of a special committee for stock conservation in the Deutsches Bibliotheksinstitut in Spring 1987 will enable progress to be made. The initiation of a study on mass conservation by the Federal Ministry for Research and Technology gives hope for further progress.

Perhaps the point in the discussion about the conservation of newspaper collections has been reached where further neglect and disregard of these long undervalued library materials will no longer be tolerated. If the Newspaper Committee of the Deutsches Bibliotheksinstitut has been able to play a small part in this development then the efforts of the circle of interested colleagues will have been worth it. Work with newspapers has been for many years in Germany the privilege - or hobby - of only a few librarians. The flow of their efforts into far reaching and overlapping endeavours in the preservation and exploitation of library materials can however not absolve interested colleagues from seeking ways of improving library work with newspapers and seeing these improvements through.

APPENDIX 1

CURRENT COLLECTION OF LEGAL DEPOSIT COPIES OF NEWSPAPERS IN LIBRARIES

Baden-Wurttemberg	Karlsruhe, Badische Landesbibliothek: 118 titles Stuttgart, Württembergische Landesbibliothek: 183
Bavaria	Munich, Bayerische Staatsbibliothek: 256
Berlin	Amerika-Gedenkbibliothek: 18 Freie Universitätsbibliothek: 8
Bremen	Staats- und Universitätsbibliothek: 9
Hamburg	Staats- und Universitätsbibliothek: 21
Hesse	Darmstadt, Hessische Landes- und Hochschulbibliothek: 80 Frankfurt, Stadt- und Universitätsbibliothek: 18 Fulda, Hessische Landesbibliothek: 2 Wiesbaden, Hessische Landesbibliothek: 49
Lower Saxony	Hannover, Niedersachsische Landesbibliothek: 98

North-Rhine Westphalia	Bonn, Universitätsbibliothek: 65 Munster, Universitätsbibliothek: 161
Rhineland-Pfalz	Mainz, Stadtbibliothek: 14 Speyer, Pfalzische Landesbibliothek: 15 Trier, Stadtbibliothek: 2
Saarland	Saarbrucken, Universitätsbibliothek: 37
Schleswig-Holstein	Kiel, Schleswig-Holsteinische Landesbibliothek: 59 Lübeck, Stadtbibliothek: 7

Complementary supra-regional collection
Frankfurt, Deutsche Bibliothek: 345 (inc 37 from GDR)on microfilm

APPENDIX 2   BIBLIOGRAPHY
(Titles mentioned in the text and other literature)

1. Collections and anthologies

'Das Angebot von Zeitungen auf Mikroformen. Referate des Seminars vom 23 März 1976'. Dortmund, Mikrofilmarchiv der deutschsprachigen Presse, 1976. 63pp.

'Die Zeitung auf Mikrofilm. Referate anlässlich des am 7 März 1972 in Bonn durchgeführten Seminars'. Düsseldorf, Agfa-Gevaert, Fachabt. Mikrokopie; Dortmund, Mikrofilmarchiv der deutschsprachigen Presse, 1972. 29pp.

Englert, Marianne and Mantwill, Gerhard (compilers), 'Dokumentation in Presse und Rundfunk. 25 Jahre Fachgruppe Presse-, Rundfunk- und Filmarchivare im Verein deutscher Archivare. Protokoll ...'. München, Saur, 1985. 250pp. (Presse-, Rundfunk- und Filmarchive, Mediendokumentation, 6).

Hagelweide, Gert, (editor), 'Mikroformen und Bibliothek'. München, Verl. Dokumentation, 1977. 471 pp.

Hagelweide, Gert, 'Zeitung und Bibliothek. Ein Wegweiser zu Sammlungen und Literatur'. Pullach, Verl. Dokumentation, 1974. 302pp.

Höfig, Willi, and Ubbens, Wilbert, (editors), 'Kooperationsmöglichkeiten für Zeitungssammelstellen'. Berlin, Deutscher Bibliotheksverband, 1978. 201pp. (AfB-Materialien, 23).

Höfig, Willi, and Ubbens, Wilbert, (editors) for the Zeitungskommission des Deutschen Bibliotheksinstituts, 'Zeitung in Bibliotheken. Bericht uber ein Stiefkind, mit notwendigen Empfehlungen'. Berlin, Deutsches Bibliotheksinstitut DBI, 1986. 388pp. (DBI-Materialien, 49).

Mantwill, Gerhard, (editor) 'Medien und Archive. Beiträge zur Rolle moderner Archive in Information und Dokumentation'. Pullach, Verl. Dokumentation, 1974. 348pp.

2. Articles and monographs

Barton, Walter, 'Bibliothek und Zeitung', in: Zeitschrift für Bibliothekswesen und Bibliographie, Vol.10, 1963. pp.1-33.

Bohrmann, Hans, 'Das Institut für Zeitungsforschung der Stadt Dortmund und seine Bestände unter besonderer Berücksichtigung Westfalens', in: Archivpflege in Westfalen und Lippe, Vol.16, 1981, pp.9-16.

Bohrmann, Hans, 'Zur Mikroverfilmung von Zeitungen. Das Mikrofilmarchiv der deutschsprachigen Presse und das Institut für Zeitungsforschung der Stadt Dortmund', in: Der Archivar, Vol.37, no.2, 1984. pp.201-208.

Hagelweide, Gert, 'Die Abteilung "Deutsche Presseforschung" an der Staatsbibliothek Bremen. Geschichte, Stand der Arbeit Möglichkeiten einer Weiterentwicklung'. Hausarbeit für die Prüfung zum höheren Dienst an wiss. Bibliotheken an der Staats- und Universitätsbibliothek Hamburg 1968. IV, 56, X S. (Masch.schr).

Hartmann, Karsten, 'Pressedatenbank: Online-Retrieval und gedruckte Register', in: Nachrichten für Dokumentation, Vol.35, no.4/5, 1984. pp.211-216.

Heide, Walther, 'Zeitungs-Sammlungen und -Sammelstellen in Deutschland. Eine inhaltliche und bibliothekstechnische Übersicht'. Berlin, Staatspolit. Verl. 1928. 28pp.

Hilsenbeck, Adolf, 'Bibliotheken und Zeitungen', in: Zentralblatt für Bibliothekswesen, Vol.37, 1920. pp.214-227.

Höfig, Willi, 'Die Behandlung von Tageszeitungen an Wissenschaftlichen Bibliotheken. Eine bibliothekarische Leitstudie'. Pullach, Verl. Dokumentation 1975. 163pp.

Höfig, Willi, 'Über die Bedeutung des Mikrofilms für Sammlung und Benutzung ausländischer Zeitungen. Das Sondersammelgebiet "Ausländische Zeitungen" an der Staatsbibliothek Preussischer Kulturbesitz Berlin. Nebst: Verzeichnis der Arbeitskopien fremdsprachiger Zeitungen auf Mikrofilm in der Staatsbibliothek Preussischer Kulturbesitz mit Titelverzeichnis und Ortsregister (Stand: Sept 1981)', in: Mikrofilm-Archiv der deutschsprachigen Presse. Bestandsverzeichnis, Vol.6, 1982. pp.37-46, 187-194.

Höfig, Willi, 'Zeitungen im Leihverkehr', in: 'Die Ordnung des Leihverkehrs in der Bundesrepublik Deutschland'. Frankfurt am Main, Klostermann, 1982. pp.110-113.

Höfig, Willi, 'Zeitungspapier und Mikrofilm. Ihre Lebensdauer im bibliothekarischen Betrieb. Literaturübersicht. Berlin, Deutscher Bibliotheksverband, 1979. V, 258pp (AfB-Materialien, 24).

Koura, Adel, 'Neues Verfahren zur Konservierung und Restaurierung von Papier', in: Zeitungstechnik, No.7/8, 1983. pp.10-14.

Hubmann, Heinrich, 'Urheberrechtliche Probleme bei der kooperativen Verfilmung von Zeitungen. Rechtsgutachten erstellt im Auftrag des Deutschen Bibliotheksinstituts'. Berlin, Deutsches Bibliotheksinstitut, 1980. 32pp (DBI-Materialien, 1).

Kekule von Stradonitz, Stephan, 'Über Zeitungsmuseen, in: Zeitschrift für

Bücherfreunde, Vol.N F 1, no.1, 1909. pp.1-18.

Kilger, Otto, 'Das pflichtgemässe Sammeln von Tageszeitungen in Deutschland, Nebst: Standortnachweisen für Sachsen, Thüringen und Anhalt'. Leipzig. Harrassowitz, 1938. VI, 179pp (Zentralblatt fur Bibliothekswesen. Beih. 71) Repr. Nendeln, Kraus, 1968.

Kühn-Ludewig, Maria, 'Zeitungsinhaltserschliessung und wissenschaftliche Bibliotheken. Hausarbeit zur Prüfung fur den höheren Dienst an wissenschaftlichen Bibliotheken'. Koln, Bibliothekar-Lehrinstitut des Landes NRW, 1975. 92 ff (Masch. schr.)

Lent, Dieter, 'Zeitungen in Archiven. Dargestellt aus der Sicht des Staatsarchivs Wolfenbüttel', in: Wolfenbütteler Notizen zur Buchgeschichte, Vol.5, 1980. pp.142-148.

Leonhard, Joachim-Felix, 'Erschliessung von Quellen zur Bibliotheks- und Buchgeschichte sowie Verfilmung historisch wertvoller Zeitungen. 2 neue Förderungsprogramme der Deutschen Forschungsgemeinschaft', (1) in: Bibliotheksdienst, Vol.20, 1986. pp.27-31. (2) in: Der Archivar, Vol.39, no.3, 1986. pp.333-342.

Leudts, Peter, 'Erfassung von Zeitungsbeständen in den Instituten für Publizistik-/Kommunikationswissenschaft'. Berlin, Deutsches Bibliotheksinstitut, 1981. 61ff.

Müller, Günther, 'Zur Massenrestaurierung von zerfallsbedrohtem Schriftgut', in: Zentralblatt für Bibliothekswesen, Vol.94, 1980. pp.226-231.

Müller, Wilfried, 'Presseausschnitte, eine besondere Dokumentationsform', in: 75 Jahre Information HWWA Hamburg. Hamburg, Deutscher Bibliotheksverband, Landesverband Hamburg, 1983. (Auskunft Vol.3, 1983) pp.254-269.

Rohwedder, Erica, 'Die Arbeit mit Zeitungen an der Universitätsbibliothek Bremen'. Hamburg, 1980. 120ff. Anlagen. Hamburg, Fachhochschule Hamburg, Hausarbeit zur Diplom-Prüfung für den Dienst an Öffentlich/wissenschaftlichen Bibliotheken, 1980.

Süle, Gisela, 'Gutachten zum Standortkatalog der deutschsprachigen Presse. Untersuchung uber die Möglichkeit seiner Überführung in die Datenbank des Deutschen Bibliotheksinstituts'. Berlin, Deutsches Bibliotheksinstitut, 1980. 24pp.

Ubbens, Wilbert, 'Zeitungen in Bibliotheken. Zum Stand der Diskussion um ein wenig geliebtes Thema', in: Zeitschrift für Bibliothekswesen und Bibliographie, Vol.27, 1980. pp.365-379.

Wächter, Otto, 'Die Erhaltung von Holzschliffpapieren. Konservierungsmöglichkeiten von Einzelblättern und Zeitungskonvoluten'. Den Haag, IADA 1983. 18 S. (Internationaler Graphischer Restauratorentag der IADA, 5).

Wächter, Wolfgang, 'Über Möglichkeiten der Mechanisierung restauratorischer Tätigkeiten'. München, IFLA, 1983. 9pp. (IFLA General Conference, Munich, 1983, 52-CON-3-G).

3. Catalogues and bibliographies

Archiv der Gegenwart. (1931/32-1955: Keesing's Archiv der Gegenwart). Zushammenstellung des Nachrichtenstoffes: Heinrich von Siegler u.a. Wien: Keesing's Archiv der Gegenwart, 1/2 (1931/32)ff.

Bogel, Else and Blühm, Elger, (editors) 'Die deutschen Zeitungen des 17. Jahrhunderts. Ein Bestandsverzeichnis ...'. Vols. 1-3. Bremen, Schunemann 1971; München, Saur 1985. (Studien zur Publizistik. Bremer Reihe. 17,1-3)

Bohrmann, Hans und Englert,Marianne, (editors) 'Handbuch der Pressearchive'. Supplement: Ubbens, Wilbert, (compiler) 'Presse-, Rundfunk-, Fernseh-, Filmarchive. Internationale Auswahlbibliographie 1971-1982'. München, Saur 1984. 265pp.

Buder, Johannes, 'Die Inhaltserschliessung von Zeitungen. Eine internationale Übersicht über Zeitungsindices und Zeitungsinhaltsbibliographien'. Berlin, Deutscher Bibliotheksverband, 1978. 119pp (Bibliotheksdienst. Beih. 133).

Gittig, Heinz, (editor) 'Berliner Zeitungen. Katalog der Zeitungsbestande bis 1932 in der Kooperations-gemeinschaft der 4 Berliner wissenschaftlichen Universitätsbibliotheken'. Berlin, Deutsche Staatsbibliothek, 1986. VI, 39pp (Bibliographische Mitteilungen, 30). Betr. Deutsche Staatsbibliothek, Universitätsbibliothek der Humboldt-Universität zu Berlin, Berliner Stadtbibliothek, Hauptbibliothek der Akademie der Wissenschaften der DDR.

Gorzny, Willi, (editor) Zeitungs-Index. Verzeichnis wichtiger Aufsätze aus deutschsprachigen Zeitungen'. Pullach, Verl. Dokumentation, 1 (1974) ff. Suppl.: Buchrezensionen, 1, 1974, ff.

Hagelweide, Gert, (editor) 'Deutsche Zeitungsbestände in Bibliotheken und Archiven'. Düsseldorf, Droste 1974. 372pp (Bibliographien zur Geschichte des Parlamentarismus und der politischen Parteien, H 6).

Internationale Bibliographie der Zeitschriftenliteratur. Abt. A: Bibliographie der deutschen Zeitschriften-Literatur. Supplement fortnightly (1921/22 monthly; 1928-1929 weekly; 1934-1944 monthly) Verzeichnis von Aufsätzen aus deutschen Zeitungen. In sachlich-alphabetischer Ordnung mit jährl. Gesamt-, Sach- u. Verfasserregister. Ed. Felix Dietrich (1938 ff. Ed. Reinhardt Dietrich). Leipzig, Dietrich. 1 (1909)-31 (1944). 1922-1927 as Bibliographie der deutschen Zeitschriften-literatur mit Einschluss von Sammelwerken und Zeitungen. Repr. Nendeln, Kraus, 1967.

Koszyk, Kurt, (editor) 'Verzeichnis und Bestande westfalischer Zeitungen'. Catalogue edited by Käthe Schröder. Munster, Aschendorff 1975. 112pp. (Veröffentlichungen der Historischen Kommission für Westfalen, 34). (Geschichtliche Arbeiten zu Meinungsbildung und zu den Kommunikationsmitteln in Westfalen, Bd. 2).

'Mikrofilm-Archiv der deutschsprachigen Presse'. (Microfilm Archives of the German Language Press.) Bestandsverzeichnis. Catalogue 6. Dortmund, Mikrofilm-Archiv der deutschsprachigen Presse, 1982. 195pp mit Beiträgen zu Zeitungssammlungen.

Munzinger, Ludwig, (editor) 'Archiv für publizistische Arbeit, Munzinger Archiv'. Informations-und Nachschlagewerk für politische, wirtschaftliche und kulturelle Fragen im Loseblattsystem. Gegr. 1913. 12. Aufl. Ravensburg, Munzinger, 1966 ff. Loose leaf.

'Pressefrühdrucke aus der Zeit der Glaubenskämpfe, 1517-1648. Bestandsverzeichnis des Instituts für Zeitungsforschung der Stadt Dortmund'. München, Saur, 1980. 247pp. (Dortmunder Beiträge zur Zeitungsforschung, Bd. 33).

Schäfer, Adelheid, (editor) 'Hessische Zeitungen. Bestandsnachweise fur die bis 1950 im Gebiet des ehemaligen Grossherzogtums und Volksstaats Hessen erschienenen Zeitungen'. Darmstadt, Verl. des Histor. Vereins für Hessen, 1978. XIII. 196pp.

Schüler, Jürgen, et al. (editors) 'Universitätsbibliothek Düsseldorf. Zeitungen und zeitungsahnliche Periodika. Verzeichnis der Original- und Mikrofilmsbestände'. Düsseldorf, Universitätsbibliothek Düsseldorf, 1986. 126pp. (Schriften der Universitätsbibliothek Düsseldorf, 1).

Schüling, Hermann, (compiler) 'Verzeichnis der bis zum Jahre 1979 in Giessen erschienen Zeitungen'. Giessen, Universitätsbibliothek Giessen, 1983. 76pp. (With locations).

'Stadtarchiv Wuppertal. Zeitungsbestände'. Wuppertal, Stadtarchiv Wuppertal, 1983. 55pp (Informationen aus dem Stadtarchiv, 2).

Sürig, Eckhard, (editor) 'Göttinger Zeitungen. Ein pressegeschichtlicher und bibliographischer Fuhrer mit Standortnachweis. Göttingen, Stadtarchiv Göttingen, 1985. 96pp (Veröffentlichungen des Stadtarchivs Göttingen, 1).

Traub, Hans, (compiler) 'Standortskatalog wichtiger Zeitungsbestände in deutschen Bibliotheken'. Leipzig, Hiersemann, 1933. XXXI, 254pp Repr. Stuttgart, Hiersemann, 1974.

Ubbens, Wilbert, (compiler) 'Staats- und Universitätsbibliothek Bremen: Zeitungen und zeitungsähnliche Periodika. Original- und Mikrofilmbestände 1 Dez. 1982'. Bremen, Staats- und Universitätsbibliothek Bremen, 1982. VIII, 196pp (Materialien der SuUB Bremen, 1).

'Universitäts- und Stadtbibliothek Köln. Alphabetischer Katalog Zeitungen'. Köln, UStB Köln, 1976. 173pp (ADV-Ausdruck.)

'Verzeichnis Berliner Zeitungen in Berliner Bibliotheken'. 2nd ed. enlarged. Berlin, Amerika-Gedenkbibliothek, 1982. 85pp.

Winckler, Martin, (compiler) 'Standortverzeichnis ausländischer Zeitungen und Illustrierten in Bibliotheken und Instituten der Bundesrepublik Deutschland und Berlin (West) SAZI'. (Catalogue of foreign newspapers and illustrated papers in German libraries.) Stand 1. Aug. 1973. Pullach, Verl. Dokumentation, 1975. 334pp.

'Württembergische Landesbibliothek Stuttgart. Zeitungsverzeichnis. 1. Ausg. Stand: Mai 1977'. Stuttgart, Württembergische Landesbibliothek, 1977. 190pp.

'Zeitschriften-Datenbank ZDB'. Compiled by the Deutsches Biblioteksinstitut and the Staatsbibliothek Preussischer Kulturbesitz Berlin (West). 16. Gesamtausdruck Herbst, 1986. Wiesbaden, Harrassowitz, 1986. Microfiche ed.

'Zeitungen im Solinger Stadtarchiv. Ein Bestandsverzeichnis. Bearbeitet von Dagmar Thiemler u.a.'. Solingen, Solinger Stadtarchiv, 1984. o. Pag. (Solinger Archivheft, 1).

GREEK NEWSPAPERS & THEIR MICROFILMING IN THE MICROFORM UNIT OF THE
GREEK PARLIAMENT

Dr Panayotis Ph. CHRISTOPOULOS

Library of Parliament, Athens, Greece

1. HISTORY OF GREEK NEWSPAPERS

The history of Greek newspapers began almost 200 years ago. In 1970, even before the establishment of the modern Greek State, the first Greek newspaper was launched in Vienna. Since then, Greek newspapers have multiplied at a very rapid rate - as of 1821 and thereafter, centred in Greece itself. Also, the centres of Hellenism scattered throughout the whole world quickly acquired their own newspapers, as did the numerous smaller Greek colonies in almost every corner of the world. The language of these newspapers is mainly Greek. However, we also find newspapers printed in one of the international languages (either in bi-lingual or multi-lingual form), including the language of the country where they are published.

We hardly need to mention that newspapers, as a cultural creation, are not in the least ephemeral. Day by day they depict the living history of the metropolis and the colonies. The highly variegated contents (political, social, cultural, economic, literary, historical and scientific - in the more general sense) are the most immediate and vivid illustration of the life of the nation. Through them we can observe the movement of ideas and various reflections of national and international news. They rouse the public's zeal and desire to learn. In fact, the public is vitally influenced and decisively moulded by the Press, which until recently, was the only means of mass information. Greek newspapers also have the following special characteristic: because of the wide dispersion of Hellenism and the lack of enough specialized scholarly journals (mainly, throughout the 19th century and perhaps to a lesser degree, during the first decades of the 20th century), significant essays and publications of historical sources were printed in numerous newspapers of that era. Most of our most important literary figures worked and printed their first texts there. This precious mine of rich information, which is only now being explored internationally as a comparatively newly discovered resource for research, has not yet revealed all its treasures.

2. BIBLIOGRAPHICAL CONTROL

Information about bibliographical access to Greek newspapers - including item identification, item description and item location - is not yet sufficiently accessible. Concerning <u>currently published newspapers</u>, we can more or less rely on the Annual of the Greek Press, which records newspapers and other serials appearing in Greece [1]. The most recent issue contains the titles of 140 daily and 1000 non-daily newspapers, as well as 850 other serials. These numbers appear disproportionately large compared to the population and size of this country [2]. Nevertheless, we can be sure that a few local and professional newspapers and journals with a small circulation are not included in the Annual. Also, the numerous publications of the Greek colonies abroad are not included. This is a very important lacuna, which is not covered by any other aid. Also, identification is not quite complete, since inter alia, it does not include: circulation, advertising rates and the exact numbers of issues printed. Furthermore, although the addresses of all the titles included are listed, item description and item location are missing. Location is absolutey necessary, since the two main deposit libraries in Greece - the National Library and the Library of Parliament - seem to have manny shortcomings in the field of newspapers.

Information concerning retrospective newspapers is extensive, although by no means complete. The relevant studies are based mainly on material which is not available in a systematic way. And as a result, they are for the most part fragmentary in character. However, there are a few thorough compilations, which constitute significant aids for the history of the Greek Press. For example, the book of D Petrakákos, "Demosiográfiovkaí Demosiografía" (in Greek, 1921); the 3 volume work of K Mager, "Istoría toũ ‘Ellēnikoũ Túpou" (in Greek, 1957-1960); and the 3 volume work of N Skiadás, "Hronkió tẽs Ellēnikís Tupografias" (in Greek, 1976-1982). There are also quite a few works, which are of a local or specialized character [3]. A useful general auxiliary work is D Gines' "Katálogos Ellēnikōn Efēmerídōn kaí Periodikōn, 1811-1861" (Athens 1967). Among existing bibliographies, I shall refer only to Constantin Zilemenos' "Contribution a l'étude de la presse hellénique" (Paris 1967, selective bibliography, on pp. 114-118) and the comprehensive bibliography of G. Koukas, "Bibliografía toũ Ellēnikoũ Túpou 1465-1982" (1982).

Printed catalogues are of course, an invaluable source for identification and location of newspaper titles. The only such catalogue for a major national newspaper collection is "Katálogos tẽs Bibliothékēs tẽs Boulẽs". A' Efēmerídes ‘Ellēnikaí B' "Periodiká ‘Ellēniká" (Athens 1900). This has now been superseded by the work of Panayótis Ph. Christópoulos, "Efēmerídes tẽs Periódou 1790-1970 stē Bibliothēke tēs Boulēs tōn ‘Ellēnōn" (in course of publication) [4].

An advantageous measure for assessing the national holdings of Greece is to compile a union list, based on published catalogues of local or minor collections, as well as the above-mentioned Catalogue of the Greek Parliament Library and the card catalogue of the National Library. At a later point, this union list may be enriched by the Greek newspaper holdings of various foreign Institutions and private collections. The preparation of such a list is a laborious process and there is no prospect of its being compiled in the near future. However, by using the Parliament's computer system to record this material gradually and create a special file, the task will proceed at a much faster pace.

3. MICROFILMING

Since the middle of 1985, the Microform Unit of the Greek Parliament, (which until then had dealt mainly with microfilming official publications on 16mm. film) began microfilming newspapers on 35mm. film. This work is now considered as the Unit's main task, aside from its work on ancient manuscripts, rare books and other serials [5].

Although there is no national programme for newspapers, the Unit proceeds as if there were such a Plan, according to international practise. The Library of Parliament possesses one of the two largest newspaper collections in

Greece, approximately the same size as the other large collection in the National Library. Neither of these collections is self-sufficient. Even if they were joined into a single unified collection, it would still be impossible to assemble a complete run, satisfactory from a qualitative point of view, even of the most important dailies with the greatest longevity. Consequently, the co-operation of other institutions and individuals is absolutely necessary, in addition to the co-operation of the newspapers themselves (those which are still in print and exist as organizations). This task is now being carried out at a national level and, as such, has the eager co-operation of all persons and institutions concerned.

The work is proceeding along two parallel lines:

3.1. Microfilming of Current Newspapers

As of January 1st, 1984, special newspaper files were established at the Unit. Every day, the papers for that particular day are collected from the newspaper agencies. They are classified, inspected and microfilmed. The originals are kept, without being bound. This procedure has been adopted for the Athens and Salonica dailies. And gradually, in the course of time, new current titles are being added to the list of microfilm material. The ultimate goal is to include all the newspapers printed in Greece, as well as Greek newspapers abroad. A continuous effort is also being made to go back to the very start of each of these current titles. Some of the current titles, which are collected and microfilmed promptly are: Akrópolis, Apogeumatiné, Augé, Auriané, Bēma, Braduné, Dēmokratikós Lógos, Ethnos, Ekklēsiasktikē Alētheia, Eleútheri Ōra, Eleútheros Túpos, Eleutherotupía, Ellēnikós Borrās, Exórmisē, Estía, Efēmerís tēs Kubernēseōs, Emērēsía, Thessalonikē, Kathērmerinē, Katholikē, Kérdos, Makedonía, Mesēmbrinē, Nea, Orthódoxos Túpos, Politikē, Pontikē, Praktikā tēs Boulés, Prōiné and Kuriákatikē Eleutherotupía, Prōti, Rizospástes, Stóhos, Fílathlos.

3.2. Microfilming of older newspapers (from 1790 onwards)

As for the previous periods of newspapers no longer in print, the procedure used is to request the best existing run for each title (best as far as completeness and state of preservation are concerned). Each such run is carefully checked, page by page. Then an attempt is made to supplement the gaps by using other runs, to repair possible wear-and-tear and restore binding if necessary. This is done at the preservation laboratory, which has been set up inside the Unit. Obviously, this whole procedure is enormously time-consuming. But only in this way, can we make sure of having a complete (or at least, as complete as possible) run of all known existing copies. There have been cases where dozens of volumes, dispersed in various collections, had to be discovered through research on one or several issues. Frequently, the search for originals in good condition is assisted by various Research Centres in Greece. In the process, they benefit directly from this work. Furthermore, special research needs of these scholarly Centres may well alter the priorities in microfilming.

Some of the previous titles already microfilmed and available in circulation are the following: Agōn (1899-1911), Athēná (1832-1864), Aiōn (1838-1891), Alēthia (1865-1881), Astu (1896-1901), Genikē Efēmerís tēs Ellados (1825-1832), Dēmokratikē (1951-1952), Ethnikē Efēmerís (1832-1833), Eleútheron Bēma (1922-1944), Elpís (1836-1868), Efēmerís tōn Suzētēseōn tēs Boulés (1862-1966), Kleió [Leipzig] (1885-1891), Kleió [Trieste] (1861-1883), Néon Astu (1901-1905), Prōiá (1925-1944), Fílos toū Nómou [Hydra] (1824-1827), Ōra (1875-1887), Izvestija [CPle] (1896-1912).

After the microfilming procedure, the film is developed and checked, frame by frame, in the reader. In this way, omissions and pointless repetitions are avoided. Also, the quality and legibility of the film are verified. All problems are dealt with without delay. Then the perfected negative film is inserted in the work log-book, where it receives a code number. A corresponding entry is provided in the indices and then copies are made on special Diazo film for the main reading-rooms of the Library. According to its policy, after microfilming, the originals owned by the Library are preserved, because of the scarcity of such material.

Because of the large quantity of material to be microfilmed, an attempt has also been made to acquire microfilms of Greek newspapers available from foreign Institutions; this has worked out quite satisfactorily. The first sets have already been purchased by the Unit and are now available for readers.

The compilation of a national register of newspaper microform masters is among the objectives of the Unit, as a contribution to compiling a World Register. In fact, this Register will include everything in the Unit's possession, as well as masters made from and owned by foreign Institutions. The microfilms produced here are also for sale. Up to now, several university institutions have acquired copies of them and continue to purchase all newly filmed titles on a permanent basis, although the Greek Unit is not yet listed in the international Directories [6].

There are progressive plans for expanding the Unit's technical equipment as soon as possible, as well as for training the appropriate staff. Also, a move to spacious new premises is planned in order to enhance the quality and productivity of the work done in the Unit.

REFERENCES

1 'Epetērída toũ Ellēnikoũ Túpou' (edited by) Genikē Grammateía Túpou.

2 Twelve decades ago, a collection of Greek serials exhibited at the International Exposition of Vienna (at the initiative of K Fōstirópoulos) consisted of 160 titles. Of these, 74 were published in Athens (69 in Greek, 2 in French, one in Italian and one bilingual in French and Greek); 43 in other parts of Greece and 18 abroad. Cf. K Fōstirópoulos, 'Notice sur la presse hellénique', Athènes, 1873 (in Greek and French).

3 Among the special studies, which are local in character, we sometimes find extraordinary frequency and completeness, as for example, in the following cases: G Láios, 'Ō Ellēnikós Túpos tēs Viénnis apó toũ 1784 méhri toũ 1821', Athens, 1961. Dínos Konómos, 'Eptanēsiakós Túps 1798-1864', in: Eptanēsiaká Fúlla, vol.5, (1964). pp. 143. Hrístos Solomōnídes, 'Ē Dēmosiografía stē Smúrnē (1821-1922)', Athens, 1959.

4 This includes more than 5000 titles, most of them in Greek.

5 Concerning this Unit, cf. Panayótis Ph. Christópoulos 'The Library of Parliament in Athens with Special Reference to its Services for Microfilming Newspapers', in: Parlament und Bibliothek, Internationale Festschrift für Wolfgang Dietz, zum 65. Geburtstag, München..1986, pp.203 ff.

6   Such as Ellen S. Wasserman (editor), 'Microform Market Place', 1986-1987, Westport, Conn., 1986; 'The Micropublishers' Trade List Annual, 1986-1987', Alexandria, 1986; the 'Guide to Microforms in Print', Westport, Conn., 1961- , or 'Newspapers in Microform, Foreign Countries. 1948-1983'. Washington DC. Library of Congress, 1984.

NEWSPAPER PRESERVATION IN HUNGARY

Beatrix KASTALY

Head of Newspaper Section, National Széchényi Library, Budapest

It was five years ago - in 1982 - when we celebrated the two hundred years anniversary of the publication of the first newspaper in Hungarian.

In Hungary most of the libraries collect the newspapers for their own profile. We cannot speak about their coordinated collection, cataloguing, storing and using; preservation is the only area where some central principles and practice are prevailing. This is due to the activity of the national library.

In the National Széchényi Library there are today about 290000 volumes of newspapers and journals. The quantity of the newspapers separately is not known exactly in spite of that in 1888 a separate division was created in the library as a Newspaper Library. But later the journals were added to it. Today the newspapers and journals belong to the basic holdings together with the books but cataloguing, storing and using of the periodicals is separated from that of books.

In Hungary newspaper preservation as such is a task which falls mostly to the share of the National Library. In other libraries those newspapers which are to be retained permanently will be bound sooner or later and they are stored in various environmental conditions. About 70% of the old - before 1952 - newspapers of the nation can be found only in the national library, in relative completeness. But the national library had never had sufficient resources for storing well and binding all the newspapers. Therefore, considerable amounts were, in the sixties, in a very bad condition; they were very brittle, crumbling, yellow and brown. To preserve the intellectual contents of the newspapers, the competent leaders of the Library and the Ministry of Culture decided on microfilming all the Hungarica newspapers of the national library. The financial, technical and personnel conditions for this work have been created. Newspaper microfilming has been performed since 1969 with four cameras and an automatic developing and printing laboratory. Preparation, microfilming, controlling and cataloguing is done by about 20 trained photographers and librarians. Between one and one and a half million pages have been microfilmed annually. The retrospective microfilming of newspapers will end in several years. The archival quality master-negatives have been preserved in an air-conditioned archive at $15-16^\circ C$ and 30-40% RH. Second negatives, however, have not been made. The positive films are kept in the store-rooms of the newspapers. The film archive of master-negatives and the stores of the original newspapers are situated in different parts of Budapest, consequently, the films can be considered not only as preservative but as safety ones too. The originals - if their positive films are ready - can be read only in exceptional cases. Paper-copies are retained after microfilming by the national library because most of the old newspapers can be found only here, and in the most cases only in one copy. In other libraries newspapers are not microfilmed.

The newspaper microfilms are regularly recorded in registers in the national library. From these registers other libraries can order microfilms against payment for completing or preserving their newspaper holdings. The microfilms made in the national library are as complete as possible as the titles which are not complete in the national library are completed with the missing parts from other libraries. The national library has also microfilmed Hungarica newspapers in the libraries both of Slovakia and Yugoslavia.

Before microfilming greater or lesser repairs have to be done on the old newspapers for achieving the best legibility. These "repairs" mean: to loosen the tight spines, to flatten the wrinkled sheets, to glue the tears and to complete the holes which are in the text and to remove the old repairing paper-strips from the pages. When the paper is very brittle we deacidify and strengthen it. This latter is done by lamination with polyethylene and Japanese tissue. These repairs before microfilming are performed by seven trained bookbinders and/or book- and paper-conservators.

The microfilming of the current newspapers will follow the retrospective microfilming. Then the repair work will reduce to a minimum, and thus the task of the conservators will change. They will deacidify and strengthen the paper of the most valuable newspapers because the national library wants to retain them permanently, or as long as possible. We have not determined yet the bulk treatment by which these aims would be achieved. The paper of most of our old newspapers is too weak and brittle and that is why impregnation with an adhesive is not sufficient for them. They would need strengthening with some fibrous material too (either cellulose fibres or some synthetic or semi-synthetic fibres). The bulk method for this purpose however is not yet known. We could think of lamination, paper splitting and applying a fibre suspension. To use these methods we have to dismantle the volumes into sheets and the operations can be done only sheet by sheet.

To reduce the vast conservation work on newspapers in the future, we have pursued experiments together with a Hungarian paper mill to develop the composition of a permanent paper for printing newspapers. The composition is adequate to the world standards, i.e. it does not contain groundwood and aluminium sulphate, it contains a synthetic sizing material and calcium carbonate, the chemical reaction is slightly alkaline and it keeps the major part of its good physical and chemical properties during ageing. As this paper is relatively thin - its weight is 50 - 55 g/m^2 -, transparency was problematical. We are continuing the experiments to create a better opacity and we are also trying to block the heavy-metal ions which catalyse oxidation of cellulose. We intend to apply this permanent paper to the copyright copies of newspapers in future.

PRESERVATION OF NEWSPAPERS: THE INDIAN SITUATION

Dr Ashin DAS GUPTA

Director, National Library of India

India does not at present have anything which can be described as its national approach to the problem of newspaper preservation. But the problem is being viewed in the broad national perspective of the preservation of India's cultural heritage as a whole. The Government of India had in the past not been concerned much with this particular problem, the only exception being the act to preserve historical monuments in 1904. Out of this enactment grew the present impressive programme of preservation by the Archaeological Survey of India. Otherwise books and periodicals were collected by the Government of India through its Press and Registration Act of 1867, but this way was mainly for Police purposes. Most of such material found its way to repositories in Britain and very little remained in Indian libraries.

Some of the public libraries of the later nineteenth century began to acquire important collections of current native newspapers. The Indian Press also lived in the Native Newspaper Reports, once again a police scrutiny to ward off sedition since the 1870s. Considering that Indian newspapers stretch back to the 1780s and most of the vernacular serials were produced domestically and catered to a very limited clientele, we must resign ourselves to the loss of most of these early printings.

At the moment the Government of India has a Committee called the National Council of Arts presided over by the Prime Minister and engaged in the task of formulating a national policy for culture. A Task Force of this Committee has the responsibility of mapping the problem of preservation in so far as it relates to books, manuscripts and periodicals. You can understand that the thinking is long-term and the most that we are trying to do is to discover the dimension of the problem. Eventually the problem of preserving India's newspapers will be seen and will be dealt with as part of the totality of the problem of preservation of cultural objects. That day, I fear, may be distant.

One other development in the recent past is also relevant to us in this context. The Government of India set up what it called a High Powered Committee to make recommendations on a National Policy for Libraries and Information Systems under a former Cabinet Minister, Professor D P Chattopadhyay. The Chattopadhyay Committee submitted its draft of a national policy to the Government last summer. This draft is now under active consideration for implementation by the Government of India. One of the major difficulties in the field pinpointed by this draft is the isolation of the Indian libraries. Libraries in India are what is called 'State Subjects' which means that they are within the jurisdiction of the constituent States of the Indian Union rather than the Central Government. The Central Government takes care of only a limited number of libraries which have been historically the responsibility of the Indian Government, as for an example the National Library itself. But all other libraries belong to the Governments of the States when they are officially supported, and all libraries of all description are within the jurisdiction of the State Governments.

The problem relating to Indian newspapers is therefore of two different kinds. One is how to locate the newspapers in scattered holdings all over the country and, only then, how to preserve them. I may say straight away at this point that in the Indian context a monolithic library of any kind will not serve the purpose. It is more important for us to learn about the holdings of the different libraries and be assured that newspapers are being properly preserved wherever they are rather than build up one national collection of vast, in fact, unmanageable proportions. This does not mean that there would not be large and representative collections of newspapers, for example, in the National Library itself, but the aim should not be to concentrate everything in one place. Given the plural context of Indian society and historical development which has seen the collections growing in different parts of the country, the decision for a monolithic library will be the wrong one to take. This position in general has been laid down in the National Policy itself which speaks of the aim of preserving the national heritage especially in the printed form at the National Library but with this effort being supplemented and complemented by sister libraries elsewhere. Particularly in the field of Indian language newspapers, the National Library would emphasise the responsibility of regional repositories to collect and preserve newspapers in local languages.

This may also be the point to emphasise that when we discuss the problem of preserving newspapers in India we usually have three different things in mind. For one thing we think of old newspapers, that is newspapers of historical interest; then we think of newspapers mainly in the English language and published in the larger cities. (I must, however, add that within this category of metropolitan publishing we also think of large-circulation vernacular dailies). In the third place we think of newspapers published in the countryside and of limited circulation only. The problem of location and preservation becomes extremely difficult with this third category of newspapers and this is where the National Library likes to remind its sister libraries of their regional responsibilities.

As things stand, Indian libraries seem to be concerned with preserving newspapers, when they do so at all, in two different ways for two different purposes. Many libraries all over the country preserve a certain number of newspapers in hard copy and in bound form, hopefully for keeping permanently. When major libraries like the Connemara Public Library in Madras do this, the aim is to preserve a respresentative selection of newspapers mainly in English, but also in some of the other major languages of the country for the library's collection. The attached list of such newspapers (Annexure-I) preserved at the Connemara Public Library will show that there is a certain overlap between the newspapers preserved there and the newspapers which are being preserved, say, at the National Library in Calcutta (This list is also attached at Annexure-I). Although information is very incomplete in the matter, we may assume that such duplication is taking place all over the country and, to some extent, it is both necessary and unavoidable. Functioning as they do in near-complete isolation from each other, the major Indian libraries must think primarily of their own collections and the demand from their own readers. It is not much consolation for Madras to know that a particular newspaper is preserved in Calcutta and vice versa. The thing we are trying to avoid through the implementation of the National Policy is primarily duplication within the same city and the same neighbourhood. The eventual aim is to have complete information on which paper is preserved where and in what condition. Unfortunately, hard copies bound for preservation deteriorate fairly soon and preservation in this form is obviously a gesture to the gods.

The second kind of preservation in microcopy is attempted by only a very limited number of libraries in the country and normally for a very specific kind of clientèle. An outstanding collection of newspapers in microfilm now comprising 145 items has been accumulated at the Nehru Memorial Library in New Delhi which is meant to serve researchers in modern and contemporary Indian history. For our purposes, we do not take into account the other outstanding collection of newspapers substantially in microform at the Indian Institute of International Affairs (Sapru House), New Delhi, as these are, very largely, newspapers produced outside India and collected to serve the purpose of Indian students of international affairs. Other than these specialised libraries, newspapers in microcopy are also preserved in some of the major newspaper offices. Researchers, however, often find it difficult to obtain access to such collections and they normally fall back either on the Nehru Memorial Library or on the National Library.

The National Library's collection of old newspapers is a very valuable one dating back to 1780 and continuing to date. A list of all English language newspapers up to 1956 is available in "Catalogue of Periodicals, Newspapers and Gazettes", but the major difference between that early period and the more recent years lies in the great accumulation of Indian language newspapers since 1956 under the Delivery of Books Act. At the moment the National Library receives 638 Indian language newspapers (List attached at Annexure-II). You may take it for granted that as the National Library throws nothing away, from the late 1950s onwards all such newspapers should be found in its collection. The Library, however, has the problem that it is unable to cope with this enormous mass of Indian language newspapers which has descended upon it in the last 40 years. The Library has made a curious compromise, preserving a selection of 25 titles in hard copy and in hard covers (List attached at Annexure-I). The selection made in the early 1970s was presumably done partly in consideration of earlier selections and partly in an effort to have one title from each State. There was also the attempt to meet local demand which is heavy in the Calcutta area. As the National Library does not discard a newspaper, our librarians are attempting to work out a compromise method of storing newspapers in loose copies under suitably prepared covers.

It is, of course, acknowledged that such preservation will not be permanent. Some hope is still entertained that once reduced to microcopies, this problem can be solved. The National Library embarked upon its microcopying programme again in the early 1970s, but because of the paucity of resources the results have so far not been very encouraging. As a result, the Library decided in recent years to concentrate solely upon the unique elements in its own collection for preservation as its first priority. We engaged the strictly honorary services of a historian who kindly surveyed our newspaper collections and compared them with the collections at the Nehru Memorial Library and the National Archives in New Delhi and also with that of the India Office Library and Records in London. The list he then drew up for our consideration is now being microcopied at the National Library (List of newspapers in microfilm attached at Annexure-III). There cannot be any doubt that we should work towards a more formal arrangement of consultation between the major libraries engaged in microcopying newspapers to prevent unnecessary duplication and to build up a national resource.

This may also be the place to mention that the National Library in spite of the paucity of resources, has to accept the task of preserving rare collections which are being lost elsewhere. Nineteenth-century libraries, like the Bangiya Sahitya Parishad in Calcutta or the Mumbai Marathi Grantha Samgrahalay in Bombay, have collections of old Bengali and Marathi newspapers. Such collections also exist in smaller libraries of the same kind while such libraries are no longer in a position to preserve them. In the recent past the National Library was kindly permitted by a sister library to the south of Calcutta to microfilm a run of sixteen years of the rare Bengali newspaper <u>Som Prakash</u>. But the thought of a survey of all such libraries is depressing.

Beyond this picture of the slowly growing resource base in India, Indian newspapers, of course, are preserved mainly in microcopies in several important repositories abroad, principally in the UK and the USA. At present there is no arrangement to work out a collaboration between collections of this kind in India and abroad. Paucity of resources obviously is a very important deterrent and I include in that not merely copying facility but proper arrangements for storage as well. But hopefully arrangements will be made so that Indian newspapers in so far as they are still available, can be preserved effectively and without avoidable duplication wherever there is interest in such material.

ANNEXURE-I
CONNEMARA (STATE CENTRAL) PUBLIC LIBRARY, MADRAS
List of Newspapers kept preserved

LANGUAGE	TITLE	PLACE OF PUBLICATION	PRESERVED FROM
Assamese	Natlin Assamiya	Dispur (Assam)	1981*
Bengali	Ananda Bazaar Patrika	Calcutta	1980*
English	Economic Times	N Delhi	1978
"	The Hindu	Coimbatore	1975
"	Hitawada	Bhopal	1984
"	Indian Express	N Delhi	1979
"	Madhya Pradesh Chronicle	Raipur	1981
"	National Herald	Lucknow	1982
"	Statesman	Calcutta	1974
"	Times of India	Bombay	1974
Gujarati	Gujarat Samachar	Ahmedabad	1982
Hindi	Arya Varthan	Patna	1982
"	Nava Bharat Times	Bombay	1982
"	Nava Jothi	Jaipur	1983
Kannada	Samyuktha Karnataka	Bangalore	1983
Malayalam	Mathru Bhumi	Calicut	1982
Marathi	Sakal	Bhopal	1982
Oriya	Samaj	Cuttak	1982
Punjabi	Ajit	Jullunder	1982
Sanskrit	Sudharma	Mysore	1982
Sindhi	Hindustan Sindhi	Bombay	1984
Tamil	Thinathanthi	Madras	1974
"	Thinamalar	Thirunelveli	1975
"	Thinamani	Madurai	1975
Telugu	Andhara Jothi	Vijayawada	1982
Urdu	Martand	Srinagar	1983*
"	Milap	Hyderabad	1983
"	Tej	N Delhi	1984*

* Irregular supply.

ANNEXURE-I

NATIONAL LIBRARY, CALCUTTA
Newspapers preserved in hard copies

Title	Place of publication
English	
1. Amrita Bazar Patrika	Calcutta
2. Assam Tribune	Gauhati
3. Bharat Jyoti	Bombay
4. Economic Times	Bombay
5. Free Press Journal	Bombay
6. Hindu	Madras
7. Hindusthan Standard	Calcutta
8. Hindustan Times	Delhi
9. Hitavada	Nagpur
10. Indian Express	Vijayawada
11. Indian Nation	Patna
12. Leader	Allahabad
13. National Herald	Lucknow
14. New York Times	New York
15. Pioneer	Lucknow
16. Search Light	Patna
17. Statesman	Calcutta
18. Times	London
19. Times Educational Supplement	London
20. Times Literary Supplement	London
21. Times of India	Bombay
22. Tribune	Ambala
Bengali	
1. Ananda Bazar Patrika	Calcutta
2. Dainik Basumati	Calcutta
3. Jugantar	Calcutta
4. Jana Sevak	Calcutta (since discontinued)
5. Lokasevak	Calcutta (since discontinued)
6. Swadhinata	Calcutta (since discontinued)
Hindi	
1. AAJ	Banaras
2. Aryavarta	Patna
3. Dainik Vishwamitra	Calcutta
4. Hindusthan	Delhi
5. Sanmarg	Calcutta

ANNEXURE-II

NATIONAL LIBRARY, CALCUTTA
List of newspapers currently received at the National Library, Calcutta

(Dailies)

	Title	Place of publication
	Assamese	
1.	Dainik Assam	Gauhati
2.	Pratidin	Gauhati
3.	Dainik Janambhumi	Jorhat
	Bengali	
1.	Ajkal	Calcutta
2.	Ananda Bazar Patrika	Calcutta
3.	Azad	Dacca
4.	Banglar Vani	Dacca
5.	Bartaman	Calcutta
6.	Dainik Basumati	Calcutta
7.	Belabhumi	Midnapore
8.	Bhabi Bharat	Agartala, Tripura
9.	Bibaran	Howrah
10.	Bharat Katha	Calcutta
11.	Dainik Chandra Bhaga	Birhum, Seuri
12.	Chetana	Kanthi, Midnapore
13.	Daily Desher Katha	Tripura
14.	Dainik Akarshan	Calcutta
15.	Dainik Bangloa	Dacca
16.	Dainik Damodar	Birhata, Burdwan
17.	Dainik Desh	Dacca
18.	Dainik Janata	Dacca
19.	Dainik Khabar	Dacca
20.	Dainik Kishan	Dacca
21.	Dainik Lipi	Asansol
22.	Dainik Mukta Bangla	Burdwan
23.	Dainik Patrika	Dacca
24.	Dainik Nava Abhijan	Dacca
25.	Dainik Sambad	Agartala, Tipura
26.	Din Duniya	Purulia
27.	Divantar	Agartala, Tipura
28.	Dainik Sangram	Dacca
29.	Ekhan Durbasha	Calcutta
30.	Ganakantha	Calcutta
31.	Ganaraj	Agartala, Tripura
32.	Ganashakiti	Calcutta
33.	Dainik Giri Darpan	Chittagong, Bangla Desh
34.	Gramer Dak	Midnapore
35.	Dainik Ittefaq	Dacca
36.	Dainik Janani	Calcutta
37.	Jagaran	Agartala, Tripura
38.	Janapad	Agartala, Tripura
39.	Jugantar	Calcutta
40.	Dainik Jugasankha	Gauhati
41.	Kalantar	Calcutta
42.	Lok Sevak	Calcutta
43.	Mahabrate	Agartala, Tripura
44.	Nagarik	Agartala, Tripura
45.	Dainik Natun Prithivi	Calcutta

46.	Natun Tripura	Tripura
47.	Paschimbanga Sambad	Calcutta
48.	Promod Varta	Agartala
49.	Sambad	Dacca
50.	Sapath	Silchar
51.	Sonar Cachar	Silchor, Assam
52.	Satyajug	Calcutta
53.	Swikriti	Burdwan
54.	Shilpabhumi	Burdwan
55.	Syandan	Agartala, Tripura
56.	Teerbhumi	Kanthi, Midnapore
57.	Tripura Darpan	Agartala, Tripura
58.	Tripura Prakash	Agartala, Tripura
59.	Uttarbanga Sambad	Siliguri
60.	Vamla Bazar	Ranaghat
61.	Vivek	Agartala

Gujarati

1.	Akila	Rajkot
2.	Bhumi	Jamnagar
3.	Bombay Samachar	Bombay
4.	Gujarat Mitra	Surat
5.	Gujarat Samachar	Surat
6.	Jai Hind	Ahmedabad
7.	Phul Chhab	Rajkot
8.	Pratap	Surat
9.	Sandesh	Baroda
10.	Sevak	Ahmedabad
11.	Naya Padkar	Anand
12.	Rakheval	Ahmedabad
13.	Jai Hind	Rajkot
14.	Jam-e-Jamshed (bi-weekly)	Bombay
15.	Janmabhumi	Bombay
16.	Jansatta	Ahmedabad
17.	Janashakti	Bombay
18.	Kutch Mitra	Kutch
19.	Loksatta	Baroda
20.	Nutan Saurashtra	Rajkot
21.	Western Times	Ahmedabad
22.	Gujarat Samachar	Khanpur
23.	Vyapar (bi-weekly)	Bombay

Hindi

1.	Adhikar	Jaipur
2.	Adhikar	Kota
3.	Adhikar	Faridabad
4.	Archna	Gwalior
5.	Aj	Banaras
6.	Aj	Gorakhpur
7.	Agradut	Raipur
8.	Aj Ka Anand	Poona
9.	Dainik Alok	Rewa
10.	Aryavrat	Patna
11.	Amrita Sandesh	Raipur
12.	Amrita Prabhat	Allahabad
13.	Aranyanchal	Ambikapur
14.	Atma-Katha	Patna
15.	Avaj	Dhanbad

16.	Balikshetra	Balia
17.	Bharat desh Hamara	Patiala
18.	Bharat bhumi	Gwalior
19.	Badri Vishal	Hardwar
20.	Banking Express	Nimach (MP)
21.	Bande-matram	Delhi
22.	Dainik Bhaskar	Bhopal
23.	Bijnor times	Bijnor (UP)
24.	Brigadier	Ujjain (MP)
25.	Chhapate Chhapate	Calcutta
26.	Chetna	Haryana
27.	Chambal Vani	Laskar (Gwalior)
28.	Dalit Pukar	Pali
29.	Dandkaranya	Jabalpur
30.	Dashpur-Darshan	Mandasaur
31.	Deshbandhu	Jabalpur
32.	Deshbandhu	Raipur
33.	Deshbandhu	Satana
34.	Dhvaj	Mandasaur
35.	Divan	Urai (UP)
36.	Gandiv	Varanasi
37.	Ganesh	Kanpur
38.	Ganga Nagar Patrika	Rajasthan, Ganga Nagar
39.	Gram Dut	UP
40.	Gwalior Samachar	Gwalior
41.	Hamarayug	Meerut
42.	Hindi Milap	Hyderabad
43.	Hindustan	New Delhi
44.	Indian Panch	Patna
45.	Indore Samachar	Indore
46.	Jagaran	Agra
47.	Jagaran	Bhopal
48.	"	Gorakhpur (UP)
49.	"	Indore
50.	"	Jhansi (UP)
51.	"	Kanpur
52.	"	Lucknow
53.	"	Meerut
54.	"	Rewa (UP)
55.	"	Varanasi
56.	Jalate Deep	Jodhpur, Rajasthan
57.	Jan Gan	Jodhpur, Rajasthan
58.	Janamat	Lucknow
59.	Jan Jagriti	Kota, Rajasthan
60.	Jan nayak	Kota
61.	Jan morcha	Faizabad, UP
62.	Jan Uthan	Gwalior
63.	Janvarta	Varanasi
64.	Javan Bharati	Satara (MP)
65.	Jan Yug	New Delhi
66.	Jay Rajasthan	Udaipur, Rajasthan
67.	Kota Samachar	Kota
68.	Karmyug Prakash	Bonda
69.	Karmyug Prakash	Urai
70.	Lucknow Mail	Luchnow
71.	Lucknow Mail	Raebareli
72.	Madhya Pratap	Gwalior
73.	Madhya Pradesh	Katani

74.	Mauna Times	Muzaffarpur
75.	Muzaaffarnagar Bulletin	Muzaffarnagar
76.	Nai Dunia	Indore
77.	Nava Bharat	Bhopal
78.	Nava Bharat	Nagpur
79.	Navabharat Times	Bombay
80.	Nava Bharat	Raipur
81.	Navabharat Times	New Delhi
82.	Navbharat Times	Lucknow
83.	Navabharat Times	Patna
84.	Navajivan	Bhopal
85.	Navajivan	Lucknow
86.	Navajvyoti	Rajasthan, Ajmer
87.	Navajyoti	Jaipur, Rajasthan
88.	Navinadunia	Jabalpur
89.	Nyay	Ajmer, Rajasthan
90.	Nayelog	Faizabad
91.	Niranjan	Gwalior
92.	Prabhat	Meerut
93.	Prabhajit	Bhilwara
94.	Pradip	Patna
95.	Prajajan	Gangapur
96.	Prakash	Howrah
97.	Prabhat Khabar	Ranchi
98.	Patliputra times	Patna
99.	Pravada Dainik	Aligarh
100.	Pariksita	Calcutta
101.	Pratha	Calcutta
102.	Punjab Keshari	Jullundar
103.	Rajdarpan	Akola, Maharashtra
104.	Rajasthan Patrika	Jaipur
105.	Rajasthan Patrika	Kota, Rajasthan
106.	Ranchi Express	Ranchi
107.	Ranturya	Ajamgarh
108.	Rastraduta	Rajasthan
109.	Rastraduta	Nagpur
110.	Rastraduta	Bikaner, Rajasthan
111.	Rastravadana	Bianora, UP
112.	Raigarh Sandesh	Raigarh, MP
113.	Sadashay	Muzaffarnagar
114.	Sahar hogi	Dhanbad
115.	Sahakar Sandarbh	Ulhas Nagar
116.	Shaladol times	Shahadol (MP)
117.	Saket Shobha	Faizabad
118.	Samay	Shahadal (MP)
119.	Sanmarg	Calcutta
120.	Sanskritik Kranti	Ghaziyabad (IP)
121.	Satna Samachar	Satna (MP)
122.	Seva Sansar	Calcutta
123.	Sainik	Agra
124.	Simavarti	Shri Ganga nagar, Rajasthan
125.	Soviety Sangh ke vichar	New Delhi
126.	Swadesh	Bhopal
127.	Swadesh	Gwalior
128.	Swadesh	Indore
129.	Swatantra Bharat	Lucknow
130.	Sutrakar	Calcutta
131.	Taruna Rajasthan	Jodhpur

132.	Tribyun	Chandigarh
133.	Udit vani	Jamshedpur
134.	Ujala	Agra
135.	Uttar Bharat Times	Bijnour, Rajasthan
136.	Vikram Darshan	Ujjain (MP)
137.	Vir Arjun	New Delhi
138.	Vishvabhramana	Indore
139.	Vishva Manav	Barailly (UP)
140.	Vishvamitra	Bombay
141.	Vishvamitra	Calcutta
142.	Vishvamitra	Kanpur
143.	Pyasa Bharati	Sitapur (UP)
144.	Yugadharm	Jabalpur
145.	Yugadharm	Nagpur
146.	Yugadharm	Raipur
147.	Yugaparea	Nagpur
148.	Yuga Times	Aligarh

Kannada

1.	Prajavani	Bangalore
2.	Kannada Prabha	Bangalore
3.	Samyukta Karnataka	Hubli
4.	Samyukta Karnataka	Bangalore
5.	Viswa vani	Hubli
6.	Mungaru	Mangalore
7.	Rajya Dharma	Mysore
8.	Mysore patrika	Mysore
9.	Sadvi	Mysore
10.	Star of Mysore	Mysore
11.	Lokavani	Bangalore
12.	Teera Nishana	Hubli
13.	Nagarika	Karnataka
14.	Nagarika	Karnataka (Dharwar)
15.	Navodaya	Karnataka (Dharwar)
16.	Brahmagiri	Chitradurga, Karnataka
17.	Chandravalli	Chitradurga, Karnataka
18.	Sahyadmi times	Shimoga
19.	Tamasoma	Shimoga
20.	Kodagu	Mercara
21.	Aruna	Mysore
22.	Chaladankarnalla	Shimoga
23.	Kolara vani	Kolara, Karnataka
24.	Dhruvandristi	Bhadravati, Karnataka
25.	Ushamahi	Shimoga
26.	Eccharike	Shimoga
27.	Lokadarshana	Belagaum
28.	Bayalu Seeme	Channapattana, Bangalore
29.	Rastra sheela	Bhadravati, Karnataka
30.	Ashoka	Musore
31.	Kodagu Dainika	Mercera, Karnataka
32.	Janatavi	Davanagere, Karnataka
33.	Nagaravani	Davanagere, Karnataka
34.	Grama Koogu	Bharama sagar, Karnataka
35.	Davanagere Times	Davanagere
36.	Shantavani	Mysore
37.	Kanthirava	Shimoga
38.	Bhadravahini	Bhadravati, Shimoga
39.	Vijaya	Mysore

40.	Vijaya vani	Tumakur
41.	Tumakur times	Tumakur
42.	Hosa diganta	Chikkamagalur, Karnataka
43.	Dronagiri	Chikkamagalur
44.	Shakti	Mercera, Karnataka
45.	Tunga Taranga	Shimoga
46.	Nadoja	Belagaum
47.	Zeal	Tamular
48.	Kanadavrutta	Kumata, Karnataka
49.	Ravi	Mercera
50.	Mysore Patrika	Mysore
51.	Vartamana	Mysore
52.	Sirasi samachara	Sirasi, Karnataka
53.	Samadarshi	Gokak, Gulbarga
54.	Nanjesh Patrika	Bangalore

Kashmiri

1. Kashmir Akhbar — Srinagar

Malayalam

1.	Anuranjanam	Kuttattukulam
2.	Coastel Express	Cochin
3.	Chandrika	Kozhikode
4.	Desabhimani (Cochin edition)	Cochin
5.	Desabhimani (Kozikode edition)	Kozikode
6.	Deepika	Kottayam
7.	Express	Trichur
8.	Eenadu	Trivandrum
9.	General	Trichur
10.	Janayugom (Quilon edition)	Quilon
11.	Janayugom (Kozhikode edition)	Kozhikode
12.	Kerala bhusanan	Kottayam
13.	Kerala dhwani	Kottayam
14.	Kerala Kaumudi	Trigandrum
15.	Kerala Nadam	Ernakulam
16.	Kerala Malav	Quilon
17.	Kerala Patrika	Trivandrum
18.	Kerala rajyam	Quilon
19.	Kerala Times	Cochin
20.	Look	Cannore
21.	Leauge Times	Calicut
22.	Malayala Manorama (Kottayam edn)	Kottayam
23.	Malayala Manorama (Kozhikode edn)	Kozhikode
24.	Malayala Manorama (Cochin edn)	Cochin
25.	Malayal Manorama (Trivandrum edn)	Trivandrum
26.	Malabara Mail	Cochin
27.	Matrubhumi (Kozhikode edition)	Kozhidode
28.	Matrubhumi (Cochin edition)	Cochin
29.	Matrubhumi (Trivandrum edition)	Trivandrum
30.	Munnani	Alleppey
31.	Patayani	Tellicherry
32.	Powran	Alwaye
33.	Prakambanam	Cannanore
34.	Cherlier Voice	Nilambur
35.	Pradipam	Calicut
36.	Priyamvade	Cochin
37.	Rastanadom	Kottayam
38.	Sadvartta	Cochin

39.	Siraj	Calicut
40.	Telegraph	Trichur
41.	Telex	Cochin
42.	Potujanam	Trivandrum
43.	Samata	Cochin
44.	Zindabad	Kottayam
45.	Veeksanam	Cochin
46.	Visvakeralam	Quilon
47.	Indian Powran	Alwaye
48.	Itival	Trichur
49.	Al Hind	Trichur
50.	Dharmna Rasmi	Malappuram
51.	Jona Keralam	Kottayam
52.	Jeevanalam	Trichur
53.	Karnataka Malayali	Bangalore
54.	Manappuram News	Trichur
55.	Dinavortta	Palghat
56.	Jonadhvani	Palghat
57.	Kerala Sree	Alleppey
58.	Joyabheri	Alwaye
59.	Jonmabhumi	Cochin
60.	Cochin Express	Cochin
61.	Keraleeyan	Cochin
62.	Day Express	Kasarkodu
63.	Calicut Times	Kozhikode
64.	Tozhilsabdam	Trivandrum
65.	Viplavym	Calicut
66.	Samanta	Cochin
67.	Taniniram	Trivandrum
68.	Tozhilali	Trichur

Marathi

1.	Agradoot	Sangli
2.	Ajintha	Aurangabad
3.	Ambejogai times	Amebjogai
4.	Adivasi-Manus	Gadchiroli
5.	Amravati Evening	Amravati
6.	Bhim-Pukar	Parbhani
7.	Bahugan-Times	Ahmednagar
8.	Bhartiya Lokshah	Hingoli
9.	Bhramar	Nasik
10.	Champavit Patra	Beer
11.	Dainik-Pukar	Chandrapur
12.	Deshdut	Nasik
13.	Deshonnati	Akola
14.	Dilasa	Parbhani
15.	Express Satara	Satara
16.	Garjana	Chandrapur
17.	Gavakari	Nasik
18.	Gavakari	Ahmedabad
19.	Godatir Samachar	Nanded
20.	Gomantak	Panaji (Goa)
21.	Hindusthan	Amravati
22.	Indrapuri-Samachar	Amravati
23.	Jivhala	Satara
24.	Janashakti	Jalgaon
25.	Juhnjar-Neta	Beer
26.	Kasari	Pune

#	Name	Place
27.	Krishival	Pazari (Kulaba)
28.	Lalkar	Sangli
29.	Lokmat	Aurangabad
30.	Lokmat	Jalgaon
31.	Lokmat	Nagpur
32.	Loskakha	Parli, Vaijanath
33.	Loksatta	Bombay
34.	Lokseva	Nagpur
35.	Lokshahi-aghadi	Nasik
36.	Lokshakti	Akola
37.	Lok Vijay	Aurangabad
38.	Lok-Yug	Ahmednagar
39.	Maharashtra Times	Bombay
40.	Mahasagar	Nagpur
41.	Matdar	Dhule
42.	Marathwada	Aurangabad
43.	Matantar	Nasik
44.	Matrubhumi	Akola
45.	Mudrika	Akola
46.	Nagar Times	Ahmednagar
47.	Nagpur Patrika	Nagpur
48.	Nava-kal	Bombay
49.	Nava-Maratha	Ahmednagar
50.	Navashakti	Bombay
51.	Prabhat	Pune
52.	Prabhat-darshan	Sangli
53.	Pratapgadache Ware	Wardha
54.	Rambhumi	Nasik
55.	Ranjhujhar	Belgaum
56.	Rashtramat	Madgaon
57.	Rashtratej	Pune
58.	Ratnabhumi	Ratnagiri
59.	Ratnagiri Times	Ratnagiri
60.	Sagar	Chiplun
61.	Sahyadri Express	Malkapur
62.	Sakal	Bombay
63.	Sakal	Kolhapur
64.	Sakal	Pune
65.	Samaj	Kolhapur
66.	Sanchar	Solapur
67.	Sandhya	Pune
68.	Sandhyakal	Bombay
69.	Sangli Samachar	Sangli
70.	Sanmitra	Thane
71.	Sarvamat	Shri Rampur
72.	Satyapabha	Nanded
73.	Satyavadi	Kolhapur
74.	Shiv-Sandesh	Phalat (Satara)
75.	Shiv-Shakti	Akola
76.	Solapur-samachar	Solapur
77.	Suprabhat	Amravati
78.	Tarun-Bharat	Belgaum
79.	Tarun-Bharat	Nagpur
80.	Tarun-Bharat	Pune
81.	Thane-vaibhav	Thane
82.	Varta	Dhule
83.	Viveksindhu	Ambejogai
84.	Viveksindhu	Solapur

85. Yashvant   Latur

Oriya
1. Dahana   Cuttack
2. Dharitri   Bhubaneswar
3. Dainika Asha   Berhampur, Ganjam
4. Agnisikha   Sambalpur
5. Hirakhanda   Sambalpur
6. Janapriya   Balasore
7. Khaharakagaja   Bhubaneswar
8. Koshala   Sambalpur
9. Pragatibadi   Bhubaneswar
10. Prajatantra   Cuttack
11. Matrubhumi   Cuttack
12. Rastraduta   Balasore
13. Samaja   Cuttack
14. Swarajya   Bhubaneswar
15. Sambada   Bhubaneswar
16. Kurukshetra   Rourkela
17. New Planner   Sambalpur

Punjabi
1. Ajit   Jalandhar
2. Akali Patrika   jalandhar
3. Alaip   Rajpura
4. Chardikala Marg   Patiala
5. Desh Darpan   Calcutta
6. Dharaledar   Patiala
7. Educator   New Delhi
8. Jag Bani   Jalandhar
9. Jag Jot   Ludhiana
10. Janpakh   Bhatinda
11. Jathedar   Jalandhar
12. Khabarnama   Sangrur
13. Lok Lehar   Jalandhar
14. Lok Ran   Rajpura
15. Mang   Ludhiana
16. Navi Prabhat   Calcutta
17. Navi Saver   Patiala
18. Nawan Zamana   Jalandhar
19. Nirbhai Leader   Ludhiana
20. Panjab Bulletin   Ludhiana
21. Panjabi Tribune   Chandigarh
22. Panthak Samachar   New Delhi
23. Puah Phatti   Patiale
24. Quami Den   Sangrur
25. Ranjit   Patiala
26. Ranjit Singh   Bathinda
27. Roop Sagar   Chandigarh
28. Senapati   Patiala
29. Sham Patika   Sangrur
30. Suraj   Ludhiana
31. Tarajman   Ludhiana

Sanskrit
1. Sudharma   Mysore
2. Samskritih   Poona

Sindhi
1. Hindu — Ajmer
2. Hindustan — Bombay

Tamil
1. Anna — Madras
2. Bharatham — Madras
3. Bold India — Bombay
4. Daily Thanthi — Madras
5. " — Cudalore
6. " — Madural
7. " — Tinucluy
8. " — Coiambatore
9. " — Salem
10. " — Tirunelveli
11. " — Vellore
12. Dina ithazh — Madras
13. Dinakaran — Madras
14. " — Coiambatore
15. Dina malar — Madurai
16. Dina mani — Madras
17. Dinasari — Madras
18. Dina Sudar — Banalore
19. Jana Sakthi — Madras
20. Malai Malar — Coiambatore
21. " — Madras
22. " — Tinichy
23. Madurai Mani — Madurai
24. Malai Murasu — Madurai
25. Malai Murasu — Coiambatore
26. " — Tirunelveli
27. " — Salem
28. " — Vellore
29. Mandra Murasu — Madras
30. Murasoli — Madras
31. Namathu India — Coiambatore
32. Thekkadir — Madurai
33. Vidivelli — Madras
34. Viduthalai — Madras
35. Malai Malar — Madurai
36. Pirugal — Coiambatore

Telugu
1. Andhra Bhoomi — Visakhapatnam
2. " — Secundrabad
3. Andhrajyoti — Vijayawada
4. " — Hyderabad
5. " — Tirupati
6. Andhrapatrika — Hyderabad
7. " — Vijayawada
8. Andhraprabha — Bangalore
9. " — Hyderabad
10. " — Vijayawada
11. " — Visakhapatnam
12. Chanakya — Kakinada
13. Eenadu — Hyderabad
14. " — Tirupati
15. " — Vijayawada

16.	"	Visakhapatnam
17.	Ganthami times	Rajah mundry
18.	Godavari times	Kakinada
19.	Gunturu Express	Gunturu
20.	Kostha vani	Raja mundry
21.	Jeevagadda	Karimnagar
22.	Mundadugu	Kakinada
23.	Poddu	Nijamabad
24.	Praja Shakti	Vijayawada
25.	Ratnagarrbha	Eluru
26.	Samacharam	Rajah mundry
27.	Samayam	Hyderabad
28.	Tadepallygudem Samacharam	Tadepallygudam
29.	Udayam	Hyderabad
30.	"	Tirupati
31.	Ujwala	Karnool
32.	Veerabhavati	Palakollu
33.	Vijayabhanu	Visakhapatnam
34.	Visalandhra	Vijaywada
35.	"	Vijayawada
36.	Warangal vani	Warangal
37.	Zameen Raitu	Nellore
38.	Andhra janatha	Hyderabad
39.	Telugu prout	Secundrabad
40.	Viswarachana	Secundrabad
41.	Nava Samaj	Palakol

Urdu

1.	Akhbar-i-mashriq	Calcutta
2.	Akkas	Calcutta
3.	Asr-i-jadid	Calcutta
4.	Azad Hind	Calcutta
5.	Azimabad Express	Patna
6.	Azaim	Lucknow
7.	Awam	Delhi
8.	Eisar	Patna
9.	Ghazi	Calcutta
10.	Hamara Nara	Patna
11.	Hindustan	Bombay
12.	Imroz	Calcutta
13.	Inquilab	Bombay
14.	Iqra	Calcutta
15.	Al-Jamiat	Delhi
16.	Khidmat	Srinagar
17.	Milap	Hyderabad
18.	"	New Delhi
19.	"	Jullundhar
20.	Nadeem	Bhopal
21.	Pratap	Jullundhar
22.	"	New Delhi
23.	Paigham-i-Nehru	Patna
24.	Qaumi Awaz	Lucknow
25.	"	New Delhi
26.	"	Jammu
27.	Quami Janj	Rampur
28.	Qaumi Morcha	Varansi
29.	Qaumi Tanzim	Patna
30.	Raftar	Jammu

31.	Rahnumai Daccan	Hyderabad
32.	Rujhan	Ludhiana
33.	Rozana Hind	Calcutta
34.	Sadaqat	Patna
35.	Sada-i-am	Patna
36.	Savera	Delhi
37.	Shan-i-Millat	Calcutta
38.	Siasat	Hyderabad
39.	Siasat Jadid	Kanpur
40.	Tej	Delhi
41.	Urdu Times	Bombay
42.	Valur	Srinagar
43.	Hind Samachar	Jullundhar
44.	Pasban	Banglore
45.	Roshni	Srinagar
46.	Sangam	Patna
47.	Ameen-i-watan	Banglore
48.	Awaz-i-mulk	Varanasi
49.	Garaj	Moradabad
50.	Chhota Akhbar	Madras
51.	Ek Waum	Patna
52.	Garm Hawa	Muzaffarpur
53.	Imarat	Jammu
54.	Jauhar-i-guftar	Balgam
55.	Kohkan	Patna
56.	Masriqi Awaz	Delhi
57.	Munsif	Hyderabad
58.	Navaid Subh	Patna
59.	Panchhi	Ludhiana
60.	Qaumi Swar	Patna
61.	Samaj	Ludhiana
62.	Sandesh	Jammu
63.	Srinagar Express	Srinagar
64.	Srinagar Times	Srinagar
65.	Taskin	Jammu
66.	Tipu Mail	Mysore

ANNEXURE III

NATIONAL LIBRARY, CALCUTTA
List of newspapers held in microfilm

Sl No.	Title	Period	No of reels	
1.	Advance	9th July 1931 to 31 Dec 1937-	34	
2.	Advocate	March 1922 to Dec 1923-	4	
3.	Anglo Indian Guardian	3rd August 1878 to 7th Dec 1912-	3	
4.	Bande Mataram	August 1906 to Oct 1908-	7	(Pos. only)
5.	Bengal Harkaru	1824 to 1866 (with gaps)	55	
6.	Bengalee	1863 to1932 (with gaps)	163	
7.	Bombay Courior	1798 to 1800-	2	
8.	Behar Herald	20th July 1898 to 31st Dec 1910	7	
9.	Calcutta Chronicle	1792-1793	1	
10.	Calcutta Courior	April 1832 to 1842	9	

11.	The Calcutta Spectator	2nd Aug 1913 to 19th Aug 1914	1
12.	The Calcutta Morning Post	23rd Feb 1810 to 27th Dec 1811	4
13.	Christian Herald	8th March 1923 to 20th Dec 1923	1
14.	Carnatic Telegraph	13th May 1858 to 26th Dec 1860	2
15.	The Englishman	May 1837 to Dec 1840	7
16.	Friend of India	January 1838 to Dec 1883	45
17.	Hindu Patriot	April 1854 to Aug 1923 (with gaps)	57
18.	The Indian Daily News	a) 3rd Aug 1864 to Dec 1872	10 (in progress)
		b) 10th Jan 1896 to Dec 1898	14
19.	Indian Mirror	Jan 1883 to Dec 1923 (with gaps)	49
20.	The Indian Nation	5th Jan 1891 to 19th Dec 1910	9
21.	John Bull	January 1824 to Dec 1832	13
22.	The Mussalman	4th Jan 1907 to 18th Sept 1933	20
23.	New India	12th Aug 1901 to 20th Feb 1904 and 3rd Oct to 31st Dec 1921	2
24.	Reis and Rayyat	Jan 1882 to 31st Dec 1910	10
25.	Rangoon Times	April 1886 to June 1908	8
26.	Reformer	1833	1
27.	The Star of India	17th Aug 1932 to 1st Feb 1936	17 (in progress)
28.	Times of India	Jan 1863 to Dec 1907 (with gaps)	88
29.	Voice of India	1883 to 1886 and 1902 to 1904	7
30.	Agra Ukhbar (Urdu)	3rd Feb 1844 to 28th March 1846	4
31.	Some Prakash (Bengali)	Bengali Era 1263 to 1293 (with gaps)	11

A SHORT HISTORY OF THE NEWSPAPER IN INDONESIA

Hardjo PRAKOSO

Director, National Library of Indonesia, Jakarta

1. INTRODUCTION

The Indonesian newspaper is becoming more and more thoroughly integrated into the daily life of the Indonesian community, though in comparison with developed countries like the USA, for instance, it is much less widely disseminated.

2. NEWSPAPERS IN THE COLONIAL PERIOD

The first newspaper in Indonesia was published in the early 17th century. At that time, several regions of Indonesia were controlled by the Dutch East Indian Company (Vereenigde Oost-Indisch Compagnie). From 1615, news from Europe was received by Jan Pieterszoon Coen, the founder of Batavia, and after being edited by his office, was sent to the Ambon government under the title Memorie de Nouvelles, copies being made by hand.

On August 7, 1744, the first printed newspaper was published in Batavia and called Bataviase Nouvelles. An officer of the Secretariat of Governor-General Imhoff, J. E. Jordans, was responsible for its publication. Only a few copies of this newspaper were published, and the paper's lifespan was a brief one, only two years.

Thirty years later the Government published the Vendu Nieuws, which contained official announcements of the company's offers, advertisements or private auctions of real property and so forth. The paper, of which only a few copies were published was strictly censored like other printed materials.

Among the services of the Governor-General Daendels, besides sweeping reforms in almost every field, was the founding of the second official newspaper in the Netherlands East Indies which appeared for the first time in Batavia on January 5, 1810 and was entitled Bataviasche Koloniale Courant.

The paper, its type and its make up were far from excellent. It did not last long since in August 1811, when Great Britain occupied the Netherlands East Indies, it ceased publication. In its place the British Government published the Java Government Gazette from February 1812, it was published in English, the official language of the moment. This newspaper contained among other things news of Napoleon's fatal march to Moscow, and government notifications, decrees and regulations. News from Europe came so irregularly that a large number of local residents had heard what was happening through the gossip of traders before the reports reached the editor of the newspaper. Historians can find in the 234 numbers of the Gazette valuable information relating to the colonial life of the day. The Gazette also had a short existence because the agreement in Europe that all Dutch colonies be returned to the Dutch Government in 1814 included the Netherlands East Indies.

After the establishment of the Dutch rule, they published an official newspaper called the Bataviaasche Courant. This is now one of the best sources for the history of Indonesia. The General-Secretary was instructed to invite all people, who were qualified or willing to contribute anything that was of interest to statesmen, seamen and merchants, so that it could form a medium for the improvement of the general knowledge of the citizens. The invitation was welcomed by the intellectuals, and important articles by historians, naturalist, sociologists, and others were published besides the daily news. In 1829 the name Bataviasche Courant was changed to Javasche Courant. It was publised three times a week, and contained official documents, regulations and decrees of government. It continued until World War II when the Japanese occupied Indonesia.

The Javasche Courant and other administrative publications were published by the Government Press in Batavia from the beginning of the 19th century. From 1825 to the first quarter of 1827 there was also a Bataviaasch Advertentieblad (Advertiser), but five years later this newspaper was merged with Javasche Courant; Multaluli (Edward Douwes Dekker), a well known Dutch author, who wrote about the condition of the Indonesian people during the colonial period, was a loyal contributor to the Javasche Courant. In addition to the Government Press, there was also a press belonging to the Batavia Society of Arts and Sciences, and it was intended for publication of literary and scientific works.

Surabaya has a small press, where the Soerabajasch Advertentieblad was printed. A press in Semarang, Oliphant & Co, turned out the Samarangsch Advertentieblad and the Samarangsche Courant, besides some school books and some printing for private use.

There was no freedom of the press. In order to facilitate the supervision of printing presses in the Netherlands East Indies, the Press Act of 1856 included a regulation by which printers and publishers were obliged to submit to the Law Officer an unsigned copy of all manuscripts before publication Printers and publishers also required a licence. Only the editor of the Tijdschrift Voor Nederlandschindie, W.W. Hoevell, was not required to submit a copy of his journal although it contained articles on the political administration of the Dutch East Indies. Because of his position and standing he conducted himself according to the Government regulations. On the other hand as the publisher of Samarangsch Advertentieblad he had to obtain permission from the Law Officer to publish each day's issue.

There were several articles in the Indische Vaderland, written by the editor himself, which sharply criticized the Government. The printers of this newspaper, Van Dorp & Co at Semarang lost the licence and the firm was closed. This was death blow to the Indische Vaderland, one of the best East Indies newspapers at that time. After Van Dorp & Co presented a protest to the Governor-General the company was allowed to publish again, provided it printed nothing "insulting" to the Government.

Although criticism came from Dutch Liberals, the Governments did not change the Press Act. And it was then by the Royal Decree of 1906, announced in the Indische Staatsblad, that these provisions were removed from the Press Act and freedom of the press won. However, at least two copies of every publication still had to be sent to the seat of local government. The press became a medium for ideas and opinion of certain groups in the community.

Newspapers which were published in Batavia from 19th century to World War II were: Java-Bode, while Bataviaasch Handelsblad, Nieuw Bataviaasch Handelsblad, het Algemeen Dagblad van Nederlandsch-Indie ceased a long time before that. There were two other newspapers: The Bataviaasch Nieuwsblad and the Nieuws van den Dag voor Nederlandsch-Indie. The Bataviaasch Nieuwsblad grew in importance because of the editor's articles, but J F Scheltema had to resign as he was sentenced to three months imprisonment for a sharp article about the publicity of the Government's opium policy. But Scheltema continued his writing and published it in Holland as a pamphlet entitled: De Opium Politiek der Regeering en de Vrijheid der Drukpers in Nederlandsch-Indie (The opium politics of the Governments and the freedom of the printing press in the Netherlands Indies).

In other big cities like Semarang and Surabaja newspapers were also published during the 19th and 20th century, continuing unitl Indonesia was occupied by the Japanese in World War II. These newspapers were: Samarangsche Courant de Locomotief, Het Algemeen Handelsblad voor Nederlandsche-Indie and Het Soerabaiasch Handelsblad. Not only in these Javanese big cities, but also in other cities in or outside of Java newspapers in Dutch were published among others: De Nieuw Vorstenlanden (Sala, 1872), Mataram (Jogja, 1877), De Preanger Bode (Bandung, 1896).

Wellknown newspapers published in Sumatra were the Deli Courant (1885) and Sumatra Post (1899). Newspapers published in other island included Borneo Advertentieblad, 1914, and Celebes Courant, 1881 from Banjarmasin, Makassar and Menado.

During World War I a Press Bureau was set up in Batavia under the name ANETA (Algemeen-General-Nieuws en Telegraf Agentschap), which had upgraded news coverage and which was useful for receiving and spreading news of world events. Indonesian journalists also felt the need of a national source of information. And in 1937 a national Press Bureau was established, called ANTARA, founded by the journalist Sipahutar.

The European community was engrossed in its own affairs and had little interest in the needs of the country. This was reflected in the narrow coverage of the Dutch language press which disseminated news of interest to this part of the community, rather than information of general concern.

Besides newspapers in Dutch, from the middle of the 19th century newspaper in Indonesian languages were also published. The first was started in Surakarta. The oldest of these included: Bromartani (Soerakarta, 1855), Soerat Chabar Betawie (Betawie, 1858), Bientang Timoer (Soerabaja, 1862), Djoeroe Martani (Soerakarta, 1864), Bianglala (Batavia, 1867), Bintang Djohar (Betawi, 1873), and Retno Dhoemilah (Jogjakarta, 1895). Although the languages used were in Indonesian languages and some of them were with Javanese script, in general the editors were still Dutch.

Between 1902 and 1930 the number of newspapers published by Indonesians themselves increased steadily, the Indonesian-Chinese as well as the Indonesian-Arabic. In addition, newspapers of a distinctly Javanese script appeared in Java.

After the national awakening in 1908, and with the founding of Boedi Oetomo by the Indonesian students, the Indonesian press became a medium to express the feelings, of a colonialized nation. The Dutch press, however, remained uncontrolled and there were often articles insulting everything which was native, causing relations between the colonizer and the colonized people to deteriorate. Among several nationalistic and radically oriented Indonesian newspapers published in Java were: Darmokondo (Solo, 1904-liberal), Oetoesan Hindia (Soerabaja, 1914-radical), Neratja (Batavia, 1917-radical), Boedi Oetomo (Djokja, 1920-nationalist), Sri-Djojobojo, (Kediri, 1929-radical Islam), Sinar Hindia (Semarang, 1921-communistic). Other published outside Java included: Tjaja-Soematra (Padang, 1914-liberal), Benih Mardika (Medan, 1919-radical Islam), Hindia Sepakat (Sibolga, 1920-radical nationalist), Oetoesan Islam (Gorontalo, 1927-radical Islam) and Oetoesan Borneo (Pontianak, 1927-liberal).

Among the Indonesian pioneers in journalism was Tirtoadisoerjo, who improved printing, journalism and the national press. His experience had been obtained during his work at Bintang Betawi, before he became editor of the newspaper Medan Prijaji, published in 1907. It was issued before Boedi Oetomo was founded.

The best known newspapers published by the Indonesian-Chinese in the 20th century were: Ik Po (Solo, 1904), SIN PO (Batavia, 1910), Tjhoen Tjhioe (Soerabaja, 1914). A Chinese newspaper, which showed interest in the Indonesian national movement and considered itself as part of the Indonesian press was Sin Tit Po (Soerabaja, 1929). Only one of these, Ik Po, was published in Chinese, the rest were in Malay.

Newspapers in Arabic whose editors were Indonesian-Arabs were Al-Achbar (Padang, 1913), Al-Ahbal (Soerabaja, 1914) and Boro Boedoer (Weltevreden, 1925).

Persatoean Indonesia, which was published in Batavia in 1928 comprised a complete report of the Indonesian Youth Congress. At the second Youth Congress the unification of the Indonesian youth was proclaimed in a solemn oath, and the Indonesian Raya was sung for the first time. It became the Indonesian national anthem. The Sin Po published this same song, composed by Soepratman, in its issue of October 1928.

According to the 1920 census Indonesia had a population of about 50 million people, of which 170,000 were Europeans. Between 1920-1930 the Europeans were served by 32 Dailies in Dutch, while in the same period there were 39 Dailies in Indonesian. About 20% of the Indonesian people could read Dutch at that time the total circulation of all Dutch dailies were estimated 6,000 to 9,000 copies, including free copies, exchange and specimen copies. Indonesian newspapers had a circulation of less then 1,000 copies daily.

3. THE JAPANESE OCCUPATION

During World War II, when Indonesia was occupied by the Japanese military from 1942-1945, all Dutch and most Indonesian publications were banned. A few still were permitted to continue publication, including: Pemandangan from Jakarta (1933-1958) and Express from Surabaja, in the Javanese language (1939-1956). The Japanese military government published newspapers in Japanese and Indonesian, though the number of these was small in comparison with that of the Dutch period. Among these newspapers were: Djawa Shinbun (Djakarta), Asia Raya (Djakarta), Madioen Sjuu (Madiun), Sinar Matahari (Jogjakarta), Sinar Baroe (Samarang), Soeara Asia (Sutabaja), and Tjahaja (Bandung). They no longer appeared after Indonesia proclaimerd its Independence in August 1945. Instead, newspapers appeared entirely published by the Indonesians themselves.

When the Japanese were still occupying Indonesia, an underground press in

Surakarta published <u>Merah Putih</u>. This newspaper was comprised of articles which encouraged the Indonesian people to prepare for Independence.

4. NEWSPAPERS SINCE INDEPENDENCE

In 1947-1949 the Dutch launched their first and second military actions in Indonesia, and occupied several regions. They again published newspapers, and some Indonesian newspapers were banned. Several of these were continuations of the Dutch newspapers before World War II, others were new ones like <u>Berita Solo</u> (Surakarta) and <u>Suluh Rakjat</u> (Semarang). But these newspapers did not last long either, for when the revolutionary war was over these newspapers ceased publication.

During the revolutionary wars, the Indonesian underground press was active again and published: <u>17 Agustus</u>, <u>Pantjasila</u> and <u>Yuddha</u>. News was obtained from ANTARA.

At the beginning of Indonesian independence, the distribution of Indonesian newspapers had reached a level much higher than previously. Two newspapers in Jogja printed 10,000 copies daily, while in the Dutch colonial period all Indonesian newspapers taken together printed about 1,000 copies. The format was small, only half of the common size, and the paper used was strawpaper, because there was no other paper available from 1945-1950.

In 1946, when Indonesia faced a critical moment with the return of the Dutch, some Indonesian journalists felt the need of a union, and in the same year the Newspaper Interprise Union was founded. Beside this union the Indonesian journalists had an association, called the Association of Indonesian Journalists (Persatuan Wartawan Indonesia, PWI), which was also established in 1946. Earlier the Indonesian journalists had an association when the Dutch still colonized Indonesia, this association's name was PERDI (Perstoean Djoernalis Indonesia), founded in 1933.

Today there are well over one hundred newspapers publishing in Indonesian and other regional languages, each reflecting opinions of various sectors of Indonesian society. They are the result of over three centuries of growth and experience in the field of publication.

BIBLIOGRAPHY

Batuputih, J, 'Ratu dunia'. Djakarta, Noordhoff-kolff, no date.

Faber, G H von, 'A short history of journalism in the Dutch East Indies'. Sourabaya, Kolff, no date.

Regering Voorlichtings Dienst. Afd. Documentatie, 'Perslijst Indonesie'. Djakarta, 1949.

Serikat Penerbit Suratkabar, 'Garis besar perkembangan Pers Indonesia'. Djakarta, SPS, 1971.

Zwemer, S M, 'The native press of the Dutch East Indies', in: <u>Moslem World</u>, vol.13, 1923. p.39-49.

NEWSPAPER CONSERVATION IN IRAN

Dr Mehrdad Niknam VAZIFEH

Librarian and Member of the Research Group, National Library of Iran

1. HISTORICAL BACKGROUND IN IRAN

The first printed newspaper was published under the supervision of one of the Qajar Kings (Nasser-e-din-Shah) in 1837 in Tehran. This newspaper had no special title, it was titled Kaghaz-i-Akhbar which is equivalent to the word newspaper. Unfortunately none of its issues exist in Iran; however two of its issues are kept in the British Library. This newspaper was completely under the control of the King and the government used to publish controlled news. Fourteen years later in 1851 another newspaper, Vaghayeh Ettefaghieh or "daily events" was published by the order of the King. This newspaper was more popular than the first one and started its work with only one reporter. The circulation of this newspaper was 1150 copies. Synchronously, La Presse was published in France with the circulation of 78000 copies and the English newspaper Daily Telegraph was published in England with the circulation of 141000 copies. At about the same time an Asyrian newspaper was also published in Ourmieh, one of the cities of Iran in the north west. Our first private newspaper was published in 1875. The title of this bilingual newspaper (Persian and French) was Vatan/La Patrie. Shortly after this many newspapers began their work in different cities of Iran like Tabriz, Esfahan and Shiraz, and even 22 Persian newspapers were published in foreign countries like Turkey, England, Egypt, India and France. The first Iranian daily newspaper was published on 31 October 1898 under the title of Kholassat-al-Havadess or "Summary of events". Many other newspapers appeared in Iran, but they did not last long. The first daily evening paper in Iran is Ettalā'āt or "Information", which was founded in 1920 and its first issue was published on 11 July 1920, in Tehran. This newspaper is one of the regular evening papers which has been printed regularly up to present. It has an English (Tehran Journal) and a French (Journal de Téhéran) counterpart too. Another major Iranian newspaper is Kayhān and its publication started in 1941 in Tehran. It has also an English counterpart under the title Kayhān International. Still another regular Iranian newspaper, Alik is printed in the Armenian language and was founded in 1930 in Tehran. This newspaper began with a circulation of 1000 issues.

The "Directory of Iranian Newspapers" [1] shows that in 1969, one hundred and twenty one (121) newspapers, were published in Iran. However during the next three years (up to 1971) most of these newspapers did not get permission to be published any more and only 43 of them were able to secure a publication permit. The most important ones are :

Morning Papers	Evening Papers
Jomhouri Eslāmi	Kayhān
Abrar	Ettelāāt
	Ressālat

2. CONSERVATION OF NEWSPAPERS

Now there are several thousand newspapers which are published throughout the world. As time passes, some new ones appear and others disappear. Some of them have a very low circulation, but you may find newspapers with the circulation of two or three millions and even more. Copies of these newspapers enter library collections and are treated according to their various policies. Some libraries keep them for a short period and then throw them away or give them to other libraries free or by exchange. But some libraries keep them for ever. Most people buy newspapers to look through them for an announcement, an advertisement or an article and then throw them out. Only a few people keep the newspapers in their own collection.

However, regardless of whether newspapers are kept in libraries or at homes in private collections, they must be conserved properly; otherwise they will soon perish.

Newspapers, in spite of their short life, must be permanently preserved in national and research libraries and archives as records of their times.

Newspapers should be kept in dark stacks which are lighted by incandescent light. The lights should be on only when we are referring to a certain issue for finding some information. For air conditioning, proper filters should be used to let the air enter the stack after proper filtration. Temperature and relative humidity should be controlled in the stacks. Of course binding newspapers will protect them from wear and tear. But newspapers should preferably be deacidified before binding, because the existing acids will cause them to deteriorate almost as rapidly as in the open air. Microfilming is also a good solution for problems existing in connection with the care of filed newspapers. But we should not forget about preservation of the originals even after they have been filmed.

It is obvious that deacidification and strengthening of newspapers is the best way to preserve them. In this connection some countries have started to take some steps and in some cases they have made good progress.

The Bibliothèque Nationale in Paris has experimented on the application of paste and tissue to large printed sheets such as newspapers.

The chemical section of the Research Laboratory of Lenin State Library in Moscow has conducted extensive experiments on using polymethyl acrylate emulsions which have enabled it to strengthen old newspapers and make them resistant to moisture.

Americans have also conducted different experiments in this field; for example the Barrow Laboratory offered American librarians a low cost interim answer for acid deterioration in books, boxed manuscripts and other bulk paper material.

The Conservation Laboratory of the Austrian National Library has developed a suitable process by which newspapers (bound or unbound) can be subjected to wood removal, delignification, deacidification and buffering. In this system they impregnate the text block in a vacuum chamber (by a strengthening, neutralizing and buffering solution) and then by subsequent freeze-drying, they prevent the sheets from sticking together during the drying process.

Other countries may also have experimented or started to experiment in this field. In Iran, as I stated before, the first newspaper was published in

1837; during these 150 years, with the low circulation and short life span of
most newspapers, we do not have very large collections of newspapers in Iran.
The National Library of Iran and our Parliament Library (Ketābkhāneh Majlis
Showrāye Eslāmi) have the largest collections of newspapers in Iran. The
National Library has 1400 titles (in more than 5000 volumes) and the Parliament Library holds 1174 titles. The National Library receives two copies of
any newspapers published in Iran legally; and has published a catalog of its
holding of newspapers. With great sorrow I must inform you that it is only
for the last 15 years that the question of conservation and preservation of
library materials has been put forth by our librarians. Some effort has been
made in this respect. The National Archive of Iran has its own small laboratory of preservation and restoration of documents and maps. The Parliament
Library has started to establish a preservation and restoration workshop. The
National Library of Iran too has a small binding and preservation workshop.
There are also a few other preservation and restoration workshops existing in
Iran but they are mainly concerned with documents, manuscripts and books. No
serious effort has been made about the conservation, preservation and restoration of newsprint. No special stack has been built with proper air conditioning facilities and lighting. Most of the libraries use water-coolers in
summer time. There, no devices exist for temperature and humidity control in
libraries. Taking Xerox copies from newspapers is very common in many libraries. But some recent efforts have been made by some librarians in order to
reduce the losses of our cultural heritage. For example, the National Library
of Iran has prepared microfilm copies of 40 old Persian newspapers and users
of the library are only permitted to use these copies. Taking Xerox copies
from old newspapers is not allowed and the National Library has microfilm
services for old newspapers.

Reprinting old important newspapers and magazines is also a method that reduces the use of the originals. During recent years some of the old newspapers
and magazines have been completely reprinted. Two of our most important daily
newspapers (Ettelā'āt and Kayhān) have started to reprint their collection in
book form and reduced size. Ettelā'āt has started this from the past (1941)
coming forward and Kayhān has started it from recent times (1978 or Islamic
Revolution period in Iran), eventually going backwards.

This was a bird's-eye view of the history of newspapers and the present situation of their conservation in Iran. I hope this has been enough to show our
serious need for technical assistance and information. I believe that papers
presented in the seminar and the conclusion of the discussions could be useful
guidance for countries such as mine, in order to take proper steps for preservation of newspapers, these pages of historical and cultural heritage of a
nation, or even the whole world.

REFERENCES

1   'A directory of Iranian newspapers, 1969'. Compiled by Parvin Abuzia,
     Tehran, Iranian Documentation Centre, 1970.

BIBLIOGRAPHY

Cunha, George Martin, 'Conservation of library materials; a manual and bibliography on the care, repair and restoration of library materials'. 2nd ed.
Metuchen, N J, Scarecrow Press, 1971.

Mohseniyān-e Rād, Mehdi, 'Moqaddameh'i bar jāme'h shenāsi-ye matbū'āt-e Iran'. (An introduction to psychology of the Iranian press). Tehran, Khabargozari-ye Johmhuri-ye Eslami-ye Iran, (1365=) 1981.

Molana, Hamid, 'Syr-e ertebātāt-e ejtemā'i dar Irān. (History of mass communication in Iran). Tehran, Daneshkadeh-ye 'Olum-e Ertebatat-e Ejtema'i, (1358=) 1979.

Mosahab, Gholam Hosseyn, 'Dā'erat-ol-ma'āref-e Fārsi'. (Persian Encyclopedia). Tehran, Feranklin, (1345=) 1966.

Sadr-e Hashemi, Mohammad, 'Tārikh-e jarāyed va majallāt-e Iran'. (History of Persian periodicals). Esfahan, Kamal, (1363, 1327=) 1984.

'Seyr-e takāmol chapkhaneh va matbū'āt dar Iran'. (Development of printing houses and press in Iran). Tehran, Vezarat-e Ettelā'āt, Edāreh-ye Koll-e Matbu'āt, (1351=) 1972.

Swartzburg, Susan G, 'Preserving library materials: a manual'. London, Scarecrow Press, 1980.

Wächter, Otto. 'Paper strengthening: mass conservation of unbound and bound newspaper'. Vienna, National Library of Austria, Institute for Conservation, 1986.

THE NATIONAL LIBRARY OF IRELAND, DUBLIN

Donal O'LUANAIGH

Keeper, National Library of Ireland, Dublin, Eire

As this Library holds files of approximately 1600 newspaper titles, current and non-current, it is the principal newspaper repository in Ireland. The greater number of these titles, dating from the early eighteenth century, are Irish newspapers, but there is also a substantial collection of English newspapers, (mainly dating from the early nineteenth century to the First World War period). Most of these non-Irish newspaper volumes have had to be placed in offsite storage owing to pressures on storage space in our main building.

For the past twenty years or so, it has been the policy of the Library to acquire newspaper files on 35 mm. positive microfilm. We acquire microfilms of all the current Irish national dailies and most major Irish weekly papers. The hardcopy issues of all current newspapers in the Republic of Ireland are acquired by us under the terms of our copyright legislation. Also, we acquire, either by purchase or donation, copies of all newspapers currently published in Northern Ireland. Microfilms of current newspaper holdings are acquired through a commercial microfilming bureau, with the co-operation of the newspaper proprietors. All our hardcopy issues are bound by us, but only those of which we have no microfilm copy are available for consultation.

Our Library has for many years held a large hardcopy collection of Dublin newspapers from the earliest days of the press, but our hardcopy collection of Irish provincial papers mainly covers the late nineteenth century onwards and in some cases dates only from 1927 (when the Irish Copyright Act came into force). For this reason it has been our policy to supplement our holdings of Irish provincial papers by acquiring 35mm. positive microfilms from the British Library at Colindale. We are most grateful for the continuing co-operation of the British Library in this project. For reasons of economy we endeavour, whenever possible, to make a joint purchase of sets of these microfilms with Irish academic and public libraries.

We supply photographic copies of pages of our bound hardcopy newspaper files, and we also supply printouts of pages of our newspapers on microfilm. At present we do not have sufficient conservation facilities, and therefore the microfilming of as many titles as possible remains an urgent necessity.

Newspaper files may be consulted on application to the Assistant Keeper on Duty.

NEWSPAPER MICROFILMING IN JAPAN

Akio YASUE

National Diet Library, Japan

I am not the newspaper librarian but very briefly I would like to describe one of our newspaper microfilm projects which has been carried out over thirty years, very successfully and satisfactorily.

In 1953 the National Diet Library, which is the National Library of Japan, made a contract with Japan's Newspaper Publisher's Association for a current newspaper microfilming project. This is a co-operative and cost sharing programme and at present covers 41 newspaper publishers, that is, 59 titles of newspapers, participating in this project framework. This coverage of 59 newspapers means that this covers all major or nationwide distributed newspapers in Japan.

I would like to add one or two practical points, that is, specialities. Each newspaper publisher sends their newsprint through the Japan Newspaper Publisher's Association to our Library. These newspapers are printed on normal white book paper on one side only. This is in order of course to have a better image, a better quality of microfilm image, and from that is made one master negative and three positive films. The master negative is deposited in our Library together with one positive film for our public service. A second positive film is given to the Association and a third one to each newspaper publisher. And from this the Association reproduce as many as they want to sell these microfilm to university libraries and public libraries and so forth.

What I would like to point out is that co-ordination and co-operation among our libraries and archives for newspaper microfilm is of course essential and necessary and this is what we are doing for the retrospective newspaper microfilming project. But also I think that co-ordination and co-operation between libraries and newspaper publishers can be sought, particularly for the case of current newspaper microfilming, because I believe that many newspaper publishers are very much concerned to preserve their own product, that is, newspapers.

NATIONAL APPROACHES TO NEWSPAPER PRESERVATION: NEW ZEALAND

Penny GRIFFITH

Deputy Director, Alexander Turnbull Library
National Library of New Zealand

1. INTRODUCTION

The last five years have seen a significant change in the policies relating to newspaper preservation in New Zealand. In effect this should be interpreted as a significant change in the policies of the National Library of New Zealand - a change at least partly due to effective lobbying, including (appropriately) through the press itself. But it also coincided with the beginning of the period in which accountability for the use of public funds, for analysing results, for consensus, have all become increasingly important, especially for centralised government organisations. Commonly these are regarded with a mixture of frustration, mistrust and envy by their colleagues, who are usually at least partly dependent, while at the same time are expected to co-operate, contribute and concur, when they would really prefer to have the power themselves.

However, it is fair to say that the changes in policies relating to newspaper preservation and retention have engendered considerable goodwill towards the National Library, and enabled it to make positive contact with a wide range of organisations and people that otherwise would not have occurred.

The author's review, completed in 1984, which was adopted as official policy, established two guiding principles for the National Library's newspaper programme - that it should:
(a) have as its prime objective for the national newspaper resource the provision of the highest quality microfilms. Consistent with this, it should ensure that the microfilming process does as little damage to the original as possible.
(b) collect, retain, and preserve as complete a file as possible of all New Zealand newspapers. Access to filmed papers to be available only where bibliographical or technical need to use the hard copy over microfilm can be proved.

The major specific achievements, in summary, are:
* clearly stated general policy
* active collection-building
* long-term filming programmes based on agreed priorities
* retention of hard copies after filming
* Newspaper Librarian position established
* complete survey of newspaper holdings/physical condition
* union list of newspapers published
* list of microfilms for sale published
* upgrading of equipment for both filming and use
* vault for remote, secure storage of archival master negatives due for completion February 1988.

These achievements are now enhanced by the facilities provided for both storage and use of newspapers in the new National Library building, which opened to the public on 1 July 1987. The separate newspaper research room is expected to be heavily used by genealogical and other research workers, and a current newspaper service (New Zealand and overseas) is a new service which will be carefully monitored.

Government support, through funding, has been critical to the success of the National Library's programme for newspapers. Approval for increased resources over the last ten years is indicative of the high profile of this national information (and heritage) resource. The Trustees of the National Library have also provided funding (for the newspaper survey of 1983) and their endorsement of the recommendations of the review were valuable when the subsequent proposals were put before Government.

2. NEWSPAPER RESOURCES

New Zealand is a small country (roughly the size of mainland Italy) as far from Europe as one can go. Its indigenous Maori population, which had a solely oral tradition before missionary and colonial settlement, has been there for about 900 years. Colonisation, almost exclusively by the British, began in earnest in the 1840s in half a dozen places on the two main islands, whose ruggedness of terrain and climate can still create communication difficulties.

From this brief summary it can be seen that New Zealand has a very recent newspaper history, but that almost all this resource falls within the period that ground woodpulp has been used in their production. Therefore almost all newspapers present the serious conservation and preservation problems with which we are familiar.

The pattern of settlement lead to strong local communities and the establishment of local newspapers, a trend which (despite takeovers) continues today; the first national daily newspaper began only in June 1987. This powerful sense of local identity can be seen in the proliferation of local authorities, historical societies and museums. These together with newspaper proprietors, major metropolitan public libraries, university libraries and central government institutions share the responsibility for the national newspaper resource. In practice this responsibility is met by widely varying degrees of care, and a range of attitudes to centralised repository functions, even though this may be the most economic and effective solution.

Maori language publications present different reasons for their scarcity - there have been very few; their language has been 'foreign' to institutions and librarians; they were produced in smaller numbers and often in more difficult circumstances, at times falling within the category of 'protest' publications, especially during the turbulent mid-nineteenth century.

2.1. Major collections

Since 1839 some 1500 New Zealand newspapers have been published, a total of roughly 35 million pages. About 2% of these titles are Maori language publications, but because most were short-lived, they comprise a much smaller percentage of the total physical resource. Currently 125 titles are produced, with an annual output estimated to be 475,000 pages or 25 linear metres - the equivalent of 755 reels of 35 mm microfilm.

The most recent union list (1985), covering locations of newspapers to 1939, records the holdings of 815 titles in 165 institutions. Many holdings are unique, incomplete, and there are also some valuable items in private hands. While the total resource is scattered, by far the major collection (7,500 volumes and 17,500 reels of microfilm) is that belonging to the Parliamentary Library, which was established in 1857, and was part of the National Library between 1966 and 1986. The major gaps in its holdings of hard copies are for the period 1953-1984, when microfilming programmes were under way but there was no complementary programme for the retention and preservation of hard copy.

It is planned to transfer a large proportion of the bound volumes and microfilms from the Parliamentary Library to the National Library during 1987. These transfers will be added to the 6,000 volumes and 7,000 reels of film already in the collections of the Alexander Turnbull Library, its division with responsibility for New Zealand collections of last resort. This will be the nucleus of a national newspaper collection for permanent preservation. The policy is to build a comprehensive collection of New Zealand newspapers, by retrospective acquisition where possible, and by retaining the current output - in addition to microfilms of all titles (as and when they become available) which will be the primary medium for public use.

Other significant collections, tending to reflect local and regional interests, are found in the major public and university libraries - the most notable being at the Hocken Library, University of Otago. Frequently the most complete holdings of individual titles are housed by the proprietors themselves, or in local council offices which often can provide space when the public library runs out. Museums, including those run by local historical societies, also often keep copies of early newspapers, as do a number of individuals. In some cases the smallest institutions have the only known copies of short-lived publications. One of the major difficulties, when the project of surveying the national holdings of newspapers got underway, was in identifying all these repositories in order to make contact with them.

The major repositories for Maori language material are Auckland Public Library, Auckland Institute and Museum, Alexander Turnbull Library (National Library), and the Hocken Library (University of Otago).

2.2. Overseas newspapers

While a number of large public libraries subscribe to overseas papers, these are generally not retained beyond six months. The major holdings of overseas newspapers are in university libraries (especially on microfilm) and in the Parliamentary Library. Holdings of Pacific newspapers are strongest in Auckland and at the Turnbull and Parliamentary libraries.

The National Library is still refining its policy for the acquisition of overseas newspapers, though it has been recognised in principle that it should reflect the overall acquisition policy. It proposes to subscribe to about ten overseas titles by airmail at an annual cost of some $NZ20,000 as a means of increasing resources needed for its own information services, and not to establish a public-library type newspaper reading room.

One of the difficulties with overseas newspapers is that we need airmail copies in the short-term while in the longer term microform would be better. The combined cost of these is prohibitively high.

2.3. Legal deposit

Legal deposit functions were formerly carried out by the Parliamentary Library, but in 1987 transferred to the National Library. Newspapers are covered by the statute, and consequently the National Library will be receiving this material. As in the past, most current newspapers will be microfilmed as soon as practicable for reasons of space; the Newspaper Publishers Association has been generous in transferring the copyright rights of microfilms of papers over one month old to the National Library for those titles which it is filming.

3. BIBLIOGRAPHIC CONTROL

New Zealand has maintained a high standard for national bibliographic control of monographs. It is possible to find in a published volume or (for more recent material) on a microfiche and online a complete record from the earliest publication (1663) noting our discovery by Tasman to the latest novel or economic edict. Unfortunately we have not yet been able to do as well for our serials and newspapers.

There have been, however, some major contributions to information on the history and holdings of newspapers which will provide a good basis for the development of a detailed newspaper bibliography. The only general history attempted, by Scholefield in 1958, is remarkably comprehensive for the period it covers. More recently, the necessary groundwork for Harvey's two surveys (1983 and 1987) covering all holdings of New Zealand and overseas newspapers (including microform) resulted in the most complete and up to date information on titles and dates of publication that we have. Early Maori language newspapers are more fully recorded, with Williams' bibliography setting high standards of accuracy and detail.

The best published source of information on holdings of New Zealand newspapers is Harvey's "Union List" (1985), but this covers papers only up to 1939. Gully's "Union List" (1961) supplements it to some degree, though neither publication lists the holdings of individual collections. It is hoped that a full union list based on both of Harvey's surveys will be published this year, thus providing information on holdings of all newspapers up to 1985. It is not intended at this stage to provide a location/collection index but, as the information is in machine-readable form, it would be straightforward to do so.

4. USE AND ACCESS

4.1. Services in the National Library

The new National Library building, which opened to the public in 1 July 1987, provides good facilities for the national newspaper collection, including separate stacks of horizontal compact shelving (490 bays) for bound volumes of broadsheet papers. For historical reasons, many tabloid size newspapers will continue to be housed as part of the library's serials collection on horizontal static shelving. The stack areas are designed to provide a physical environment of 13° Celsius and 40% RH. Microforms are housed in a separate air conditioned storage area.

Access to the current issues of selected papers (both New Zealand and overseas) will be provided through the Reference & Interloan Services division's serials reading room. Hard copy will transfer to the Alexander Turnbull

Library for preservation once the microfilms have been received.

The Turnbull Library, being primarily a research library, will provide access to the microfilms and unfilmed older papers - and the hard copy of the filmed papers - when it can be shown that there is a real need which cannot be met by microfilm. These services will be provided in a separate Newspaper Research Room seating 12 people which will have 5 pieces of equipment for microfilm use (2 reader-printers, 3 readers); a prototype adjustable table providing an angled surface for the use of bound volumes is also being produced.

At the time of writing the newspaper collections (apart from microfilm) have been inaccessible for 18 months due to stock relocations before moving to the National Library building. As a result, patterns of use are not yet known. However, it is expected that the two previous main groups of users - genealogists and historical researchers - will continue to be the heaviest users, reflecting the need to consult primary documents more frequently in societies with recent histories and shorter historiographies. Statistics of researchers solely using newspapers are not available.

4.2. Staffing

While newspapers will be consulted in a separate reading room, this is primarily for practical reasons of handling and storage. The staff servicing the room will be part of the Turnbull Library's Reference Section, and newspapers have always been considered as just another source of information - users are usually wanting answers, not access to newspapers as such. Indexing and clipping of papers is thus usually part of the wider programme for indexing and not kept separate, though there are a couple of exceptions to this.

However, the National Library does have a specialist Newspaper Librarian - a position approved by Government in 1985. The initial responsibility for the position was the completion of surveys of holdings newspapers; now that that has been done, the major tasks are:
* cataloguing the National Library's collection
* assisting with bibliographical aspects of the National Library's microfilming programme
* building the national newspaper collection
* liaison with other organisations and individuals to ensure awareness of the importance of the newspaper resource and its conservation
* input into indexing programmes, including proposals for co-ordinated automated indexing.

4.3. Interloan

Microfilms are available for interloan, both within New Zealand and overseas, with copies of National Library films being run off for interloan as the need arises. Hard copy is not available, though it may be possible to meet some needs through photographic reproduction - but not by photocopying, which presents conservation problems.

5. PRESERVATION

5.1. General

While the temperate climatic conditions of New Zealand are more kind to library materials than some other environments, conservation and preservation issues, especially those relating to storage and use, are of major concern.

The National Library itself has begun a major conservation review (due for completion in 1987), to identify the policy, procedures and resources needed for the proper storage, handling and conservation of all its collections, and not just those for which it has a specific statutory responsibility.

The New Zealand Library Association's Library Resources committee has also initiated discussions and policy development relating to the identification, preservation and surrogate copying of scarce and high demand New Zealand items. Another professional group, the Archives and Records Association of New Zealand, has become active in working towards preservation policies, and was instrumental in stimulating the quite public debate which saw the National Library reconsider its policy for newspapers. The review which was carried out also sought submissions, 33 of which were received.

In this context it is important to recognise the contribution made by many of the other curators of newspapers in New Zealand - whether libraries, newspaper or council offices, or individuals. Some, on the other hand, are not able to provide even basic conditions for the material in their care. The Library recognises that its concern for the preservation of material may not always be well received, and that its advice or willingness to accept material may be misinterpreted.

5.2. Newspaper preservation in the National Library

As indicated earlier, the Library has taken a leadership role in acknowledging its responsibility for building, maintaining and preserving a comprehensive collection of New Zealand newspapers. The core of this collection will be in place when the major transfers of older material from the Parliamentary Library take place in 1987, and is continuing with the systematic retention of papers aftr filming which began in 1985. The policy of acquiring copies of retrospective titles not already held (particularly for the period 1953-1984) is a longer term project.

The major way in which the National Library is ensuring the long-term preservation of newspapers is by having as its prime objective the provision of the highest quality microfilm, so that the hard copy is not used. Hard copy will be available for consultation only when it can be proved there is some specific need which microfilm cannot meet. Papers are shrinkwrapped (but not vacuum packed) after filming with storage being provided at present in the new National Library building. In due course it is envisaged that remote storage will be necessary.

As the microfilms themselves take on a critical role as the prime medium for public use, attention is paid to the archival quality of the master negatives, and appropriate storage for them. When microfilming began in 1952, the need for this was not foreseen, and some 6,000 original negatives produced between then and 1972 were in regular use until 1983. Their condition is of concern and duplicates are being run off on demand to protect the originals, which are the best we have.

A secure air-conditioned vault is being built at one of the National Library's regional centres, some 150 km from Wellington; this should be completed by February 1988. The type of equipment used for filming copies (especially bound volumes) is also a preservation matter and we are currently in the process of upgrading this so that as little damage as possible is done. The National Library's Conservation Officer is involved in all decisions where it seems necessary to remove bindings in order to obtain good images.

One of the day-to-day problems we have not yet solved is how to provide photocopies (or equivalents) from original hard copies, especially bound volumes. The delays and expense of getting proper photography done will generally preclude this method. Some images have been produced by using a hand-held polaroid camera and then enlarging them on a photocopier, but they are not very good.

It is, of course, impossible to set about building a comprehensive collection of newspapers, or carry out a long term microfilming programme, or to start to analyse the extent of the problem (and resources to meet it) without knowing:
* what the titles and dates of publication were
* where they are held
* what condition they are in.

The importance of the two surveys which Dr Harvey carried out cannot be overemphasised in terms of information for the basis of planning a strategy. As far as I know, these are the only surveys of newspapers which have specifically quantified (on a numerical basis) the physical condition of newspapers, so that it is possible to carry out a filming programme which will ensure that papers in the worst condition get filmed first.

6. MICROFILMING

While there are a total of 5 microfilming operations in New Zealand (3 in the private sector) experiences with commercial filming of newspapers have not been very satisfactory. The National Library, which is keen to increase its own microfilming output (especially of manuscript material), has recently reconsidered the use of other producers, but concluded that it was necessary to retain responsibility for filming of newspapers to ensure quality control. It would appear to be one of the benefits of the manageable proportions of the total newspaper resource that it is able to be centralised in this way, at least in terms of quality control. A commercial organisation, is, however, being used by Massey University in its project to film scarce New Zealand periodicals, and yet another by a library and a newspaper publisher who wanted a title filmed which did not come within the National Library's revised priorities for filming.

It should be noted here that, while other new technologies were on the horizon (and still are), at the time of the review (1984) it was concluded that microfilming would continue to be the main medium to which newspapers would be transferred for the foreseeable future, ie 10 years. There seems no reason to modify this assumption at this stage, and the ability of small libraries to afford access to more sophisticated systems will affect decisions on future applications.

The Microfilm Production Unit of the National Library has the following priorities for filming:
* newspapers identified in the surveys as being in urgent need of filming due to physical deterioration. (This meant a score of 30 out of a maximum of 48; half the papers published before 1939 came into this category - some 7 million pages).
* current newspapers (apart from 6 major metropolitan dailies).

The goal is to have finished filming all New Zealand newspapers by the year 2000, both current and retrospective, and the programme's priorities will adjust as progress is made.

While it might be desirable to film only older papers, it was also necessary to continue filming current papers for space reasons. A compromise was made in the case of 6 daily metropolitan papers which the Parliamentary Library intended to continue keeping in bound volumes, even if they were filmed - this ensured that copies would be available for filming in the future, and allowed a greater proportion of time to be spent on older papers. This decision, not to film 6 of the metropolitan papers, was the one which did cause some problems for both libraries and newspaper publishers, however worthy the guiding principle.

Sixty per cent of the Microfilm Production Unit time is spent on filming older papers, and forty per cent on the current titles, with a total of about 100 master negatives being produced each month (plus intermediate positive films for generating copies, and copies as required). A three-year programme is followed, with the Library negotiating for the loan or donation of holdings of older papers for filming, and making all the arrangements for the transport of material to Wellington. Copies of the films are provided free of charge to those who supply older papers.

The standards for filming which have been followed since 1977 are Library of Congress Specifications for Microfilming Newspapers in conjunction with ISO 4087, whichever is the more specific in any given instance. Two processors are installed which achieve archival standards and pass the methylene blue test requirements.

The type of film produced are:
* silver halide (polyester based): for master negative, intermediate positive, and copies (as required)
* diazo: for copies.

A catalogue of films of newspapers produced by the Microfilm Production Unit available for sale is available from the National Library, and a proposal to establish a union catalogue of master negatives is being considered.

7. FUTURE DEVELOPMENTS

The major issues which are likely to affect newspaper programmes in the next 5 years are:
* direct access to on-line texts of newspapers
* alternatives to microfilming for providing surrogate copies
* co-ordination of newspaper indexing on automated databases.

As more microfilms become available in more libraries, the level of local and regional use is likely to increase. There is no reason to expect that the importance of newspapers as a valuable primary source of information for historical research will diminish. One of the keys to increased use will be improved bibliographical control, and one of the benefits should be better access to information through increased indexing.

8. SUMMARY

Date of first New Zealand newspaper: 1839
Total number of newspaper titles published 1839-1985: 1500
Total number of pages printed 1839-1985: 35,000,000
Number of pages in urgent need of filming: 7,000,000
Equivalent number of 35 mm microfilm reels: 11,500
Number of titles produced annually: 125
Equivalent number of 35 mm microfilm reels: 755
Major repositories of newspapers:

Parliamentary Library (7,500 vols approx plus 17,500 reels microfilm)
Alexander Turnbull Library, National Library of New Zealand (collection designated the national newspaper collection; 6,000 vols approx plus 7,000 reels microfilm)
University libraries, especially Hocken Library, University of Otago
Metropolitan public libraries
Newspaper publishers' offices
Local Authorities' offices

Legal Deposit repository: National Library of New Zealand
Medium for public use: microfilm (35 mm) when available
Retention after microfilming: shrinkwrapped for permanent preservation in remote storage; access only in exceptional circumstances
Number of microfilming operations (nationally): 5 (of which 3 are private sector)
Number of filming newspapers to archival standards: 1 (Microfilm Production Unit, National Library of New Zealand)
Standards followed: Library of Congress Specifications for Microfilming Newspapers & ISO 4087
Microfilm produced:
    Master negative: silver halide (polyester based)
    Intermediate positive: silver halide (polyester based)
    Distribution copies: diazo, silver halide (polyester based)
Number of staff: 12; number of cameras: 5
Number of reels produced annually: 1200
Copies made for sale: Yes; catalogue is available

BIBLIOGRAPHY

Griffith, P A, 'Review of Microfilming Policy for Newspapers'. Wellington, NZ, National Library of New Zealand, 1984. (National Library Bulletin no 24) Reviewed in: Microform Review, Vol.15 no.3, Summer 1986. p.194.

Gully, J S, 'A Union Catalogue of New Zealand Newspapers Preserved in Public Libraries, Newspaper Offices and Local Authority Offices'. 2nd ed. Wellington, NZ, General Assembly Library, 1961.

Harvey, D R, 'The 1983 survey of New Zealand newspapers', in: New Zealand Libraries, Vol.44 no.7, September 1984. pp.117-120.

--- 'Second Survey of New Zealand Newspapers; final report'. Wellington, NZ, Alexander Turnbull Library, National Library of New Zealand, 1987. 2 volumes. Unpublished report covering holdings of New Zealand newspapers 1940-1985, overseas titles, and all microforms.

--- 'Survey of New Zealand-Newspapers [to 1939]; Final Report'. Wellington, NZ, Trustees of the National Library of New Zealand, 1983. 3 volumes. Unpublished report.

--- 'Union List of New Zealand Newspapers before 1940 Preserved in Libraries, Newspaper Offices, Local Authority Offices and Museums in New Zealand'. Wellington, NZ, National Library of New Zealand, 1985.

--- 'An Unsuccessful Attempt at a Bibliography of New Zealand Newspapers', in: New Zealand Libraries, Vol.45 no.1, March 1986. pp.11-14. Discusses a 1920s proposal.

'New Zealand Newspapers on Microfilm; a list of titles available from the National Library of New Zealand'. Wellington, NZ, National Library of New Zealand, 1986. Catalogue of microfilm for sale (available from National Library of New Zealand, Private Bag, Wellington, New Zealand)

Scholefield, G H, 'Newspapers in New Zealand'. Wellington, NZ, Reed, 1958. The only attempt at a comprehensive history.

--- 'A Union Catalogue of New Zealand Newspapers Preserved in Public Libraries, Newspaper Offices, etc.'. Wellington, NZ, Government Printer, 1938.

Williams, H W, 'A Bibliography of Printed Maori to 1900 and Supplement'. Wellington, NZ, Government Printer, 1975. Reprint of works first published 1924 and 1928.

NEWSPAPER PRESERVATION AND ACCESS IN NIGERIA

Dr Gabriel B ALEGBELEYE

Lecturer, Department of Library, Archival and Information Studies, University of Ibadan, Nigeria

1. INTRODUCTION: THE NATIONAL CHARACTER OF NIGERIAN NEWSPAPERS

It is a truism to state that the Nigerian newspaper has a character peculiarly its own. The Nigerian press is usually regarded as perhaps the most outspoken, volatile and witty in Black Africa. Its criticisms of government and the private sector are far ranging and pointed. As the government's watchdog, Nigerian newspapers have often attacked the conspicuous extravagance and profligacy of government. The <u>Nigerian Tribune</u> of 10 July 1975, for example, in condemning extravagance of government, referred to the importation of Shire horses from Britain:
> 'When Governor Blake of Kano State bought 12 durbar horses which were flown on a charter plane in preparation for the grand durbar at the Black Arts Festival, he certainly could not have thought he was buttressing a programme in a socialist state. The cost of each horse was N800.00. With their flight the figure could not have been less than N100,000. The twelve horses all died in a month and N100,000 evaporated like the puff of smoke from a near smoker. It hurts when one thinks that till today, under 5 per cent of Kano State school children are in school.' [1]

The ability to poke fun and ridicule is an essential and often used weapon of the Nigerian press. Ten days after the coup of 1975 a <u>Sunday Chronicle</u> article stated:
> 'So we had the Third coming in which the order which had grown nauseatingly old was bloodlessly changed and we have on our hands new prefixes to go along with. We are thus ex-this, ex-that, ex-these, ex-those, the former, the erstwhile ... Even if you were yearning for the men in 'agbada' and you woke up one rainy day to fund another set of men in khaki, and you have no choice, your may want to give them a chance ... If someone said that the new men need some luck, someone else would say that they need it plenty.' [2]

Yet the Nigerian press could equally be sarcastic. Speaking on the indigenisation exercise which had received much critical comment from a cross section of the Nigerian society for not having done anything of the sort, the <u>Sunday Times</u> of 3 August 1975 opined:
> 'Nigerians were successfully (and thanks to the power that be then) entrenched to take over the sale of gari, palm oil akara leaves, tuwo and other specialized jobs that required primitive brawn and native intelligence.' [3]

In a rather uncharitable appraisal of Gowon, a writer in the same paper said:
> 'For my own part, I am sorry to see General Gowon miss a golden opportunity for immortalising his name. He ran a beautiful race but pulled a muscle as he was approaching the tape. He prepared a

delicious dish but overturned the pot at the service table. He wrote an excellent speech but lost his voice at the time of delivery.' (3)

Osundare [4] reported that obituaries, 'in memoriam' and other forms of announcing bereavement are a constant genre of newspaper content in Nigeria. At the end of his illuminating paper, Osundare wondered what Nigerian newspapers would be like without mortuary advertisements. On most days:
> 'The space allocated to mortuary advertisements in the 'Daily Times' is more than the space allocated to international and world news and almost equal to that apportioned to national news.' [5]

The English of Nigerian newspapers has a vigour and style all its own that will distinguish Nigerian English from the original in the same ways that idioms of American English have grown apart from the original. Nevertheless, Nigerian newspapers constantly deal with major themes of public life - education, agriculture, corruption, commerce, industry, the quality of life, the need for political direction including international affairs. Banjo [6] has however argued that international affairs have played a less prominent role in many Nigerian newspapers.

2. THE GENESIS OF NIGERIAN NEWSPAPERS

The origins of newspaper publication in Nigeria dated to 1859 when a printing press established in that year at Abeokuta started production under the leadership of the venerable Rev. Townsend. Rev. Townsend was a missionary of the Anglican Mission who was sent to Badagry and Abeokuta so as to minister to the spiritual and educational needs of Sierra-Leonian immigrants who had settled in both places after the end of the slave trades. Iwe Irohin, a bilingual newspaper, was the title of the new publication. The publication of Iwe Irohin was regarded by the Missionaries as a satisfactory way of slaking the appetite of the products of CMS schools that had reached about 3000 people at the time. The information disseminated by this early newspaper covered Church matters such as marriage, announcements, church news but according to Azikwe [7] it also included "post office notices, advertisements, trade reports, cotton statistics and general news." This early newspaper in collaboration with the Anglo-African launched an unrelenting attack on the nefarious slave trade which continued to thrive clandestinely in what was later known as Nigeria. The early Nigerian newspapers had a chequered history. The newspapers were also characterized by their high mortality rate. Table 1 shows the mortality rate of the early Nigerian newspapers. It must be noted at the outset that the high mortality rate cannot but have some bearing on the problem of access to be discussed later in this paper.

The second phase in the history of the press in Nigeria was marked by the arrival of Payn Jackson from the Republic of Liberia in 1890, who in conjunction with Herbert Macaulay founded what Azikwe [8] called "a school of iconoclasm in the political arena of Nigeria." It should be recalled that this was the period of colonial regime at its zenith. The newspapers during this period launched a vehement attack on the socio-economic evils of the day. Among the issues the newspapers discussed were the water rate, the building of a colonial church with public funds and the exclusion of Nigerians from worshipping there, the flogging of Nigerians particularly in the North, illegal traffic in liquor, nationalization of native courts, the establishment of indirect rule, the amalgamation of Northern and Southern Nigeria, the formation of the Nigerian Congress of the British West Africa, agitation for amendment to the Nigerian Constitution, the organization of pressure groups and the formation of political parties. In other words, the Nigerian newspapers mirrored the times.

The third phase, 1945-60, belonged to what Nduka [9] described as "a pulsating period in the history of Nigeria." It was a period when political agitation by colonialists reached its apogee. With the granting of independence to India, Nigerian newspapers of the period turned their attention to the ceaseless agitation for a better deal from Britain. The attention of the newspapers was directed not only to political agitation but also to social and economic and educational matters. This was the situation till 1960 when Nigerian was granted independence.

The fourth phase, from 1960 to the present is marked by an unprecedented growth in the number of newspapers in Nigeria. The issues discussed by the papers continued to be a reflection of the times. Regarding the proliferation of newspapers in the post independent Nigeria, Banjo [10] noted that between 1978 when party politics was restored after thirteen years of military rule and 1984 when the military regime was reimposed, no less than 32 newspapers were established in Nigeria. Table 2 shows the growth of Nigerian newspapers between 1978 and 1984.

	NAME OF PAPER	YEAR ESTABLISHED	YEAR DISCONTINUED
1	The Anglo-African	1863	1865
2	The Lagos Times	1880	1883
3	Lagos Observer	1882	1888
4	Eagle and Lagos Critic	1883	1888
5	The Mirror	1887	1888
6	African Messanger	1921	1926

TABLE 1
The mortality of some early Nigerian newspapers

1	Business	(82)	17	Sunday Concord	(80)
2	Daily Nation	(82)	18	Sunday Graphic	(83)
3	The Democrat Weekly	(84)	19	Sunday Herald	(82)
4	The Guardian	(83)	20	Sunday New Nigerian	(82)
5	The Hope	(83)	21	Sunday Post	(83)
6	The Telegraph	(83)	22	Sunday Satellite	(82)
7	Morning Focus	(83)	23	Sunday Spotlight	(83)
8	National Concord	(80)	24	Sunday Stamp	(82)
9	The Nationalist	(78)	25	Sunday Sun	
10	Nigerian Call	(81)	26	Sunday Telegraph	(82)
11	Nigerian Newsweek	(83)	27	Sunday Triumph	(82)
12	The Premier	(83)	28	Weekly Eagle	(81)
13	The Satellite	(82)	29	Weekly Echo	(83)
14	The Spotlight	(83)	30	Weekly Focus	(79)
15	Sunday Advocate	(83)	31	Weekly Freedom	(82)
16	Sunday Call	(82)	32	Weekly Trumpet	(83)

TABLE 2
Nigerian newspapers established between 1978 and 1984

Source: Banjo, A O, "Problems in the storage and dissemination of newspaper information: a Nigerian Example". Paper delivered at IFLA General Conference, Nairobi, 1984, p12.

3. NEWSPRINT PRODUCTION IN NIGERIA

Although today there are a few paper mills in Nigeria, the one that is relevant to our present discussion is the Nigerian Newsprint Manufacturing Company at Oku-Iboku (NNMC) because the largest proportion of newsprint used in the production of newspaper is supplied by this company. It is however believed that small quantities of newsprint are still smuggled into the country in spite of a fairly tight government control.

According to Akachuku [11] NNMC at Oku-Iboku was to receive 20,000m^3 of dry pulpwood from the Forestry Division of the Ministry of Agriculture and National Resources, Cross River State, in 1981 for the test run of the mill before starting the main newsprint production the following year. This quantity was to be increased to 310,000m^2 per annum when in full production by 1988. Table 3 shows the pulpwood requirement of Oku-Iboku paper mill.

YEAR	VOLUME 1000 m^3
1981	20
1982	200
1983	235
1984	250
1985	250
1986	265
1987	265
1988	310
1989	310

TABLE 3
Pulpwood requirements of Oku-iboku

Source: Banjo, A O, "Problems in the storage and disssemination of newspaper information", (as above)

For the supply of wood to feed the Oku-Iboku paper mill, reliance is placed primarily on the short fibre Gmelina Arborea. Gmelina Arborea is a hardwood that was introduced into Nigeria from South East Asia because of the suitability of its wood for paper manufacture. The pulping process of the Oku-Iboku paper mill is semi-chemical. The newsprint is manufactured from acidic pulp and has a low surface finish, a characteristic that Nigerian newspaper publishing houses deplore. The short-fibred Gmelina Arborea is supplemented with long-fibred pulp imported from abroad. The resulting newsprint from Oku-Iboku newspaper mill is consequently inherently weak and unstable. Because of the paper's instability it cannot be preserved for an indefinite length of time without special treatment.

4. OBJECTIVES OF THIS PAPER

The primary focus of this paper is: (a) to examine the problems as well as methods of newspaper preservation in Nigeria. Additional objectives are: (b) to investigate methods of providing access to Nigerian newspapers and (c) to provide suggestions for better access to as well as better preservation of Nigerian newspapers.

4.1. Methodology

The instruments used in collecting data for the paper consisted of a questionnaire developed to elicit the views of librarians as to their methods of newspaper preservation as well as their methods of providing access to the backfiles of their newspaper collection.

The questionnaires were mailed to Nigerian university libraries. The reason for selecting Nigerian university libraries rather than other library types is because they are research institutions which not only collect newspapers but also preserve them and endeavour to provide avenues for their proper exploitation. It is also conjectured that Nigerian university libraries are in many respects Nigerian libraries writ large.

Although the study is limited to Nigerian university libraries an attempt has been made to include other libraries in Nigeria noted for their newspaper collections. These include for example the National Library of Nigeria, the National Archives of Nigeria and the Nigerian Institute of International Affairs. Thus, 24 questionnaires were mailed to all the existing university libraries in Nigeria. Responses came from 18 university libraries, thus providing a 75 per cent response rate.

4.2. Data analysis

Data analysis was conducted on all responses. Frequency distributions were used to provide the basic summary statistics for the study.

5. RESULTS OF SURVEY

5.1. Nature and size of newspaper holdings in university libraries

All Nigerian university libraries with the notable exception of Sokoto University attempt to have a national coverage in their newspaper collection. Most universities acquire not less than eight different newspapers per day. In the case of Sokoto University, its coverage include "every daily newspaper available within Sokoto town." The oldest university in the country – the University of Ibadan – has newspaper collections dating back to 1948. The National Archives of Nigeria is the repository of copies of newspapers from the beginning of journalism in Nigeria, when _Iwe Irohin_ was published in 1859. The collections of older newspapers for example include:

    The Lagos Times, Lagos 1888 – 1891
    Lagos Observer, Lagos 1883
    Lagos Weekly Times, 1890
    Nigeria Daily Times, 1926 –
    The West African Pilot, 1937 – 1968
    The Eastern Nigerian Guardian, Port Harcourt 1940 – 1945
    The Nigerian Tribune, Ibadan 1947 –
    The People, Port Harcourt 1950 – 55

The National Archives and the National Library attempt to be comprehensive in their newspaper collection.

5.2. Newspaper storage

All university libraries claim that their newspapers are stored separately from the rest of the collection. This probably underscores the special features of newspapers, for example their size and value to the libraries studied. It is however interesting to note the wide variety of ways newspapers are stored in the libraries studied. By far the largest number of libraries store their newspapers by wrapping them up. Binding is another method of storage often employed. A few libraries indicate that their collections are stored in archival containers. Only one library indicated that it has microfilmed a small portion of its collection.

Still under storage, one major problem of storage relates to the storage of newspapers in a controlled environment.

It is generally known that the storage of newspapers in a controlled environment minimizes their deterioration. Atmospheric moisture, for example, often causes the lignins and other impurities in paper to produce acids which weaken paper stability and strength. The photochemical effect of direct light leads to oxidation of lignins and paper cellulose thus hastening the process of deterioration.

Temperature is another environmental factor which is particularly relevant in Nigeria where temperatures are high all the year round.

It is generally agreed for example that the rate of chemical reactions in cellulose doubles for each 5° C (9° F) rise in temperature. The chemical reaction that takes place under the high temperatures of Nigeria is left to the imagination of the reader.

There is of course the effect of airborne pollutants. In view of the importance of the foregoing environmental factors, it was necessary to find out under what conditions newspapers are preserved. The majority of libraries studied preserve their newspapers under environmental conditions that are far from congenial. Indeed, only one university reported storing its newspapers in an air-conditioned room. The value of air-conditioning in tropical and subtropical countries, of which Nigeria is a typical example, is that it effectively eliminates high temperature extremes while stabilizing the temperature and humidity at the same time warding off airborne pollutants and other particulate matter.

5.3. Measures against pests, insects and rodents

It is a truism to state that tropical countries swarm with insects, pests and other micro-organisms. Indeed Plumbe noted some years back that of the over 1,200 species of cockroaches extant, the majority of them are to be found in tropical countries. In view of the prevalence of insects in tropical countries in general and Nigeria in particular, it was necessary to find out whether libraries take any measures against their ubiquitous presence.

From Table 4, it would be seen that quite a number of libraries, 8 out of 18 or 44%, take no measures against insects, pests and other micro-organisms. Most libraries report that the method of checking pests etc include the use of chemicals although no specific names are mentioned but it is quite clear that a number of libraries use sprays such as "Raid" etc. Interestingly enough only one library mentioned the prohibition of food from the library as an important method of checking insects etc. This might suggest that not enough emphasis is yet placed on housekeeping methods in order to ward off insects in libraries.

	N	%
Measures against insects, pests etc	10	55.6
No measures against insects, pests etc.	8	44.4
TOTAL	18	100

TABLE 4
Measures against insects, rodents etc.

5.4. Disaster prevention in university libraries

Disasters, particularly man-made, are likely to be more common in univeristy libraries than other Nigerian libraries. This is because universities in Nigeria are usually in the throes of one crisis or the other. Libraries in these institutions are often at high risk. But besides fire, floods from leaking roof, etc., are common features. At least one important Nigerian library has been ravaged by fire. In view of these possible disasters it was necessary to find out what measures libraries take to combat disasters. Table 5 shows the statistics of libraries that take precautions against particular types of disasters and those that do not.

	YES		NO	
	No	%	No	%
Precaution against fire	12	66.7	6	33.3
Precaution against flood	5	27.8	13	72.2
Precaution against theft	14	77.8	4	22.2

TABLE 5
Precaution against disasters among Nigerian university libraries

It must also be added that the commonly reported methods of combating fires include the following:

(a) the use of fire extinguishers
(b) prohibition of the exposure of naked fire
(c) the switching off of all electric appliances and
(d) the prohibition of smoking in libraries.

However, in a different study [12] on disaster planning yet to be completed by the author it is clear that majority of libraries in Nigerian are yet to take even the most elementary precautionary measures against disasters. For example, the majority of library personnel in Nigeria are ignorant of how to use fire extinguishers which are often conspicuously placed in these libraries. The major methods of preventing theft as reported by respondents include: (a) the enforcement of a closed access system and (b) the use of guards.

5.5. Other methods of newspaper preservation

(a) MICRO-REPRODUCTION
This is a method that is often used in lieu of keeping the ink print files. Microform as a method of preserving the intellectual content of the originals also enjoys the advantage of saving space. Unfortunately,

the use of microform for the preservation of the new intellectual content of newspapers is still very restricted in Nigeria. Only two university libraries for example among those studied reported that they have converted small portions of their newspaper holding to microform. However, a majority, approximately 15 university libraries out of 18 or 82% of the libraries studied, are rhapsodic about converting their backfiles of newspaper into microform. There is however no indication on the part of these libraries that they are aware that microfilming, desirable as it may be, involves a rigid adherence to established standards if they are to produce archival-quality film.

(b) DEACIDIFICATION

Only the National Archives of Nigeria engages in the deacidification of portions of its collection as a method of preserving the newspapers in their original format. The method of deacidification employed in Nigeria involves the use of magnesium bicarbonate.

A solution of magnesium carbonate ($MgCO_3$) is made up by adding 1.5g of $MgCO_3$ to 1 litre of distilled water. Carbon dioxide is then bubbled thorugh the solution to produce a solution of magnesium bicarbonate ($MgCO + CO_2 + H_2O \rightarrow Mg(HCO_3C_2)$). It deacidifies by reacting with sulphuric acid to produce magnesium sulphate plus water and carbon dioxide ($Mg(HCO_3)2 + H_2SO_4 \rightarrow MgSO_4 + 2H_2O + 2CO_2$). The residual buffer is magnesium carbonate, this buffer reacts with sulphuric acid to produce magnesium sulphate ($MgCO_3 + H_2SO_4 \rightarrow MgSO_4 + H_2O + CO_2$).

As for encapsulation, this method of giving maximum physical protection to frequently used materials, is not practised at all in Nigeria.

(c) LAMINATION AND ENCAPSULATION

Newspapers in Nigeria are neither laminated nor encapsulated. The National Archives of Nigeria practices lamination using Ademco tissue and cellulose acetate film. Lamination in the National Archives of Nigeria is however only applied to documents. However, lamination when preceded by deacidification and alkaline buffering process may be desirable for a sizeable portion of Nigerian newspapers.

(d) PRESERVATION OF NEWSPAPER CLIPPINGS

Newspaper clippings are very popular with Nigerian librarians. At least 16 university libraries out of 18 or approximately 89% of the libraries studied engage in the practice of making clippings. Most of these libraries also mount their clippings on papers or boards that are non-alkaline. In other words no care is taken as to the quality of the paper on which the clippings are mounted.

A related problem is the adhesive used by libraries that mount their clippings on papers or boards. In almost all cases, glue sticks, gums and pressure-sensitive tapes are used rather than alkaline adhesives such as rice or wheat starch. The result is the rapid deterioration in the quality of Nigerian newspapers subjected to this kind of treatment.

6. PROBLEMS OF EXPLOITATION AND ACCESS TO NIGERIAN NEWSPAPERS

The effective exploitation of Nigerian newspapers should be regarded as a joint responsibility of both the library and the newspaper publishing house. Mr Banjo, Director of the Nigerian Institute of International Affairs, has provided copious examples of how the full exploitation of newspapers is hamp-

ered by the very nature of the content of the newspapers. The following inhibiting factors were noted by Banjo [6]:
(a) the overemphasis of Nigerian newspapers on politics and politicians with the near-total neglect of human interest stories
(b) the paucity of the coverage of foreign affairs
(c) problems of inaccurate reporting, denials and rejoinders of political stories
(d) the high mortality rate of the newspapers particularly the early ones to which we refer in Table 1.

The erection of obstacles in the way of untrammelled and unrestricted access to newspaper information should be regarded as a joint responsibility of libraries and newspaper publishing houses. To date, only two Nigerian newspaper publishing houses have encouraged the indexing of their newspapers - these are the Guardian and the Concord.

The creation of what Wilson calls bibliographic instruments is in Nigeria unfortunately left to librarians and other information professionals to shoulder in spite of the fact that newspaper publishing houses are in a better position financially and otherwise to support the creation of such bibliographic instruments. In the absence of comprehensive indexes to Nigerian newspapers information retrieval is like finding a pin in a haystack. In the absence of the more comprehensive type of indexing described above, librarians and other information professionals have resorted to the creation of the less laborious and expensive means of access such as the making of newspaper clippings and arranging them by subject or some other form of classification. Other practices in vogue include the use of the UDC. The Nigerian Institute of International Affairs library (NIIA) uses a straightforward alphabetical arrangement of the subject headings.

Perhaps we should end our description of the exploitation and access to newspaper information in Nigeria on a more cheery note by referring to the success story of the NIIA library. This library's newspaper collection is specifically referred to because of the deserved plaudits it receives both from local and foreign scholars. This success story is the more impressive in view of the numerous problems libraries face in Nigeria in their efforts at facilitating accessibility to and exploitation of their resources. Some of the problems faced by Nigerian libraries include administrative inertia, financial difficulties and the paucity of top-flight professionals to mention only a few. The NIIA newspaper clippings grew at a phenomenal rate from 257 clippings in 1964 to 182,110 by 1983, covering some 5,500 subject headings. The subject headings decided upon are alphabetically arranged. Strenuous efforts are made to prevent a proliferation of subject headings. The NIIA Library, conscious of the weakness of a straightforward alphabetical arrangement particularly in separating related subjects, mitigates this by the provision of cross-references.

7. CONCLUSION AND RECOMMENDATIONS

It appears clear from this study that the condition of newspaper production, preservation and access in Nigeria leaves much to be desired. As we have shown in the study, part of this problem is outside the purview of librarians, archivists and other information professionals. Archivists, librarians and other information professionals cannot control the quality of materials used in newspaper production. As can be seen in Fig 1, the newsprint manufacturers determine the quality of newsprints. Unfortunately these newsprints already have the seeds of their own deterioration before they got to the hands of librarian and archivists etc.. What options are open to librarians, archivists, etc.?

First, there is need for newspapers to be stored in a controlled and monitored environment since this, if vigorously pursued, will minimize deterioration. By a congenial controlled and monitored environment, one has in mind a storage where (a) the atmosphere is unpolluted and (b) there is low relative humidity and temperature. This, unfortunately, is not yet the situation in many Nigerian libraries.

Secondly, in many libraries in Africa where newspaper backfiles are in advanced stages of deterioration and where there is no demonstrated need to preserve the original, micro-reproduction might be a possible option. This option has the added advantage of saving space which librarians could then use for other library-related activities. This option is to be recommended in view of the fact that archival-quality, safety base, silver halide film has a useful life potential of several hundred years, particularly when properly processed, stored and handled.

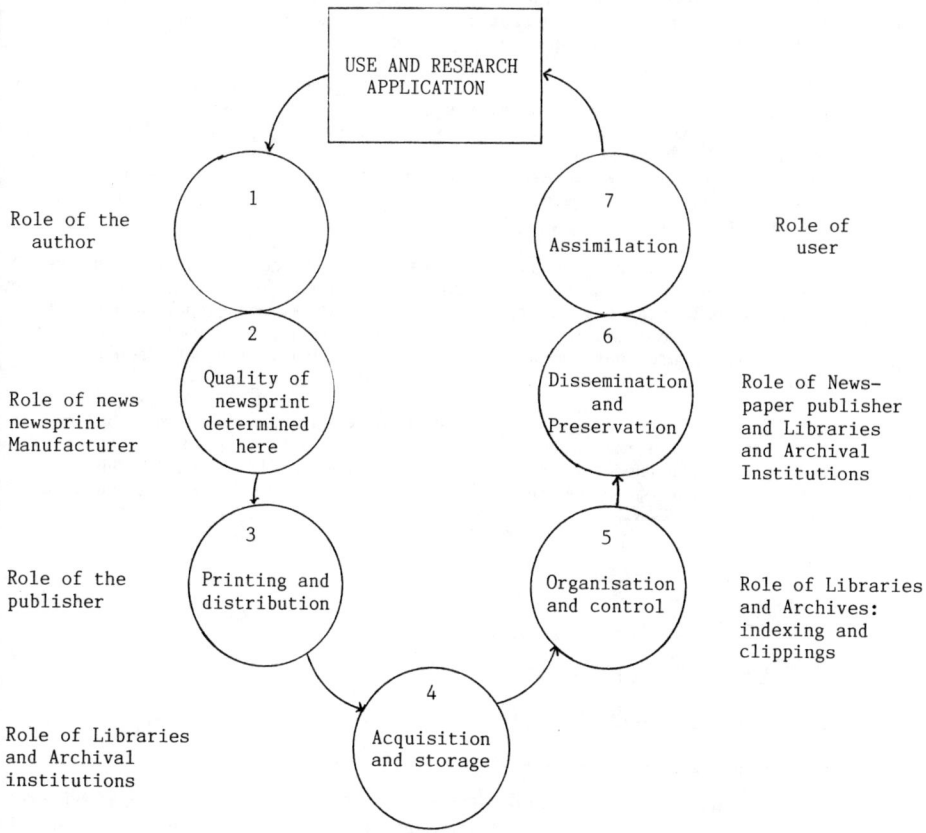

FIGURE 1
The transfer of information by newspapers

In many cases, however, the newspaper might need to be preserved in its original format. This might involve more sophisticated treatment. As we have shown in this study only one institution, the National Archives of Nigeria has the facility for deacidification and lamination. Polyester film encapsulation which is an alternative method of providing maximum physical protection for newspapers is not practised at all.

Since a number of methods utilized for the protection, reproduction and treatment of newspapers are fairly sophisticated and in view of the fact that in many African countries few libraries have the financial resources as well as the technical skills for embarking on many of the methods and techniques described above, it is advisable for these countries to consider the establishment of regional conservation centres which would be capable of dealing with deteriorating and brittle materials on a fairly large scale as well as offering workshops and advice to libraries and archival institutions. Resources, skills and energy which would have been dissipated on a myriad of minuscule conservation projects in Nigerian libraries could be channelled to much more strengthened and well-funded regional centres.

The problem of the bibliographic control of Nigerian newspapers is still to be squarely tackled. At the moment, the situation still leaves much to be desired. Since only two newspaper houses in Nigeria have so far encouraged the indexing of their newspapers, the trend might be for the rest to fall in line. The remaining newspaper houses that are yet to encourage the indexing of their collection would need gentle prodding by librarians and other information professionals.

On the part of librarians and archivists, there is need for consciousness-raising concerning conservation needs and problems. To cite just one example, libraries collecting newspaper clippings in Nigeria are neither aware of the need to mount their clippings on good alkaline paper, nor are they aware of the need to ensure that unmounted clippings are deacidified and given an alkaline reserve to arrest further deterioration.

The Nigerian Library Association might need to set up a task force on the preservation of library materials whose goal would be to prepare a conservation policy for the country. Like in many other fields, there is need for international co-operation in the area of research staff training and information dissemination.

REFERENCES

1   Nigerian Tribune, 10 July 1975.

2   Sunday Chronicle, 10 August 1975.

3   Sunday Times, 3 August 1975.

4   Osundare, N, 'The Rhetoric of Lament: A Sociocultural Stylistic Study of Obituary and In Memoriam in Nigerian Dailies'. Seminar paper delivered at the Institute of African Studies.

5   Op. cit. p.33.

6   Banjo, A O, 'Problems in the storage and dissemination of newspaper information: a Nigerian example'. Paper delivered at IFLA General Conference, Nairobi, 1984.

7   Azikiwe, R, 'Pioneer Heroes of the Nigerian Press', in: Daily Times, Vol.17, 1987.

8   Op. cit. p.5.

9   Nduka, O, 'Western Education and Nigerial Cultural Background'. Enugu, OUP, 1964.

10 Op. cit. p15.

11 Akachukwu, A. 'Pulpwood Requirements of Papermills', in: Nigerian Tribune, 23 December 1986, p.6.

12 Alegbeleye, G O, 'Disaster planning in Nigerian libraries'. (in progress)

NEWSPAPER PRESERVATION AND ACCESS: NORWAY

Anne Grete HOLM-OLSEN

Head, Norwegian Dept., Royal University Library, Oslo, Norway.

The Royal University Library, Oslo, is also the National Library. According to Norwegian legal deposit law all documents published in the country should be delivered to this library. Newspapers and periodicals are to be submitted as they appear.

Newspaper publishing in Norway began in 1763. The first daily newspaper, Morgenbladet, started in 1819 and is still published.

The library has an almost complete collection of Norwegian newspapers from the beginning. The collection consists of about 60,000 volumes. We now have 200 newspaper titles, covering all types from daily newspapers down to some appearing once a week.

Preservation effort has tended to concentrate on microfilming. Filming of Norwegian newspaper started in the 1940's. The whole collection is now available on microfilm and today's papers are filmed currently. Two copies, one positive and one negative plus a master negative are produced for the library. Copies of films are available for purchase. The papers are bound after filming and remote storage of original copies has been necessary. For conservation reasons bound volumes will not normally be made available to readers: only in exceptional circumstances, i.e. if photographs are required, can original volumes be retrieved for use in the library.

BIBLIOGRAPHY

'Norske aviser 1763 - 1969' (Norwegian Newspapers 1763 - 1969). Oslo, 1973-74. 2 vols. (The bibliography was compiled by Tom Arbo Høeg and edited by the Royal University Library. It includes 1650 titles).
Vol.1: Titles in alphabetical order with full information about the history of the paper.
Vol.2: Index of persons (editors and personal publishers) and Index of places.

BRIEF HISTORY OF NEWSPAPER COLLECTIONS IN SOUTH AFRICA WITH SPECIAL REFERENCE TO PRESERVATION

P R COATES

Chief Librarian, South African Library, Capetown, South Africa

1. ORIGINS OF THE PRESS

The first newspaper published in the subcontinent was The Cape Town Gazette and African Advertizer, begun in August 1800 as a private venture but very soon taken over by the Government to become its official organ. The next private venture was The South African Commercial Advertiser; this commenced in January 1824 and continued for many years after winning a fierce struggle against government attempts to suppress it.

Newspapers were established later in other parts of the subcontinent, in the Eastern Province of the Cape in 1831 (Graham's Town Journal), in Natal in 1844 (Natalier), the Orange Free State in 1850 (The Friend) and the Transvaal 1862 (De Emigrant). All these early papers catered for the interests of the European colonists. The first proper newspapers for the indigenous population were Isigidimi Samaxosa (1870) and Imvo Zabantsundu (1884).

As a result of the struggle for the freedom of the early press, the government of the day attempted to control the circulation of newspapers by imposing a heavy tax on paper (Ordinance 26 of 1826), the paper being stamped in Cape Town. This made newspapers expensive in Cape Town and almost impossible to produce in the remote districts. Very rapid development of the newspaper press followed the abolition of this tax by Ordinance 2 of 1848.

2. COLLECTION BUILDING

Throughout the period between the early and mid-nineteenth century, while newspapers were infrequently issued (e.g. weekly or semi-weekly) and printed only on a single sheet, private individuals collected and bound their own files of newspapers. Many such private collections have now passed into public possession. Perhaps the largest private collection was that of the Cape Town attorney J H Redalinghuys (fl. 1840-1870). Local libraries and Chambers of Commerce also formed collections which were more or less complete for their area of interest. It is thanks to these earliest collectors that such complete files of early newspapers survive today.

The commencement of a national newspaper collection began in 1829 when Ordinance 60 ("For preventing the mischiefs arising from the printing of newspapers... by persons not known") provided in Section 14 for the deposit of copies of each issue with the Government. Publishers were paid for the newspapers so deposited. The law lapsed in 1848 but the practice continued. Registration was again legislated for by Cape Act 29 of 1884 and legal deposit was implemented by Cape Act 4-1888 which remained in force in the Cape until the national Act 9 of 1916 came into force, since which time the several "legal deposit" libraries have been in receipt of all newspapers published in the state.

The most comprehensive collection was formed in Cape Town by the Colonial Office (i.e. Department of the Interior) receiving papers under the Ordinance of 1829 and purchasing papers from all the other colonies and states in Southern Africa. These were bound by contract and the volumes have not proved very durable. When the colonial period ended in 1910 the Colonial Office transferred its collection of 3310 volumes to the South African Library. After that date bound volumes of Cape papers only were delivered by the Department of the Interior to the South African Library, and in the other provinces to their respective State Archives Depots. This arrangement ended in 1926.

Subsequently the South African Library has maintained the largest collection of newspapers with an emphasis on the Cape Province. The State Library in the Transvaal also began a good local collection in 1887, while the Natal and Orange Free State Archives continued their local collections until 1986 and 1978 respectively. All archives are transferring their newspapers to libraries willing to accept them.

A very large collection of volumes was maintained by the Cape, and subsequently South African, Parliament but this was discontinued in 1979 and the collection is now housed in the South African Library, which has also accepted many other large collections. The South African Library's stock was estimated to be about 30000 volumes in 1980. Since 1981 all South African newspapers are preserved. Over 900 bound volumes are added to stock annually.

With the increasing bulk of collections and the rapid rise in the cost of storage accommodation, newspaper collections have been centralized to a considerable degree in the legal deposit libraries. Only the South African Library is statutorily required to retain newspapers in printed form, and is committed to receiving from other libraries original newspaper not already in stock provided these are in a reasonable state of preservation.

3. PRESERVATION

South African printers adopted low-grade wood pulp paper in the 1880s. This paper has deteriorated rapidly, and in many instances can no longer be handled. Restoration is unthinkable considering the quantity of paper involved.

Microfilming was recommended as a solution in 1940 and work was commended in 1946 by the state-run National Film Board at the South African Library. Eleven of the most heavily-used titles were filmed. A commercial organization, Microfile Ltd., was established in about 1946 to film South African papers. Systematic in-house microfilming of newspapers was commenced by both the State Library (which has by far the largest establishment) and the South African Library in the late 1960s. To date the State Library has produced some 4000 masters, the South African Library 2000 and Microfile 11000. The British Library is also engaged in filming such South African titles as have been preserved only in that Library.

The South African Library policy on preservation of originals is that they shall be stored as long as they are in storable condition. All titles are bound when new. Little-used titles are not rebound after microfilming but stored wrapped in acid-free parcels. It is also intended that duplicate sets which have been received over the years will be discarded after checking for completeness. The State Library now binds no newspapers, but stores the loose parts in cardboard files. The Bloemfontein, Johannesburg and Natal Society

Public Libraries all have a selective ongoing binding policy.

4. INDEXING

At present the position is very unsatisfactory. For the past decade and a half, the Institut for Contemporary History has run a clipping service linked to a broad-based computerized index which does not provide in-depth analysis. Computerized indexing is being investigated by Die Burger which hopes to cover not only their own titles but other newspapers as well.

Most current access is through the clipping files of the larger newspapers' libraries. The Argus-group clippings can be purchased on microfilm. The Star experimented with a computer-assisted indexing project in 1969 but this was discontinued after six months through lack of support

Retrospective indexes have been started from time to time but have met with little success. A local index to Graham's Town papers was attempted but abandoned after one year. The first published newspaper index in South Africa was A Raybone's Index to The Graff Reinet Herald, 1852-1854. This project ended disastrously when several years of cards awaiting typing were destroyed in a fire. The only other restrospective index at present is The Cape Town English Press Index, compiled by P R Coates. At present indexes for the years 1871 to 1873 have been completed and published and 1874 is in the process of compilation. This project is being undertaken privately without financial assistance. CEPIX is a detailed index to all African news appearing in the titles indexed. Each part is published on microfiche by the South African Library.

Two other indexes to newspapers and other publications must be mentioned. They are firstly a vast card index compiled by W F Fairbridge from the earliest times up to about 1920, whose drawback is that its coverage of the publications was unsystematic and unreliable. Secondly there is the very extensive card index to events relating to the South Eastern Cape compiled by Peter Crail. Both of these card indexes are in possession of the South African Library.

NATIONAL APPROACHES TO NEWSPAPER PRESERVATION; THE UNITED KINGDOM

Eve JOHANSSON

Head, British Library Newspaper Library, London, UK

1. THE PATTERN OF PROVISION IN THE UNITED KINGDOM

One newspaper collection in the United Kingdom is pre-eminent - that of the British Library. Its newspaper Library has the only comprehensive legal deposit collection, although there are gaps before 1844 and some current titles are not at present deposited. Five other UK libraries have the right of legal deposit of newspapers, but the British Library is the only one to enforce it comprehensively. The others confine themselves to the national newspapers and those of their region; for instance the National Library of Scotland concentrates on Scottish newspapers and the Bodleian Library on those of Oxfordshire. Academic libraries in general do not have extensive collections even of the national newspapers, and few take their local newspapers. The British Library is the only source for the user seeking the complete range of the national papers, or the local papers of more than one area, or a combination of the two.

The collection development policy of the British Library for foreign newspapers covers the world, aiming to collect at least two titles from every country in such a way as to reflect its political range and periods particularly important in the development of the country. (Newspapers in Oriental scripts are however selected, stocked and serviced from the Oriental Collections in central London by the language specialists.) No other library in the UK collects on a similar scale, though some academic libraries servicing areas of specialisation in post-graduate research have important collections.

Public libraries, with their important tradition in the UK, make an invaluable contribution, collecting the newspapers of their areas, typically locating them in their local studies or local history departments, and often undertaking indexing projects of great local value. Their newspaper holdings are heavily used, they are the first port of call for the majority of UK users, and they hold some unique materials not held by the British Library.

Newspaper publishing offices often have files of their own titles, and some of these are accessible to the public: in addition there are important news libraries maintained by newspaper offices and media services, providing cuttings and indexing services (often with a great deal of duplication of effort) for journalists. These services are not usually available to the outside user, though those that are run by librarians will often give help to other libraries through the networks of informal contacts that always exist within a profession.

There is no single professional or other forum where those working with newspapers in libraries in the UK can meet. In the public library sector, the Information Services Group (formerly the Reference, Special and Information Section) of the Library Association and the Local Studies Group are the two most appropriate bodies. Two associations of media librarians and those working in news libraries have been formed recently: they are not affiliated to the Library Association or any other umbrella body.

In spite of the predominance of the British Library Newspaper Library, the emphasis in the UK is on co-operation between libraries of all kinds and other organisations, as I hope will become apparent.

Newspapers in UK libraries are universally heavily used, and a most popular research material. Two developments of the second part of the twentieth century have contributed to encourage their use : the growth of higher education in the UK, the USA and the English-speaking Commonwealth, and a popular interest in local history and family history. This combined with the deterioration of wood-pulp based newsprint since the late nineteenth century and the sheer housekeeping problems associated with large formats has made newspapers the problem material that they are for most libraries.

2. THE BRITISH LIBRARY NEWSPAPER LIBRARY

The Newspaper Library is a completely integrated service for all the aspects of newspapers, being responsible for their legal deposit, collection development, cataloguing, public services, storage and preservation policy within the framework of British Library policy generally.

It houses 18 miles (29Km) of bound newspaper volumes or parcels, and 228,000 reels of user positive microfilm, and reading rooms with 100 reader seats including microfilm reading machines. Newspapers must be read there: they are not delivered to other reading areas of the Library. 3,000 titles are taken currently, about 75% of this intake being UK legal deposit materials. The rate of growth is currently 500 linear feet (160 m) per year. There are some gaps in the current legal deposit intake: an estimated 500 "free" newspapers are not at present acquired, and not all local editions, nor all the "time" editions of national papers. There are also some gaps in the historical sets caused by losses in wartime bombing.

There is a microfilm unit of 33 cameras all dedicated to newspaper work, and a specialist conservation and binding unit also dedicated to newspapers. The staffing complement is 150 and its annual budgets, including accommodation and overheads, add up to over £1.75 millions. It is almost certainly the largest such library in the world.

The newspaper stock of what is now the British Library has been housed on the present site ten miles out of central London, at Colindale, since 1905, in a purpose-built building of splendidly functional appearance, and the range of its responsibilities has grown during the twentieth century. The newspapers were the first category of the British Library's stock to be moved out of the British Museum building - the process of outhousing to off-site storage has gone on ever since. In 1900 the Trustees of the British Museum sought to 'transfer their files of local newspapers or other material, of dates not earlier than 1837, to the charge of boroughs or counties in England and Scotland' and 'to destroy any valueless material, whether duplicate or not, not earlier than 1660'. The move was a reaction to the space problems with which the British Museum building has always been bedevilled. Under the terms of the British Museum Act, this would have necessitated legislation, and a bill was in fact introduced into Parliament in 1900. A lobby was mounted, successfully, to stop the bill, and the Museum's solution was to purchase land for offsite storage. The site was a green-field one and the <u>Hendon and Finchley</u>

Times, the local newspaper, of 24th August 1906, records the purchase. Initially, the building operated as a store, from which the newspaper volumes were delivered to the reading rooms in the Great Russell Street building. In 1932, a reading-room, bindery and additional stack space were added, and in 1948 the first microfilm cameras were acquired to make good losses from wartime bombing by microfilming damaged volumes and some borrowed from other libraries in order to be filmed in London. The microfilming unit developed apace and did a great deal of work with Kodak, its principal supplier, to develop the archival microfilming of newspapers before the international standards evolved. Microfilm began to meet the library's space-saving needs in the 1960's: foreign newspapers began to be filmed and the originals sent to off-site storage (or, a policy which operated from 1964 to 1975, and was reinstated in 1986, disposed of). In the 1960's, the space and preservation needs of other libraries began to be partly met from microfilm supplied from the Newspaper Library, which remains one of the largest suppliers of microfilm in the world.

Within the context of a large, general research library, the Newspaper Library has the inestimable advantage of specialisation and vertical integration of functions. Decisions rest with a relatively small number of people, constantly in touch, and aware of all the aspects of the library. For example, the programme for preservation microfilming is closely integrated with the provision of public services in the reading rooms where microfilm reading machines must be provided and maintained, and with the conservation workshop, the planning of accommodation and the marketing of microfilm. Paradoxically, it may have been the fact that in 1900 the Trustees of the British Museum undervalued their newspaper stock as a research resource that has enabled the Newspaper Library to develop the specialist expertise and the level of service that it offers today.

The microfilm unit is possibly the largest of its kind. It microfilms to the highest archival standards, using polyester base film and almost exclusively 35mm silver halide roll film. Master negatives of all film are stored in a basement store constructed in 1961 which provides the correct environmental controls. Roughly half the microfilming capacity is taken up with work from outside customers, and there is a published sales catalogue of available microfilm. At the same time it performs a juggling act with other priorities which compete for attention: microfilming of volumes borrowed from other libraries to fill gaps in the British Library's set, microfilming of deteriorated volumes withdrawn from circulation because of their physical state or of whole categories of the stock, and microfilming of press cuttings collections are examples.

The conservation workshop employs 9 staff and is dedicated to work on newspapers. It has a specially built spray deacidification unit, the only one of its kind in intensive use for newspaper conservation: the deacidification agent used is magnesium methoxide. Lamination and rebinding are carried out in the same workshop. The laminating tissue used is Crompton's tissue, a long-fibre, lignin-free natural cellulose tissue and the adhesive used is a mixture of Texicryl and Poloid, which is heat-set and archivally acceptable. The lamination process used is completely reversible, and was introduced in 1972-73 after intensive research carried out by the former HMSO and British Museum conservation laboratories. The research has not been published.

The workshop has a capacity of about 4,000 - 4,500 volumes per year.

Use of the Newspaper Library is high: all reader seats are taken and queues form on more than one day in three. There are 26,000 reader visits per year. About 30% of users (this figure is an estimate based on surveys) are readers in other parts of the British Library: the remainder are using newspapers only among the British Library's collections. About 40% are from overseas. Concentration of use is on UK newspapers (about 80% of users are using only UK titles) and on the twentieth century (63% of readers request only twentieth century dates, and 14% are using newspapers of the last ten years). Newspapers of very recent date are not delivered to the public until either bound or microfilmed, so there may be a delay of three months to two years before they are available: the Newspaper Library works with public libraries in London to ensure that titles are available elsewhere until its own are ready for use.

Research interests are as varied as they could be. A profile of users' subjects of study dating from 1975/6 suggests the following:

History of particular themes and events	20% of readers
History of places and institutions	18%
Reviews and articles on the arts	13%
Biographical and critical material on persons	11%
History of technical development	8%
The press	7%
Family history	6%
Sport	5%

The pattern is not thought to have changed greatly, though the staff would feel that local history and family history are increasingly popular as subjects of study.

Neither bound volumes nor newspaper microfilm are available on inter-library loan from the British Library, nor from any other library in the UK, at present.

The Newspaper Library has complete catalogues by title and place of publication, on cards and in sheaf form respectively. They were published in eight volumes by British Museum Publications Ltd. as of 1971, and are heavily used in other libraries. The catalogues are not at present automated but there are plans to automate them after 1970, when the published catalogues stop, and to make them available in MARC format on the British Library's main systems (including BLAISE). The cataloguing rules are the Newspaper Library's (formerly the British Museum's) own.

There is on-line access to the principal indexing and full-text services such as Textline and World Reporter though these are not at present available to users on a full-scale charged basis. The library does not carry out any indexing or cutting of newspapers, although it holds two important collections of press-cuttings acquired from other services.

3. PRESERVATION POLICY FOR NEWSPAPERS IN THE UK

There is no central authority for library policy-making in the UK, and no direct governmental sanction for the policies that are adopted. Nevertheless the British Library does not make its own policies in a vacuum, but seeks to take into account the contribution made and the requirements of other kinds of libraries and it and other library bodies aim to achieve co-operation in the interests of the best use of the available resources.

3.1. The British Library Newspaper Library

The preservation policy of the Newspaper Library has evolved over time, and at present is undergoing change as a result of major reviews of the Newspaper Library and of all the British Library's preservation activities that took place in 1976 and 1986. The salient features of the policy may be summarised as follows:
- (a) the use of microfilm as the medium of use and preservation of all UK provincial and foreign newspapers
- (b) the systematic use of microfilm for the preservation of defined categories of deteriorating UK newspapers
- (c) the purchase of microfilm from other sources wherever film of adequate standard is available, and the avoidance of duplication of microfilming
- (d) the selective use of conservation of the original for certain categories of UK papers only
- (e) the development of a national role for the British Library Newspaper Library in planning its priorities and making its experience and expertise available to other organisations as widely as possible

In the early 1970's the then British Museum recognised that it had in the newspaper stock what began to be talked of as a time-bomb. The review of 1976, which resulted from this realisation, still provides the Library with a good deal of the basic data for its planning. It was estimated that 31,000 volumes in all were in need of re-binding or full conservation, that they were being added to by about 500 per year, and that 7,500 of them were "urgent" cases. From the period of worst deterioration, 1860-1920, the Library holds about 100,000 volumes or 65 million pages, which in due course will join the "urgent" category.

Until the middle of the 1970's, the Newspaper Library relied on binding of all current UK intake. Bound volumes were delivered to the user. Foreign intake was purchased originally in microfilm wherever possible (and still is), and microfilmed if not available on film from another source. The conservation workshop treated deteriorating older UK bound volumes, but over 90% of its capacity was taken up with current binding and it barely kept up with the rate of deterioration of the stock. In spite of this, conservation of the original tended to be preferred for UK materials and microfilming was not systematically used to replace volumes in poor condition.

The 1976 review recommended, among other things, the microfilming of all current UK intake, the more systematic use of microfilm to replace deteriorating UK originals, and a switch in the orientation of the conservation workshop to more specialist conservation of originals in defined categories. It has taken until now to effect this recommendation, but it is believed that it will provide a more effective use of the resources available, and a better overall treatment of UK legal deposit materials.

From the end of 1985, all UK intake has ceased to be bound and there is a programme, to be implemented by the end of 1990, to microfilm or buy microfilm of all UK provincial newspapers. Microfilm will be bought where possible, or if microfilm of suitable standard cannot be acquired it will be made by the library. The originals, which are the legal deposit copies (legal deposit does not cover microforms at all under the present state of the law in the UK, and the Library's interpretation of its obligations under the law is that it is obliged to keep the originals in viable form) will be preserved by wrapping them in acid-free paper and storing them horizontally in the correct environmental conditions where they will only very exceptionally be delivered to users. This will secure the survival of the original more effectively than the policy that operated up to now. Newspapers deposited by law from countries of the Commonwealth or former colonies will be similarly treated.

Microfilm will also be used more consistently for the archival preservation of materials after 1870. It will be used systematically for individual volumes that are withdrawn from use because of their poor physical condition, and for defined categories of material. Examples are the holdings of Irish newspapers before 1900, which are in an exceptionally poor state owing to their large size and the conditions in which they were stored before the Newspaper Library was created; some 500 Scottish newspapers of which the unique titles survive in the Newspaper Library; and unique holdings being identified by the NEWSPLAN programme (see section 3.3 below).

Preservation by microfilming is considerably more economic than conservation of the originals, and savings achieved here have justified an increase in the microfilming capacity of the Newspaper Library.

Ceasing to bind the current UK newspapers has released more capacity in the conservation workshop for the preservation of the originals of older volumes. The workshop will henceforward concentrate on UK national papers, magazines etc. in which the use of colour is important, and pre-1850 titles of which the paper is more robust. In this way it is hoped to catch up on the backlog of those 31,000 volumes.

The development of the Library's national role is an important component of these changes, and it is further discussed below in section 3.2 and 3.3. The Newsletter of the Newspaper Library makes an important tool for increasing awareness and communicating the expertise that has been built up, as are the programmes of visits and open days for library professionals.

3.2. Other libraries

Other libraries and organisations, including local archive offices and newspaper publishers, have made and are making an important contribution to the national preservation effort. It is difficult to summarise the position, and this paper will come closer to providing a national picture than anything yet published. The British Library has carried out, with co-operation from others, two recent studies which provide much of the available data.

In 1983-5 a study was carried out, originally proposed by the South-West Regional Library System and with their co-operation, into the archival microfilming and current policies in this, one of the ten library Regions of the UK. It was funded by the British Library (Reference Division) and the report was published as "NEWSPLAN: report of the pilot project in the South West", by Rosemary Wells (British Library Research and Development Department, 1986, LIR 38), ISBN 0 7123 3057 7. Libraries, record offices, museums and private collections in the Region were visited, and the state of preservation and the amount of microfilming and standards of microfilm used of all local papers of the region were visited, and the state of preservation and the amount of microfilming and standards of microfilm used of all local papers of the Region were examined.

Very considerable efforts have been made by the library authorities of the Region, who with the newspaper publishers have microfilmed about 40% of the output of local titles. Microfilm has been preferred over the preservation of the original in almost all cases. Priorities have been systematically assessed, based on the experience of local librarians over many years of deterioration of their files, and most libraries have long-term programmes for microfilming. Priorities are the most seriously deteriorated sets, the most heavily used titles, and the most important titles. Libraries in many cases co-operate with other local organisations, including newspaper publishers (though not all are interested to hold microfilm), to share costs or to establish a complete file of a title. Commercial microfilm bureaux have been used and some have acquired extensive experience of the requirements of newspaper filming. The British Library has been the largest supplier. About half of the microfilm made is not up to standard or has been made from incomplete sets when a more complete microfilm could have been achieved. Budgets for microfilming are inadequate, though libraries do their best and are fully aware of the preservation needs of their newspaper collections. Storage conditions are often inadequate, and the newspapers receive very heavy use. In many cases it was found that the sets in the British Library Newspaper Library are in much better physical condition than those held locally, for this reason.

A second study was carried out by the Newspaper Library in October 1986 to March 1987 into the microfilming of current UK newspapers country-wide. The results have only just been collated and are not yet published. It has been found that about 720 current titles out of 1853 being published are being microfilmed - rather more than had been anticipated. Of these the British Library films 144 titles. Others are filmed by bureaux, for library authorities and newspaper publishers who in a small number of cases are co-operating to share costs. 31 commercial bureaux were identified as filming newspapers, and 13 public library authorities and 9 newspaper publishers have their own microfilming facilities. 61% of titles are being filmed to the British Standard. 25 cases of duplication of microfilming effort were identified - in one case, for instance, the British Library was filming for the local library while the newspaper office was using a bureau without being aware of the interest of the local library in its titles.

Two libraries were using microfiche for their newspapers, and a number of respondents to the survey questionnaire indicated an interest in obtaining fiche. Colour microfilm was not being used at all - the general opinion appeared to be that the use of colour (while it may be historically important for the British Library to capture for the future the results of the present-day changes in the techniques of newspaper production) was not important to record.

The object of the British Library is to use the results of these two studies in planning the extension of the policy described above, of holding microfilm of all current UK intake. It will wherever possible avoid duplication of microfilming and will purchase microfilm being made elsewhere to acceptable standard. It will seek to extend the amount of microfilming being done by bureaux and others in order to increase the total microfilming capacity nationally, and in doing so will hope to co-operate with other libraries by sharing the costs of new microfilming contracts: the number of examples where this has been done is encouraging. It will in all cases encourage the observance of the correct standards and the preservation of master negative in the proper conditions. Where it adds titles to the 144 at present being filmed on a current basis by the British Library, it will publicise the fact and seek standing orders for its microfilm from libraries and others. Finally, it is building up a central record of all the information gleaned, including details of the titles it microfilms, in order to create a data-base which could provide the foundation for a future national register of microform masters of newspapers.

3.3. NEWSPLAN

NEWSPLAN is a programme for the preservation of all UK local newspapers, archival and current, on archivally permanent microfilm, with the British Library, local libraries and others acting in co-operation to
- identify the priorities
- establish action plans
- seek additional resources
- publicise the need.

It began in 1985 with the publication of the report by Rosemary Wells, mentioned above, and has been extensively publicised through the library profession and the newspaper industry. It has had warm endorsement, and is a high priority in the British Library's strategic plan.

The study in the South West indicated the size of the task facing the libraries (and other organisations) of the country as a whole. If the South West is typical in the volume of its newspaper publishing and the amount of microfilming already achieved, there are about 350-400 camera years of work to be done to film all UK papers up to the end of 1985. (It must be emphasised that this figure is an estimate.) This is a massive task and not one that could be carried out on the resources of the British Library alone, but it is achievable on a time-scale of 10-15 years. The foreword to the report of the pilot project, by Mr J Beard, Hampshire County Librarian, recommended that public library authorities should allocate 1% of their book budgets to newspaper microfilming. If they come near to this target, it will make an appreciable contribution to the resolution of the problem.

The NEWSPLAN programme envisages two phases - research and implementation. The research phase take as its model the study done in the South West which proved that a systematic assessment of needs and achievements to date can be done. It is hoped to cover the whole of the UK (including incidentally the Republic of Ireland, whose newspapers are subject to legal deposit in the UK and whose newspaper titles prior to 1922 cross the border in ways that could make their exclusion difficult) with similar research projects. Studies will work through the library Regions, and with British Library (Humanities and Social Sciences) providing some financial support. Studies have begun in three other Regions, the North West, the East Midlands, and the North, and approaches have been received from all the remaining Regions. The total cost of the research is likely to be about £250,000.

The raw data collected will be compiled into action plans: this has already been done in the South West, where categories for action have been identified, depending on the physical state of surviving sets, the importance of titles, and their degree of use. Examples of the categories are:
- title must be filmed by the British Library because it holds unique originals or its set is in better condition. It places title on its list of priorities for in-house filming
- title can be filmed by a bureau, and British Library and local sources seek a cost-sharing contract
- a complete set can only be made up from the British Library and the local sets: British Library borrows volumes and establishes complete microfilm
- the best set for microfilming is held by a newspaper office. British Library and local libraries will approach the owner and seek a cost-sharing arrangement for microfilming.

An implementation committee for the South West has been formed, under the chairmanship of N Higham, Librarian of Bristol University, and the British

Library has already begun some additional filming, taking into account the priorities of local libraries. Six authorities in the Region have already committed additional funds to newspaper filming and it is hoped that the actions taken will develop into a model for co-operation in other areas.

A central data-base of information about microfilming identified by the research or undertaken as part of the programme has been begun (modestly, on Kardex) at the Newspaper Library and like the information on current microfilming may form the basis for a national register of microform masters in the future.

The elements of co-operation and publicity are felt to be particularly important. It is clear that the British Library's own capacity will not be sufficient to meet the national need: similarly in assessing its own priorities it needs to take into account those of the areas where newspapers originated and where they are most heavily used. The advice of the local collections is invaluable at the centre. At the same time the value of a national proramme with a title and the support of the national library can only help to secure the badly needed additional resources for newspaper preservation.

4. BIBLIOGRAPHIC CONTROL

It would be fair to say that in general preservation has taken priority over the need to secure improved bibliographic control over British newspapers and the newspaper holdings of British libraries.

There is no complete or authoritative bibliography of UK newspapers at present. There exists a valuable project of the Library Association's Information Services Group to compile the "Bibliography of British newspapers" which is edited by Charles Toase and is designed to be published in one volume per county. The British Library has undertaken the publication of the volumes but the editorial work is being carried out on a voluntary basis, and progress is slow and likely to remain so unless financial support for the project can be found.

The published catalogue of the Newspaper Library provides an important basis for the identification of titles, and there are several important directories, but there is no complete holdings or locations list for UK libraries. Examples of useful sources produced to date are:
"Directory of Scottish Newspapers". Edinburgh, National Library of
    Scotland, 1984
"Northern Ireland newspapers: checklist with locations".
    Prepared and published by the Joint Working Party on Resources for
    Local Studies of the Library Association, Northern Ireland Branch
    and the Public Record Office of Northern Ireland (rev. ed. Belfast
    1983)
"World list of national newspapers". (A holdings list of natinal
    newspapers in UK libraries. London, Butterworth for the Standing
    Conference of National and University Libraries, 1976 (updating
    supplement published by the British Library Newspaper Library as a
    supplement to the <u>Newsletter</u> 1985)
and many list of the local papers of their area produced by local libraries and archives. The reports of the NEWSPLAN studies, which the British Library hopes to publish, will provide lists of all the titles identified in the relevant regions, and will make a contribution, but they will not provide a single source. It does not all add up.

One of the principal problems in the exploitation of newspapers is the absence of indexes, but significant progress has been made recently in identifying those that do exist. The Newspaper Library has completed a survey of the newspaper indexing activities of other libraries and local studies organisations, and has publicised the results through a seminar. The proceedings of the seminar have been published in the <u>Newsletter</u> no.8 of the Newspaper Library, and it is hoped to publish the resulting list. 805 indexing projects were discovered, of very varying scope and quality, maintained by very different institutions including libraries, archives, newspaper offices and retired individuals pursuing an enthusiasm.

5. SUMMARY AND CONCLUSIONS

Four themes can be identified which characterise the picture of library provision of newspapers in the UK and preservation effort.

First, UK libraries have given priority to the preservation of newspapers on microfilm rather than to the preservation of the original.

Second, preservation has received a higher priority than assuring full bibliographic control.

Third, preservation is being approached from both ends, as it were - both archival microfilming of older materials and the current microfilming of newspapers, which will anticipate the problem, are receiving attention.

Finally, preservation is seen as essentially a co-operative business. The contribution made by local libraries has been of the very greatest importance, both to the promotion of preservation programmes and to the development of policy.

SCOTTISH NEWSPAPERS

Dr Ann MATHESON

Keeper of Printed Books, National Library of Scotland

The total number of Scottish newspaper titles is around 1,200. The earliest surviving Scottish newspaper is <u>Mercurius Scoticus</u> published in Leith, near Edinburgh, in 1651. Up to the year 1800 there were approximately 40 newspaper titles issued in Scotland. Scottish newspapers of this period present relatively few problems for librarians or researchers. Their format is generally small-scale, and they are printed on paper made from rag which produces a sturdy resilient paper that stands up well even to heavy consultation. Scottish newspapers of this period also enjoy a reasonable level of bibliographical completeness. The National Library of Scotland has probably the most extensive collection of pre-1800 Scottish newspapers in existence, the majority of them obtained contemporaneously; the Mitchell Library, Glasgow, is also well endowed, particularly with West of Scotland titles. Researchers who seek access to Scottish newspapers of this period may thus do so conveniently and without significant difficulty.

However, the position of newspapers of the 19th and 20th centuries is very different. From 1800 to the present, approximately 1,150 newspaper titles have been published in Scotland; and Scottish newspapers from the 1840s onwards are subject to the same deterioration that manifests itself in other UK newspaper titles of this period. There is, however, an additional complication in Scotland in relation to coverage of 19th- and early 20th- century Scottish newspapers. For historical reasons, the Advocates' Library, the private library that was the forerunner of the present National Library of Scotland, did not claim, through the legal deposit privilege, the Scottish regional newspapers that began to be issued in the 19th century, and, consequently, the National Library's coverage of newspapers of this period is relatively poor. The most complete coverage of Scottish newspapers of this period is to be found in the British Library Newspaper Library.

In 1984, in response to the marked increase of interest in Scottish newspapers, among researchers and librarians, the National Library of Scotland set up a Committee on Scottish Newspapers to examine the situation of Scottish newspapers and to make recommendations. The Committee's first priority was to examine how Scottish newspapers could be preserved, or their deterioration at least arrested, and how more titles could be made available conveniently for use by researchers in Scotland.

A union listing of Scottish newspapers - the <u>Directory of Scottish Newspapers</u> - was published by the National Library in 1984, and this was a useful tool to assist with the measurement of the problem. The results of the measurement were a cause for concern. On the evidence available, 35 per cent of Scottish titles could not be assembled in a complete file; and 53 per cent of all titles were extant only in a single complete file. In a number of cases, the single file is held by the newspaper proprietor and is, therefore, at possible risk in the event of a change of ownership.

The Committee on Scottish Newspapers produced a Report in 1986: <u>Scottish Newspapers: A Programme for Microfilming Scottish Newspapers</u>. This Report recommended large-scale microfilming to archival standards as the proposed solution to the preservation problems of Scottish newspapers, and recommended the setting up of a dedicated microfilming unit for Scottish newspapers in the National Library of Scotland. This unit, which will be modelled on the British Library's newspaper microfilming unit, will liaise closely with Colindale in order to ensure that limited financial resources are spent in the most effective way and not wasted through duplication of filming. The Scottish Office, which funds the National Library of Scotland, has asked the Library to seek public support to raise the capital sum necessary to establish the unit, and a public appeal will be launched this autumn to try to raise the necessary capital.

Other projects under examination by the Committee on Scottish Newspapers at present are: a listing of Scottish newspaper indexes; a manual for librarians on how to deal with Scottish newspapers in their collections; and an examination of the possibility of creating guidelines for the preparation of Scottish newspaper indexes.

NATIONAL APPROACHES TO NEWSPAPER PRESERVATION - WALES

Beti JONES

Assistant Librarian, National Library of Wales

1. INTRODUCTION

The first steps towards the eventual establishment of a National Library of Wales, were taken in the middle of the 18th century at about the same time as the British Musuem itself was being brought into being. The Cymmrodorion Society, set up by a group of Welshmen living in London, provided by its constitution of 1753 for a library to be set up in the Welsh School at Clerkenwell Green, which would seek to procure copies of all books, past, present and future, printed in Welsh, as well as manuscripts and books in other languages deemed to be relevant to the Society's needs. Much was accomplished by the Society during the following years, but by the end of the century, it had been dissolved and the collection of books and manuscripts amassed by it were stored at the Welsh School.

By 1843 a decision had to be taken as to the future of the collection, and as no Welsh National Library existed, they were donated that year to the British Museum, where they still remain. However, the aim of setting up a Welsh National Library was not abandoned and after years of campaigning, it was finally achieved in 1907 when a Royal Charter was granted, which ordained that the National Library for Wales should be founded at Aberystwyth with the object of "preserving and maintaining works of all kinds in Welsh or any other Celtic languages, or relating to Wales or Celtic peoples, as well as works in any language in any subject which might help the furtherance of higher education and research". The granting of the right to legal deposit copies of nearly all British and Irish publications by the Copyright Act of 1911 has proved of vital importance in the Library's attempt to fulfil this second object.

2. NEWSPAPERS

The first weekly newspaper to be published in Wales was The Cambrian, an English language publication which appeared in 1804. This was followed ten years later by a Welsh language weekly newspaper, known as Seren Gomer, both papers being published in Swansea. These early newspaper, together with others, were later procured for the library from private collections and other sources, but needless to say, much material of this kind published during the last century, - which saw a rapid increase in Welsh publishing,- and up to 1911, only exists in the British Library collections.

3. PRESERVATION

Though the NLW had collected newspapers from its foundation and had claimed legal deposit copies of all published in Wales from 1912 and had in 1937 produced a detailed list of its holdings, an all out effort to collect and preserve all newspapers relating to Wales - national, local, weekly, daily -

only from the beginning of the 1970's. At that time BLNL at Colindale toyed with the idea of decentralizing its local archives, in which case the NLW would have been the natural home of the Welsh Collection. Accordingly the purchase of microfilms from the BLNL to fill gaps in our collections was delayed.

In the meantime, however, much has been accomplished in this field. We have borrowed newspaper files from newspaper offices and filmed them at the Library. In so doing advantages accrued to both sides as proprietors who in the past had had to provide space for those wishing to research their files, could henceforth refer them to the National Library. Many files thus borrowed were stored under highly unfavourable conditions and it is just as well that they are now on film. Other sources were also tapped to fill our gaps e.g. a number of titles in collections of the Welsh University College Libraries have been microfilmed – in particular the collection of University College of North Wales, Bangor where the assistance of a local MSC was recruited, together with the items from the collections at the Cardiff Central Library and the Glamorgan Record Office. The Library has also co-operated with other Welsh Libraries, Record Offices and newspaper publishers in purchasing files from the BLNL, with the costs being shared among the different participants. Films of newspaper published for the benefit of Welsh communities in America and other countries have also been bought by us.

There are newspapers of course, which unfortunately are not to be found in any library or archive, and it has been the Library's practice in the past to rely on local knowledge of any private collections held, but with the passing of time, this becomes increasingly more difficult.

Resources have, however, never been available to build up a comprehensive collection by systematic filming of all extant titles. We have therefore concentrated on making good the most obvious deficiencies in our existing collection,

　i. by attempting to increase our holdings relating to areas or localities not well represented in NLW,

　ii. by filling gaps in our holdings of certain newspapers frequently requested by readers,

　iii. by procuring microfilms of a few titles which are heavily used and deteriorating rapidly.

It is hoped that the scope of this work can be widened in the near future.

In 1988 for example we hope to embark on a NEWSPLAN project for Wales, and since a process of compiling a detailed bibliography of periodicals and newspapers in Welsh language, and of general Welsh interest up to 1900, is already under way, it is hoped that both projects will be complementary, and to each other's mutual benefit.

NLW claims legal deposit copies of only a few major British Newspaper publications outside Wales. Up to and including 1986, it was the NLW's custom to bind all UK national newspapers that were then current, but most are now purchased on microfilm, except the Welsh material (which is still bound) as is the case with foreign newspapers. The originals are then wrapped and stored. We would prefer if possible, in the case of Welsh newspapers in both languages to have them bound as well as microfilmed, but this will have to be decided by the amount of money available: of these papers we receive 7 daily and 61 weekly titles as well as 51 monthly community newspapers.

THE US NEWSPAPER PROGRAM

Jeffrey FIELD

Assistant Preservation Officer, Office of Preservation,
National Endowment for the Humanities, USA

1. INTRODUCTION

The US Newspaper Program (USNP) is a co-ordinated, national effort to identify, to preserve, and to make available to researchers newspapers published in the United States from the eighteenth century through the present. Through grants from the National Endowment for the Humanities (NEH) and with technical management from the Library of Congress (LC), fifty states, the US Trust Territories, and eight national newspaper repositories will enter bibliographic and holdings records into the OCLC/CONSER database for an estimated 250,000 newspaper titles and preserve on microfilm those titles most important for research. This paper is an account of the origins of the Program, its development, its organization and management, its current status, and its future expectations.

2. ORIGINS: THE RESEARCH NEEDS OF HISTORIANS

Newspapers have long been of interest to researchers for their rich documentation of civic and cultural life, particularly on the local and regional levels. For Alexis De Tocqueville, the famous commentator on mid-nineteenth century American democracy, the immense number and wide variety of local American newspapers were testimony to a vibrant, pluralistic society. But beyond their immediacy in the day to day intercourse of American cities, towns, and territories, De Tocqueville saw in newspapers the chief record for posterity of transitory and often inadequately documented local or regional life and affairs. He wrote, "The only historical remains in the United States are the newspapers; if a number be wanting, the chain of time is broken and the present is severed from the past."

If De Tocqueville's observation is an exaggeration, it is nonetheless the case that newspapers are among the most comprehensive of historical sources for the study of local and regional history. For example, Clarence S Brigham wrote in the introduction to his "History and Bibliography of American Newspapers, 1690-1820": 'I doubt whether any contemporary expression of printed opinion and fact, both for national and local history measures up to the newspaper. No history of a town or a city can be written without recourse of its newspapers. In the eighteenth and early nineteenth centuries even the advertisements have unique value in social and economic study.'

De Tocqueville and Brigham underscore the importance of newspapers for purposes of historical research. And it was in the interest of researchers that the Endowment became involved in the US Newspaper Program. The idea for the Program grew out of the work of the committee on Bibliographical and Research Needs of the Organization of American Historians. Under the chairmanship of the late Walter Rundell, the Committee proposed to the OAH in 1969 that a revision of Winifred Gregory's "American Newspapers, 1821-1936" was badly needed. Shortly thereafter, the Endowment requested that the American Council of Learned Societies provide a list of the research tools most needed by its constituents. A revision of Gregory was high among the priorities of the Organization of American Historians, the American Historical Association, and the Society of American Archivists.

With Endowment grant support during 1973 through 1975, the OAH hired Dr Gale E Peterson to determine what it would take to update the Gregory volume. Although the OAH began with the idea that another printed bibliography would suffice, it soon became apparent to Dr Peterson that an adequate newspaper reference work would have to contain far more information than reported in Gregory. In addition, that work should allow for easy updating. Furthermore, even as Gregory and her researchers had noted, newspapers were fast disappearing, not simply through neglect, but through deterioration of their wood pulp paper. A fully adequate newspaper programme would, therefore, have to involve preservation as well as bibliographic control.

As a historian, Dr Peterson concerned himself with the adequacy of points of access to newspapers provided by earlier bibliographies. He advised that the absence of subject information in Gregory should be remedied by introducing such identifiers as "Republican", "Democratic", "Knights of Labor", that were found in bibliographies produced by the Ohio Historical Society and the Rhode Island Historical Society, among others. Any revision of Gregory ought to contain subject access to the newspapers.

3. DEVELOPMENT: THE IOWA PILOT PROJECT

From OAH's earliest deliberations in 1973, it was planned to follow Gregory's methods of organizing project activities on a state-by-state basis. The logic of this strategy is clear, for collecting, preserving, and providing access to newspapers has traditionally been a responsibility of a state library, state historical society, or state university.

Development of the CONSER national serials data base and the concurrent development of the MARC-S format suggested the possibility of building a national newspaper data base. To aid the historians in following these library developments, the OAH invited the Library of Congress to become affiliated with the endeavor. Don Wisdom, Chief of LC's Serial Division, became the Library's liaison to the OAH project.

To test the feasibility of operating in a state and to explore the use of computerized records, the OAH conducted a pilot project in Iowa during 1977-1978. The project was conducted through the Iowa State Historical Department and it involved the collection of data through a mail survey sent to some 1,200 potential newspaper repositories. Project staff learned that 700 of these institutions maintained permanent newspaper files. Data from these institutions were entered into an in-house computer, in a MARC-like format, based on a draft version of newspaper cataloguing rules in preparation by Elaine Woods.

The Iowa pilot project's principal product was a printed union list, containing information on Iowa newspapers held both within and outside the state. Realizing the incompleteness of the bibliographic information, the project director, Alan Schroeder, remarked that 'a truly comprehensive catalog of Iowa newspapers in out-of-state repositories must await the completion of the proposed national program of state bibliographic projects.'

4. TOWARDS A FEDERAL PROGRAM

At the conclusion of the Iowa project in 1978, the Endowment was persuaded that a national Program could proceed. The Iowa Pilot Project had demonstrated the feasibility of state-by-state newspaper survey activity and had provided the final impetus for a truly federal endeavor; that is, an undertaking dependent upon the voluntary participation of each state and territory, guided by a central management body and following a common set of rules and procedures.

To devise project procedures and Program guidelines for the bibliographic and preservation microfilming components, the Endowment solicited the advice of newspaper librarians and microfilming specialists. During 1978 and 1979 advisory meetings were convened in Washington to sketch out the guidelines for the US Newspaper Program. It was also during this time that Elaine Woods, under a Carnegie Foundation grant to the OAH, completed work on a first draft of the newspaper cataloguing manual.

In 1981 the Endowment contracted with Dr Pearce Grove, Director of the Library at Western Illinois University, to aid agency staff in developing the final stages of the Program. Dr Grove had participated in several of the project's advisory meetings and had recently produced a bibliography of New Mexico newspapers. In 1982, the Endowment concluded negotiations with OCLC and the Library of Congress to provide for CONSER entries by US Newspaper Program participants. Having OCLC/CONSER serve as the host data base not only provided the Program with an on-line cataloguing facility, but also with a means for long-term up-dating of the records by the project participants.

The USNP was launched in August 1982 by NEH grants to six repositories with extensive holdings covering the fifty states. The initial six participants included the American Antiquarian Society, the Center for Research Libraries, New York Historical Society, Kansas State Historical Society, the State Historical Society of Wisconsin, and Western Reserve Historical Society. The Library of Congress joined the effort as a seventh national repository, though not with Endowment grant funds, since NEH is prohibited from making grants to other federal agencies. Collectively, these repositories were estimated to hold over 40,000 US titles. Entry of their records would allow the database to be built quickly and furnish a large body of bibliographic records to which state projects would merely add holdings [1].

As it turned out, many of the holdings at the national repositories are either very short runs or single issues. State projects have had to enhance a large number of existing records and some anticipated cataloguing efficiencies have been lost. Nonetheless, there was an important outcome of the work of the initial repository projects beyond the creation of records.

Cataloguing rules for newspapers were only formulated with the advent of the US Newspaper Program, and until their use by the initial national repository projects, the rules existed in a vacuum. Implementation of the rules demanded agreement among project participants on interpretation. To refine the rules became one of the major tasks of the initial projects, and several special meetings of the repository project cataloguers were held at the Library of Congress to arrive at common solutions to cataloguing questions.

Even before cataloguing began, project participants meeting for training at OCLC in January 1983 discussed the crucial need for subject access to newspapers. They agreed to use the "intended audience" field of the local data record for this purpose and to employ as their subject authority a listing prepared by the State Historical Society of Wisconsin. The group also agreed that the primary point of access to newspapers should be geographic rather than by title. The Wisconsin list was superseded in 1987 by the use of Library of Congress subject headings.

5. NATIONAL MANAGEMENT ARRANGEMENTS

The crucial arrangements to ensure that the state and repository projects work in tandem according to clearly articulated national standards were formalized in 1984 in an Interagency Agreement between the Endowment and the Library of Congress. The Library of Congress determined to take an active management role in the Program not only because it monitors the CONSER database, but also because of the interest of the Deputy Librarian of Congress, William J Welsh, in national preservation programmes. Mr Welsh was keenly aware that the immense bibliographic effort of the USNP will provide the basis for nationally co-ordinated preservation microfilming of endangered and deteriorated newspapers deemed important for research. The Library of Congress has assisted local newspaper microfilming efforts since 1948 when it began publication of Newspapers in Microform.

The Interagency Agreement between the Endowment of LC stipulates respective management responsibilities for the two agencies. The Endowment's responsibilities include policy formation and general programme management, grantmaking and monitoring, co-ordinating with the Library of Congress and other appropriate organizations, the long-range plans for carrying out and completing the Program.

The Library of Congress is responsible for development and implementation of technical procedures, initiating and co-ordinating CONSER membership mechanisms for new Program participants, providing training and technical guidance to participants, ensuring adherence to appropriate national and international standards, co-ordinating ongoing quality control measures relating to bibliographic data and interpretations, system enhancements or modifications.

To carry out its management responsibilities, LC established the position of USNP Technical Co-ordinator in its Serial Record Division. Robert Harriman was appointed to this position in 1985 and he has been the guiding hand behind the USNP projects ever since. Mr Harriman had produced in 1984 the Newspaper Cataloging Manual, CONSER/USNP Edition, which refined the manual produced by Elaine Woods by incorporating changes and additions and rule interpretations worked out during the first two years of the USNP's operation. During 1985 Mr Harriman, in co-operation with OCLC staff, developed the USNP/OCLC Training Workshops, which are the chief means of training new project cataloguing staff. The duties of the USNP Technical Co-ordinator also involve project oversight. During 1986-1987, Mr Harriman has made several visits to USNP projects in order to resolve cataloguing and organizational difficulties. Mr Harriman's work demonstrates the centrality of the Library of Congress in the management of the USNP.

The co-operation of the On-Line Computer Library Center, Inc (OCLC) has also been crucial in developing the USNP. To accommodate the very large number of repositories adding local data records to the bibliographic record, OCLC has modified its union list software. OCLC hosts the USNP/OCLC Training Workshops and its staff take part in training the USNP project cataloguers. In addition, OCLC staff keep each of the OCLC regional networks informed of USNP developments.

In June, 1985 OCLC announced the availability of a <u>USNP National Union List</u>, containing records for some 25,000 titles, in five volumes, with three index volumes, providing access by subject or intended audience, place of publication, and date of publication. The Summer, 1987 edition of the Union List contains records for over 56,000 titles and is available on microfiche. In addition to the national union list, OCLC produces state newspaper union lists for each of the projects. These lists will be the primary off-line means of providing researchers with access to titles and holdings within each of the states.

6. CONDUCTING PROJECTS IN THE STATES

USNP activities are conducted primarily through co-operative efforts organized on a state-by-state basis. Responsibility for project administration must be assumed by a single institution. Usually, this institution maintains the largest collection of newspaper holdings in the state and has staff who are experienced in serials cataloguing and union listing procedures and in preservation microfilming of newspapers.

State projects proceed in phases. The first phase involves planning. The principal activity of a planning project is a survey by mail of repositories to establish newspaper holdings locations within a state, to provide a count of titles of both in-state and out-of-state newspapers, and to provide information on the preservation condition of holdings, both in hard copy and in microform copy. Planning project staff then analyze this information in order to develop a plan for cataloguing and preservation microfilming [2].

Implementation of a USNP project involves cataloguing newspapers throughout a state or territory or in a national repository and entry of bibliographic and holdings records into the CONSER database through the OCLC system. Holdings of both in-state and out-of-state imprints are recorded. Preservation microfilming of important deteriorated newspaper files for present use and future access constitutes the ultimate goal of the Program.

Implementation projects will vary in size and duration according to the estimated number of titles to be catalogued and microfilmed. For the Virgin Islands, cataloguing encompassed 53 titles and took six months. In Delaware, there are an estimated 600 titles to be catalogued in a one year project. Montana produced records for 1,121 titles and microfilmed 320,000 pages of newsprint in a two year period. In Iowa, there are 6,500 titles to be catalogued and 6.5 million pages to be filmed in a five-year effort. Pennsylvania estimates cataloguing over 10,000 titles and filming over 3 million pages in a five-year project. New York State may have as many as 25,000 titles. This project may require from eight to ten years to complete.

For cataloguing purposes, each project is designated as a self-authenticating CONSER member for the duration of the project. Training for project staff in cataloguing and union listing procedures is conducted at OCLC headquarters in Ohio. A senior serials cataloguer or equivalent project staff member is responsible for quality control for the state or repository projects. Final responsibility for quality control rests with the USNP Technical co-ordinator at the Library of Congress [3].

While much of the cataloguing is done in a few repositories with a large number of holdings, each of the state projects also involves cataloguing of holdings found in local historical societies, public libraries, county court houses, museums, newspaper offices, and college and university libraries throughout a state.

Not all cataloguing sites are hospitable to cataloguing work. For example, in Moundsville, West Virginia project cataloguers were led to a room under the roof of the building which houses the offices of the Moundsville Daily Echo. There, stored in fertilizer sacks, were newspapers collected on the editor's travels around the world and more complete collections, suffering from storage conditions, of papers published closer to home. In north-central Pennsylvania, cataloguers from Penn State University climbed an extension ladder into a garage attic to find, among the stacks of newspapers stored there, a number of previously undocumented titles. In yet another attic, in an abandoned farmhouse in Iowa, cataloguers found a store of nineteenth-century newspapers that had been left to the birds and the weather. Such circumstances as these provide an element of adventure and offer rewards of discovery not available in routine cataloguing work.

A report from the USNP project in Pennsylvania illustrates the effectiveness of the Program's fieldwork in locating titles and holdings. For four counties in central Pennsylvania, previous bibliographies cited 210 titles. Holdings had been located for only 89 of these titles. The project fieldworkers discovered an additional 103 titles and found holdings for a total of 142 titles.

Similar discoveries have been made even in states having fairly good bibliographic control over holdings that have been centalized, such as those in the Montana Historical Society. The Montana USNP Project originally estimated approximately 900 titles. The final count was 1,121. The Indiana USNP Project originally estimated holdings for 3,600 titles; however, the project staff found in the state library an entire room full of newspapers that had been overlooked in the planning project survey. The current estimate for Indiana is 5,500 titles.

7. PRESERVATION MICROFILMING

Newspapers were among the first items to be reformatted onto microfilm during the 1930s, when preservation microfilming first came into use by such institutions as the New York Public Library [4]. Since that time, newspaper repositories in nearly all states have done a large amount of microfilming. In the Western states, such as Montana, Utah, Idaho and Nevada, the major newspaper repository in the state has microfilmed nearly all state imprints. In other states, particularly in the East, microfilming has not been comprehensive. The USNP project in Pennsylvania, for example, seeks to microfilm some 3 million pages. For some states, microfilming of all state imprints is a goal that has not yet been accomplished. For example, in Iowa, the USNP project will microfilm some 6.5 million pages (including recopying of numerous poorly produced microfilms). This effort will preserve only 30% of Iowa's extant newspapers. For other states, microfilming will be fairly selective.

In fact, USNP projects are asked to be selective in the use of project funds for preservation microfilming. Funding could not possibly support comprehensive microfilming in many states, nor do research needs require saving every newspaper. In making a decision about what titles to microfilm, each project must adhere to a set of general criteria that include research importance and condition of the original. The following list, used by the USNP Pennsylvania project, is a good illustration of the selection criteria:

1. Research importance: In selecting from among several newspapers published in the same community at the same time, greater weight will be given to

the papers which published legal notices, gave broader coverage to local events, births, deaths, marriages and regional or state government activities.

2. Physical condition: Preference will be given to papers whose fragility prohibits their use.

3. Geographic scope: at least one title, or group of titles, will be filmed for each county in the state, to provide as nearly as possible an unbroken record of newspaper publication from the earliest surviving paper of that county to the present.

4. Completeness of runs: Preference will be given to complete or nearly complete runs rather than broken runs in order to achieve geographic coverage.

5. Period of publication: Preference will be given to papers published since the late nineteenth century.

All projects must adhere to national standards in producing microfilms. First or second generation masters must be on silver halide film in compliance with ANSI/ASC PH1.28-1984 American National Standard for Photography (Film) -- Archival Records, Silver-Gelatin Type, on Cellulose Ester Base or ANSI/ASC PH1.41-1984 American National Standard for Photography (Film) -- Archival Records, Silver-Gelatin Type, on Polyester Base. The latter standard for polyester base is preferred.

Production procedures should be guided by ANSI/MS 111 American National Recommended Practice for Micofilming Newspapers on 35mm Roll Microfilm (Revised in 1985 and to be published shortly) and, where relevant, by ANSI/AIIM MS23-1983 National Standard: Practice for Operational Procedures/Inspection and Quality Control First Generation, Silver-Gelatin Microfilm of Documents.

The testing of the master film to meet archival standards should comply with ANSI PH4.8-1978 American National Standard Methylene Blue Method for Measuring Thiosulfate and Silver Densitometric Method for Measuring Residual Chemicals in Films, Plates and Papers.

Storage for first generation camera masters must be in accordance with ANSI PH1.43-1983 American National Standard for Photography (Film) -- Storage of Processed Safety Film.

Film enclosures must adhere to ANSI/ASC PH1.53-1984 American National Standard for Photography (Processing) -- Processed Film, Plates, and Papers - Filing Enclosures and Containers for Storage.

Adherence by each USNP project to these well articulated standards ensures that microfilms will be of the highest preservation quality. In effect, the standards serve as the chief means of providing quality control over an otherwise highly decentralized set of activities.

Microfilming services for the projects are provided through an in-house capability or through a vendor. Numerous state agencies have extensive in-house microfilming operations. Institutions without an in-house capability must find a microfilm vendor. Performance to national preservation standards must be stipulated in a contract with the vendor [5]. There are numerous vendors that can produce to national standards for a price that is often less expensive than many in-house operations. Prices will vary according to local circumstances, but will probably range from 10c - 20c per frame for a preservation master and one service positive.

All microfilms produced by USNP projects will be available for interlibrary loan and usually for sale as well. Early indications from the first participants in the USNP are that interlibrary loan requests for newspaper holdings are rapidly rising as titles are recorded in the CONSER/USNP database. A dramatic example of the increased accessibility of newspapers is provided by the New York Historical Society, which reported that requests for use of titles in its collections rose from 42 to 110 from 1982 to 1984, while the number of requests citing the CONSER/USNP record rose from 2 to 67 during this period.

In addition to the microfilming conducted as part of on-going state agency efforts and by the USNP projects, commercial firms also film newspapers. While most of this filming is done for currently published newspapers, the Readex Microprint Corporation is producing a microfilm set of Early American Newspapers. This commercial venture will produce a set of titles of chiefly pre-1820 newspapers, although titles whose publishing history extends beyond that date will be included. USNP projects are advised to avoid duplictive preservation efforts and they must, therefore, take the Readex venture into account in their preservation planning.

8. FUNDING SUMMARY AND CURRENT STATUS OF THE USNP

As of May 1987 there are seventeen states and one national repository involved in cataloguing and microfilming activities. Another six states are involved in planning. Three states, one territory, and seven national repositories have completed their work. (See the appendix for a complete listing). The national database contains records for over 60,000 titles. The NEH has spent to date approximately $8.3 million; non-federal contributions total $4.8 million. The NEH expects to conclude the USNP by 1995, but each project has made a commitment to maintain the database and to continue microfilming of current publications. Given these commitments, the USNP should not have to be done again.

BIBLIOGRAPHY

1 Grove, Pearce S, 'A Revolution in Newspaper Access', in: Resource Sharing and Information Networks, Vol.3 no.1, Fall 1985. pp. 101-114.

2 Hoffman, David R, 'The Pennsylvania Newspaper Project: Initial Stages', in: The Serials Librarian, Vol.10 no.3, Spring 1986. pp. 69-76. For additional information on the Pennsylvania USNP project, see articles (various) in Carter, op.cit.

3 Carter, Ruth C, 'The United States Newspaper Program: Cataloging Aspects', in: Cataloging & Classification Quarterly, Vol.6, no.4, Summer 1986. (the entire issue).

4 Bourke, Thomas A, 'The Microfilming of Newspapers: an Overview'. Microform Review, Vol.15, no.3, Summer 1986. pp. 154-156.

5   Byrne, Sherry, 'Guidelines for Contract Microfilming Services', Microform Review, Vol.15, no.4, Fall 1986. pp. 253-264.

U.S. NEWSPAPER PROGRAM PARTICIPANTS

This list reflects funds awarded by the NEH to date in support of USNP cataloging and microfilming projects. The dollar amount includes funds awarded for planning and for the continuation of multi-stage projects. The list contains both current and completed projects and provides estimates of the number of titles to be catalogued and pages to be microfilmed, and the name, telephone number and institution for the state's project director.

ALABAMA ($413,079) Cataloguing and microfilming. An estimated 3,000 titles to be located and recorded; 4.6 million pages to be microfilmed. Edwin C. Bridges, Director, Alabama Department of Archives and History, Montgomery, AL. 36130   205/261-4361.

ARKANSAS ($178,643) Cataloguing. An estimated 2,100 titles to be located and recorded. John A. Harrison, Director, University of Arkansas Libraries, Fayetteville, AR. 72701   501/575-3845.

DELAWARE ($58,787) Cataloguing. An estimated 600 titles to be located and recorded. Nathaniel Puffer, Assistant Director of Libraries for Collection Development, University of Delaware Libraries, Newark, DE. 19716   302/451-2231.

GEORGIA ($477,441) Cataloguing and microfilming. An estimated 3,900 titles to be located and recorded; preservation microfilming of 2.5 million pages. Barry B. Baker, Assistant Director for Technical Services, University of Georgia Libraries, Athens, GA. 30602   404/542-2534.

HAWAII ($49,900) Cataloguing completed, with 476 titles located and recorded. John R. Haak, University Librarian, Hamilton Library, University of Hawaii at Manoa, Honolulu, HI. 96822   808/948-7205.

IDAHO ($s63,616) Cataloguing and microfilming. An estimated 800 titles to be located and recorded; preservation microfilming of 360,000 pages. Karin E. Ford, Idaho State Library, 325 W. State St., Boise, ID. 83702   208/334-5124.

INDIANA ($453,503) Cataloguing and microfilming. Cataloguing of 5,500 titles directed by Indiana University. Sally J Rausch, Associate Dean for Technical Services, Indian University Libraries, Bloomington, IN. 47405   812/335-3403. Preservation microfilming of 600,000 pages conducted by the Indiana Historical Society. Peter T. Harstad, Director, Indiana Historical Society, 315 W. Ohio St., Indianapolis, IN. 46202   317/232-1888.

IOWA ($623,301) Cataloguing and microfilming. An estimated 6,500 titles to be located and recorded; an estimated 6.5 million pages to be microfilmed. Nancy Kraft, Directory of Libraries, State Historical Society of Iowa, Iowa City, IA. 55240   319/335-3916.

KENTUCKY ($427,078) Cataloguing and microfilming. An estimated 5,590 titles to be located and recorded; an estimated 1.5 million pages to be microfilmed. Judy Sackett, Head Periodicals-Newspapers-Microtexts Department, M.I. King Library, University of Kentucky, Lexington, KY. 40506   606/257-8387.

LOUISIANA ($236,774) Cataloguing and Microfilming. An estimated 2,300 titles to be located and recorded; 7,200 reels of preservation microfilms to be produced from existing microfilms. Sharon A. Hogan, Director of Libraries, Middleton Library, Louisiana State University, Baton Rouge, LA. 70803-3300 504/388-2217.

MARYLAND ($192,255) Cataloguing and microfilming. An estimated 1,300 titles to be located and recorded; 500,000 pages to be microfilmied. Peter H. Curtis, Curator, Maryland Room, McKeldin Library, University of Maryland, College Park, MD. 20742 301/454-3035.

MISSISSIPPI ($197,317) Cataloguing and microfilming. An estimated 2,100 titles to be located and recorded. Dale Foster, Coordinator, Mississippi Newspaper Project, Mississippi Department of Archives and History, Jackson, MS. 39205 601/359-1424.

MONTANA ($126,181) Cataloguing and microfilming completed. 1,121 titles located and recorded; 320,000 pages microfilmed. Robert M. Clark, Librarian, Montana Historical Society, Helena, MT. 59620 406/444-4787.

NEVADA ($135,315) Cataloguing completed. 975 titles located and recorded. Robert E. Blesse, Head of Special Collections, University of Nevada-Reno Library, Reno, NV. 89557-0040 702/784-6538.

NEW JERSEY ($189,208) Cataloguing. An estimated 3,020 titles to be located and recorded. Lida Sak, Rutgers University Libraries, New Brunswick, NJ. 08903 201/932-7513.

NEW YORK ($268,668) Cataloguing. An estimated 6,500 titles to be located and recorded in two of nine library regions. Patricia Mallon, New York State Library, Albany, NY. 12234 518/474-6971

NORTH DAKOTA ($215,809) Cataloguing and microfilming. An estimated 1,800 titles to be located and recorded; 2.8 million pages to be microfilmed. Gerald G Newborg, Director, State Historical Society of North Dakota, Bismarck, ND. 58505-0179 701/224-2668.

OHIO ($179,318) Cataloguing. An estimated 3,400 titles to be located and recorded. William G Myers, Ohio Historical Society, Columbus, OH. 43211 614/297-2531.

PENNSYLVANIA ($1,216,061) Cataloguing and microfilming. An estimated 9,500 titles to be located and recorded; 3 million pages to be microfilmed. David Hoffman, Director, Division of Library Services, State Library of Pennsylvania, Harrisburg, PA. 17105 717/783-5968.

TEXAS ($414,598) Cataloguing. An estimated 7,500 titles to be located and recorded. Bobby D. Weaver, Archivist, Panhandle-Plains Historical Museum, Canyon, TX. 79016 806/656-3146.

UTAH ($115,572) Cataloguing completed. 1,263 titles located and recorded. Robert P. Holley, Assistant Director for Technical Services, Marriott Library, University of Utah, Salt Lake City, UT. 84112 801/581-7741.

VIRGIN ISLANDS ($17,363) Cataloguing completed. 57 titles located and recorded. Henry C. Chang, Department of Conservation and Cultural Affairs, Division of Libraries, Museums, and Archeological Services, St. Thomas, USVI. 00801 809/773-5715.

WASHINGTON STATE ($231,143) Cataloguing and microfilming. An estimated 2,000 titles to be located and recorded; preservation microfilming of 1 million pages. Jeanne Engerman, Washington Room Librarian, Washington State Library,

Olympia, WA. 98504   206/753-4024.

WEST VIRGINIA ($185,319) Cataloguing and microfilming completed. 1,180 titles located and recorded; 460,000 pages microfilmed. Harold M. Forbes, Associate Curator, West Virginia & Regional History Collections, West Virginia University Library, Morgantown, WV. 26506   304/293-3536.

WISCONSIN ($131,415) Cataloguing and microfilming. An estimated 2,200 titles to be located and recorded. James P. Danky, Newspapers and Periodicals Librarian, State Historical Society of Wisconsin, Madison, WI. 53706   608/262-9584.

U.S. NEWSPAPER PROGRAM PARTICIPANTS: NATIONAL REPOSITORY PROJECTS

In addition to state projects, the Endowment has funded the cataloging of newspapers at eight national repositories and also funded preservation at one of the eight. Each of these libraries has extensive newspaper collections containing titles from nearly all 50 states.

AMERICAN ANTIQUARIAN SOCIETY. ($425,794) Cataloguing completed; 14,324 titles recorded. Joyce Tracey, Newspaper and Serials Librarian. Worcester, Massachusetts   01609   617/755-5221.

CENTER FOR RESEARCH LIBRARIES. ($35,845) Cataloguing completed; 1,035 titles recorded. Karla D. Petersen, Director for Technical Services. Chicago, Illinois   60637   312/955-4545.

KANSAS STATE HISTORICAL SOCIETY. ($415,844) Cataloguing completed; 10,330 titles recorded. Eugene Decker, State Archivist. Topeka, Kansas   66612 913/296-4792.

THE NEW YORK PUBLIC LIBRARY. ($609,999) Cataloguing and microfilming. an estimated 4,900 titles to be recorded; 800,000 pages to be microfilmed. Irene Percelli, Serials Department. Fifth Avenue & 42nd Street, New York, New York 10018   212/930-0639.

THE NEW-YORK HISTORICAL SOCIETY. ($298,316) Cataloguing completed, 9,080 titles recorded. James Bell, Director. New York, New York 10024   212/873-3400.

RUTGERS UNIVERSITY LIBRARY. ($140,000) Cataloguing completed; 3,000 titles recorded. Lida Sak, Rutgers University Libraries. New Brunswick, New Jersey 08903   201/932-7513.

STATE HISTORICAL SOCIETY OF WISCONSIN. ($350,912) Cataloguing completed; 7,000 titles recorded. James P. Danky, Newspapers and Periodicals Libbrarian. Madison, Wisconsin   53706   608/262-9584.

WESTERN RESERVE HISTORICAL SOCIETY. ($207,689) Cataloguing completed; 3,920 titles recorded. Kermit Pike, Director of the Library, History Library. Cleveland, Ohio 44106   216/721-5722.

NEWSPAPERS COLLECTIONS IN YUGOSLAV LIBRARIES

Dora SEČIĆ

Chief, Information Centre, National and University Library, Zagreb, Yugoslavia

1. INTRODUCTION

When in 1951 the Directorate for Information of the State administration published the first "Register of Research and Special Libraries in Socialist Yugoslavia" [1] it was stated that only 8% of the quoted libraries were not founded in the twentieth century. At that time, in the early fifties, public librarianship was in the stage of intensive development. If we take these facts into consideration it is clear that in Yugoslavia there are not many libraries with significant collections of old newspapers. The oldest daily and weekly newspapers in south Slavic countries were published in the last quarter of the eighteenth century in Slovenia and Croatia which were part of the Habsburg empire, first in foreign and then in the native languages. The other parts of the country were still under Turkish rule. The first newspapers in the liberated Serbia appeared in 1834. Bosnia and Hercegovina, at that time Turkish, got its first newspaper in 1866 and after 1878 when it was occupied by Austria journalism was developed together with the administration and political system. The first Macedonian newspapers were printed in Bulgaria at the end of the nineteenth century while the greater part of Macedonia was almost until the First World War in the Turkish empire with weak connections to Europe and underdeveloped journalism.

After the First World War Yugoslavia was created but some parts of the country, for example Istria, came and remained under Italian rule until 1945.

In a country with such a turbulent history it is natural that library collections have many gaps. But thanks to the legal deposit laws during the last two centuries many newspapers which were published in our country during the foreign rule can be found in national and regional central libraries of Austria, Hungary and Italy. Some of these titles do not exist in Yugoslav libraries or are incomplete and according to agreements about cultural co-operation some of our libraries, as for example the University Library of Maribor [2], have developed programmes of supplementing their holdings with the most important titles in microform. This is a very costly and enduring activity which will surely persist in the future.

To the previously mentioned facts we have to add one more reason why so many titles and volumes of newspapers are not available in Yugoslav libraries. During the last war a great part of the rare library collections was destroyed or plundered, the greatest loss being the major part of the rich collection of the National Library of Serbia in Belgrade which was ruined by a bomb.

The National and University Library (NUL) in Zagreb is the oldest big universal library in Yugoslavia and it remained preserved during the last war. It has a long tradition in collecting South Slavic materials and got a remarkable and adequate building in 1913 which enhanced the development of all its collections. Due to the damage to the National Library in Belgrade, a still greater part of its collections remained unique in Yugoslavia and therefore to a great extent threatened because it has been heavily used for sundry, especially research, purposes.

The new socialist country was organized as a federal state composed of six republics immediately after the war. Librarians started co-operative programmes both on the level of the new republics and on the federal level. First it was important to ascertain the state of the art in the libraries in all federal units. Where libraries were lacking they were founded. This was especially important in the less developed republics and provinces where materials had to be collected by donation and from previous private institutions. The National Library of Serbia started as soon as it was possible a programme of completing the collection of microfilmed periodicals and other publications damaged in 1941. It is a long term task which has been systematically performed for many years now [3].

Today we register about 2500 titles of newspapers of all kinds and 28 dailies. Each capital of our six republics and two autonomous provinces publishes at least two daily newspapers, with the exception of the smallest republic, Montenegro, which has only one daily. In Croatia, Slovenia and Serbia some of the regional centres publish daily newspapers as well. Other smaller regions have weeklies.

2. LEGAL DEPOSIT COLLECTIONS

In the past legal deposit collections of newspapers had existed in Slovenia and Croatia since the beginning of the nineteenth century and in Serbia since 1870 [4].

When Yugoslav countries united in 1919 the new legal deposit regulation provided for three deposit libraries in the whole state. These are the present-day National Library of Serbia, NUL in Zagreb and NUL in Ljubljana. This means that for these three republics there exists already a continuity of collecting legal deposit copies since the last century.

In 1945 the new federal Act planned a central deposit collection for each of the six republics and since 1965 and 1974 respectively two more national libraries of the autonomous provinces of Kosovo and Vojvodina were included. So today we have eight complete collections of current newspapers published on the territory of Yugoslavia in the national libraries in Ljubljana, Zagreb, Sarajevo, Cetinje, Belgrade, Novi Sad, Priština and Skopje.

In addition to the federal acts, each republic and autonomous province has its own laws which regulate the distribution of the legal deposit copies to the regional central libraries within the federal units. So for example in Croatia in addition to the NUL in Zagreb, six more libraries receive, register, store and make available copies of all materials printed in SR Croatia. Newspapers of all kinds are the material which brings about most difficulties to these libraries. The reason for this is publications which are a consequence of the development of the system of socialist self-government, communal information systems, the education system and parallel with the democratization of the society, the appearance of numerous organs of religious communities, to mention only some of the types of the numerous new serial publications which emerged during the last decades in Yugoslavia.

The great bulk of material chokes the libraries with multiple (university or public) functions and with limited financial resources. For this reason the Croatian librarians initiated in 1985 a discussion on the possible selection of some categories of serial publications to be deposited for archival purposes. The problem of space, lack of staff and minimal preservation possibilities were the main reasons which motivated the regional libraries to propose selection on the regional principle.

Discussion on the related topic of co-ordinated cataloguing of the legal deposit materials is in progress in the Association of Yugoslav National Libraries. Truly all editions of local newspapers have been fully processed only in the national library of the republic or province of publication for the same reasons already mentioned as applying in Croatia. That means that some modifications of the present federal acts will probably be necessary.

In addition we must not forget that new technology will in the future reinforce usage of microforms and other media which will enable libraries to replace huge rows of bound volumes to achieve space savings.

In many municipalities there exist local collections of old and new newspapers and during the last decades numerous new collections of that kind have been established. Library associations and central libraries support their organizing and promotion [5].

3. BIBLIOGRAPHIC ACTIVITY AND UNION LISTS

Immediately after the war Yugoslav professionals started compiling bibliographies of Yugoslav serial publications on the local level and on the level of the republics. In the fifties the Yugoslav Lexicographic Institute in Zagreb organized a great action of collecting data for a universal bibliography of serial publications covering the period from the eighteenth century to 1945. Titles were included regardless of language and, where available, location data were added so that this publication is the only union catalogue of older Yugoslav serial publications which covers the whole country [6]. Regrettably, we must state that since 1955 this project has not been resumed so that this catalogue is not fully up-to-date.

In the sixties the focus of interest of our profession was on the acquisition and availability of foreign literature so that union catalogues of foreign periodicals were published. Foreign newspapers are sometimes included, but Yugoslav libraries collect very few, only the most important foreign titles.

However, bibliographic activities have a longer tradition. The first retrospective bibliography of Yugoslav newspapers covering the whole period from the beginnings to the twentieth century was published in 1911 [7]. Afterwards, during the period between the two world wars, a few lists and annuals of current newspaper production were published. In socialist Yugoslavia since 1956 the Yugoslav Bibliographical Institute has been publishing the current bibliography of Yugoslav serial publications (journals and newspapers mixed in one series)[8]. In 1975 Ž. Stoković published a retrospective bibliography of all Yugoslav newspapers from 1945 to 1973 [9].

Additionally in many places local retrospective bibliographies and union lists have been compiled. With promotion of local collections of library materials surely new and more complete bibliographies and catalogues will be supplied because we still miss a lot of data on older serial publications.

4. PRESERVATION AND CONSERVATION

In parallel with the bibliographic activities very soon after the war, Yugoslav librarians realized that the existing newspaper holdings were partly in bad condition and that extensive action for restoration was needed. So the resolution of the Third Congress of the League of Yugoslav Library Associations passed in 1956 contains a recommendation concerning preservation and conservation of library materials [10]. E Verona coming from NUL Zagreb suggested on the same occasion that systematic microfilming of Yugoslav newspapers be organized as soon as possible. She was the person who among many other topics occupied herself with the problem of restoration of old newspapers [11]. A workshop for the restoration of library materials was established in the NUL Zagreb in 1961 and preservation by lamination of old newspapers was introduced. In 1966 the programme for conservation of old Croatian newspapers was extended to include the most valuable collections in other libraries in Croatia [12]. The programme includes both restoration and microfilming and has been carried out continually since that time.

This has been until now the only specialized co-operative programme for restoration and conservation of newspapers in Yugoslavia. Other republics which have conservation and restoration facilities include all precious materials in common programmes.

In Slovenia a co-operative microfilming project which gives priority to newspapers is planned [13].

All national libraries except those in Montenegro and Kosovo which have no microfilming programmes photocopy continually rare and damaged newspapers as finances permit. For these purposes most often 35 mm silver halide roll film is used. The filming has been performed mostly for purposes of preservation and retention and all the libraries still give originals to users in their reading-rooms. This is due to the insufficient reading equipment and causes further damage to old newspapers.

5. STORAGE AND AVAILABILITY

All national libraries except those in Belgrade, Pristina and Zagreb have inadequate space for the accommodation of newspapers. NUL Zagreb has moved its newspaper holdings to a newly adapted building in 1986. The same building houses the Centre for Micrography and Restoration of Library Materials which ought to be enlarged in the coming years. This proves that the library is conscious of its archival responsibilities as the greatest source of old Yugoslav newspapers and of the fact that its newspaper holdings are unique and essential sources of information for the present and future needs of numerous researchers.

We lack published user studies which would give us insight into the needs, demands and categories of our users of newspapers. Libraries only publish collective data on circulation of volumes and inter-library loan activity. Yugoslav libraries provide newspaper articles to remote users only in the form of microfilms and photocopies. Originals are never lent outside the reading-rooms. Statistics show that the number of requests has been increasing each year. This shows that newspapers are getting more and more interesting for research.

At their congresses and meetings as well as in professional publications Yugoslav libraries have seldom tackled the topic of newspapers in libraries. We hope that the results of this Symposium will give us impetus.

BIBLIOGRAPHY

1   'Popis naučnih i stručnih knjižnica u Jugoslaviji', in: Informativni priručnik o Jugoslaviji, Vol.10-11, 1951.

2   Hartman, Bruno, 'Mikrofilmano časopisje v Univerzitetni knjižnici Maribor, (Microfilmed newspapers in the University Library Maribor), in: Knjižnica, Vol.30 no.1-2, 1986. pp.101-102.

3   'Program razvoja Narodne biblioteke Srbije za period 1970 - 1980', in: Bibliotekar, Vol.22 no.5, 1970. pp.431-455.

4   Hergešić, Branka, 'Obavezni primjerak - povlastica ili dužnost,' (Dépôt légal - Privilège ou devoir), in: Vjesnik bibliotekara Hrvatske, Vol.12, no.3-4, 1966. pp.97-107.

5   Bikicki, Milana, 'Periodične publikacije u zavičajnoj zbirci', (Local collections in public libraries), in: Bibliotekar, Vol.22 no.3, 1970. pp.246-251.

6   Ujević, Mate, (editor) 'Grada za bibliografiju jugoslavenske periodike', Zagreb, 1955. ('Anali Leksikografskog zavoda FNRJ', Vol 2).

7   Udruženje, Srpsko Novinarsko (editor) 'Jugoslovenska štampa: referati i bibligrafija'. Beograd, 1911.

8   Bibliografija Jugoslavije. Serijske publikacije. Beograd, Jugoslovenski Bibliografski Institut, 1956- . (changed title; original title: Spisak časopisa i novina štampanih na teritoriju FNRJ).

9   Stoković, Živorad K, 'Štampa naroda i narodnosti u SFRJ 1945-1973'. Beograd, Jugoslovenski Institut za Novinarstvo, 1975.

10 'Rezolucija III Kongresa Saveza društava bibliotekara FNRJ', in: 'Drugi i treći kongres Saveza društava bibliotekara FNR Jugoslavije'. Ljubljana, 1958, pp.80-81.

11 Verona, Eva, 'Ueber die Restaurierung von Zeitungsbeständen in der National- und Universitätsbibliothek in Zagreb', in: Zentralblatt für Bibliothekswesen, Vol.77 no.10, 1963. pp.433-443.

12 Dadić, Vera, 'Program zaštite starih hrvatskih novina', (Programme for preservation of old Croatian newspapers), in: Vjesnik bibliotekara Hrvatske, Vol.24 no.104, 1981 pp.53-59.

13 Gazvoda, Jelka, 'Mikrofilmanje gradiv v knjižnično-informacijskem sistemu Slovenije: med potrebami in možnostmi', (Use of the microfilm in modern Slovenian libraries: between needs and possibilities), in: Knjižnica, Vol.30 no.3-4, 1986. pp.111-119.

CHAIRMAN'S SUMMARY

Ian GIBB

British Library, retired.

We have had a marvellous exchange of experience, which is enormously valuable. I think that everyone will have learnt a tremendous amount. Certainly, though I have been involved with newspapers over the last 10 years of my career, I have learnt a vast amount. Much of this I did not know before and I am sure that is equally true of other people. I think probably the key word that could be used if it were necessary to pick out one thing from all the presentations is co-ordination. This can happen in a variety of ways, but any newspaper preservation programme for any country has three main elements in it, which might broadly be called investigation and planning, bibliographical control and preservation. Now what exactly those contain will probably differ within each country as well as the order in which you take them and the level of importance which you give to each of those, but I think that it has come through that virtually everyone has tried to tackle these three elements in one way or another.

The solutions quite interestingly often seem to mirror the political structure, which is reasonable enough, since political structures provide money and so you have to find where the money is. It has been very interesting to see how far people lean towards a centralised solution, how far a decentralised or how far we are confused about what we are doing as Jeff Field said. We have obviously got a number of different patterns. Perhaps without wanting to be too brash about this, some of the smaller countries, for example, Sweden and New Zealand, who are doing a great deal, are pretty heavily centralised. This is partly a function of the size; the larger a project gets the more you are likely to decentralise. We in this country, of course, do have a very large newspaper library, but equally we realise how much else there is to do and the political complexity of the British Isles leads to further complications. Unusually I think, we have here regional organisations of libraries which are not based on political areas. Many countries have library organisations which relate to the divisions of their country. Take the Federal Republic of Germany or for that matter the United States and Canada, and these clearly are mirrored in the way in which the problems have been approached.

I think the one point that is the most important is, as Marianne Scott said, 'it works in their situation'. I do not think in any sense it is for IFLA to attempt to dictate. It is very useful that IFLA should be involved in standards because standards internationally help very considerably. It is very useful, as more than one speaker has said, that the interest of an international body can often be taken back to a country where it can be put in this way: "Look, we want to do something, this is what is being done internationally and these are the standards we should achieve". That is very helpful, I am sure, in trying to raise funds, so that you are not thought just to be some sort of madman who wants to do something about newspapers in your own country (and surely nobody else in the world is doing anything about that sort of thing). I can hear the administrators saying that. So, again as Marianne said, what works in your own situation is the best thing. Obviously international cooperation can be very important, particularly in those complicated political situations that history has left us with: colonial situations or countries which have been split up or merged, so that records and material are housed in a number of different places. But you may well have heard a lot this morning that has sparked off in your mind the thought 'Ah, that might help in my country' or 'someone else is doing that, I thought I was probably the only one doing something like that' and I think that that is the enormous value of the exchange of experience we have all had this morning.

ELEMENTS OF A NEWSPAPER PRESERVATION POLICY WORLDWIDE

Dr Hans BOHRMANN

Director, Institut für Zeitungsforschung, Dortmund,
and
Geschaftsführer des Mikrofilmarchivs der deutschsprachigen Presse e.V.

INTRODUCTION BY Dr BOHRMANN

Germany in former times was, and nowadays is, a very complicated area of newspaper collection, and as my colleague Wilbert Ubbens pointed out in his paper, newspaper preservation only functions through a programme of co-operation between several libraries and archives in the Federal Republic of Germany. We have the necessity to combine our resources and to co-operate in our land if we are going to be able in later times to co-operate with other countries. We have since 1930, a national library, but this national library in Leipzig has only small holdings of historical newspapers, because of the importance of the older state libraries, especially in Munich and Berlin, and because of the lack of money. The German newspaper library has never been developed anywhere. If we search for strategies of national co-operation it is necessary at first to be able to co-operate in Germany itself.

In the West German situation this means the following; you have to know where a newspaper is, in the holdings of which library. Catalogues in Germany are incomplete. Comprehensive catalogues of the Länder in the most cases omit newspapers. The Deutsche Bibliothek in Frankfurt only has holdings from May 8th 1945 and forward. The scholar is therefore forced to seek help from newspaper librarians and in libraries with big newspaper collections or in libraries specialising in newspapers. This approach is also suitable because newspapers are the sort of material which belongs as well in traditional archives as in a library and the information necessary to understand the complexity of newspaper appearance and contents is often better in archives and special libraries, than in the big libraries with the big holdings of newspapers. Western Germany has the Dortmund Institute for Newspaper Research and this is one contact point. We have a large collection of newspapers in Dortmund. Many papers are in the form of microfilm and we have a collection representative of German press history up to the beginning of the 18th century. But this collection is far from complete. We need information as to where the other papers are; we have close contact with the Bremen State Library, for instance, and other libraries specialising in this field.

For information about the foreign press located in German libraries, it is necessary to contact the Staatsbibliotek Preussischer Kulturbesitz in Berlin West. This library has large holdings of foreign newspapers. We think it is very profitable to work within a network of specialised libraries and we ask scholars to seek contact with such libraries. The international conference here in London may help us to search for the possibilities of funds to build up a complete catalogue of German newspapers. In this West German system preservation of the original is, as Wilbert Ubbens pointed out, a purpose of the libraries in the Länder and other regions, while the national library, the Deutsche Bibliothek collects only newspapers in microform. The London conference may encourage us to make the best of this really bad situation.

The microfilming of newspapers, in my opinion, is the best way to preserve the original because the user is the very enemy of the newspaper. The microfilming programmes conducted and co-ordinated by the special libraries of newspapers in the Federal Republic work within a framework of microfilm archives of the German language press. This is a way we have to proceed. This is also only the way to serve international lending of newspapers as whole runs, rolls or distinct articles. The lending of the paper original is impossible. The London conference may encourage us to convince the German Research Foundation to give further financial aid for the microfilming of newspapers.

I think the situation in Germany in the next ten years would be much better than now if we had international aid for microfilming and international help for the preparation of a national bibliography of newspapers. In my paper I listed some other ideas for elements of a newspaper preservation policy worldwide, but I think it is necessary to prepare the possibilities for a worldwide co-operation firstly in one's own country.

* * * * * * * * * * * * * * * * *

Because of the high frequency with which their issues appear and the universality of their content, newspapers are far more than a diary of general political history. From the point of view of their contents, newspapers are a whole collection of such diaries, which can be evaluated from the most diverse viewpoints. Newspapers are thus not only valuable antiquities, though they are that too, but they provide source material for very different purposes, ranging for example from family enquiries into the announcements of births and deaths to research enquiries about the development of prices of everyday objects or the development of social institutions, for example marriage.

Since newspapers have been recognised for their value as source material and have been developed by researchers into an instrument for serious and scientific use (source criticism), libraries and archives whose holdings include, or rather, also include, newspapers, must ensure that the periodic press can be preserved as a frequently tapped source and still remain usable.

This double task is made even harder to fulfil because of the fact that since the first decades of the nineteenth century newspapers, after appearing for approximately two centuries in a manageable format, went over to the large paper size which we now generally think of as newspaper format, and half a century later, also as a result of the demand for paper which had increased considerably because of the newspaper industry, they altered their production completely. Rag paper, which had good properties in relation to longevity and use, was gradually, starting in England and France, replaced by paper made from wood pulp. The large format produced problems when used because it can tear simply when the pages are turned. The wood pulp paper made the situation worse since it can, if not used, be preserved under favourable conditions for a long time, but with use it is subject to more or less speedy decay. These facts are universally valid. They become increasingly grave the warmer and damper the climatic conditions of a country are and, a factor generally connected to the climatic factors (see for example the North/South conflict), the poorer the state is, the less possible it is to take the measures necessary to guard against paper decay. The setting up and the management of air-conditioned store rooms and the conservation treatment of newspaper paper needs a considerable outlay of funds. Even if such means are available at all they are usually applied to other, more important purposes than the preservation of these witnesses to everyday life, newspapers. A library and archive policy on newspapers which desires to be effective worldwide must take this state of affairs into account if it does not want to fall prey to illusion.

With the technique of microfilming a process was slowly developed more than half a century ago which can, with a comparatively small outlay of funds, preserve newspapers for use long term. Microfilming limits the air-conditioned storage space necessary, it facilitates the making of copies and also allows for the possibility of preserving valuable paper originals of newspapers for use by keeping them separate, although the nature of the material (the acid content of wood pulp paper) militates against this [1].

Microfilming is an aid to the preservation of newspapers provided it is used regularly, even intensively, because the fragile carrier of print, the paper, is replaced by a new, durable carrier, plastic. The microfilm takes the place of the original, it can represent the original, for example when it comes to the conveying of its contents, but it is otherwise not comparable with the original. The microfilm processes have absolutely nothing of the aura of the original. Its task is the conveying of the text to the user. Problems in the reproduction emerge for example with photos, whose quality is problematic even in the original because of the graining in newspaper print which is still usually necessary for technical reasons to do with the printing, not to mention colour print, whether it be text or picture. Colour originals can frequently only be reproduced approximately on black and white microfilm. Even then they only give an impression of the original; but colour film, which is now available, is so costly to produce, so complicated to use, and so difficult to store, and thus overall so expensive, that its use is out of the question for the filming of newspapers, even when the originals are in colour. In addition a colour microfilm would only appear in black and white in a reader-printer [2].

The recognition that microfilming is a suitable means for keeping newspapers permanently available and yet also for being able to preserve them, has now spread worldwide. Starting from the industrial centres of Western Europe and North America and also Australia, it has encompassed almost all countries [3]. Nearly everywhere in the Eastern bloc countries the filming of newspapers has now been undertaken or at least the preparations for filming are well advanced. This is particularly the case in Czechoslovakia, Hungary and the DDR. But the Soviet Union and its allies are suffering particularly from the fact that in their economic area neither suitable cameras nor reading equipment nor reader-printers are manufactured, and thus that to acquire them they are dependent on the quota of foreign currency for the countries with a strong currency. In most developing countries the possibility of acquiring hardware is also a major obstacle in the way of beginning the filming of newspapers and of carrying it through [4]. Thus progress in the filming of newspapers can only be hoped for by co-operation between countries, whether through the agency of UNESCO or on the basis of two-sided agreements. This help can lie not only in the making available of hardware and the production of microfilm (silver film for archive films and diazo for the films to be used) but can also be seen in the transmission of user copies from each library's filming of certain of its own titles. Thus the large national libraries and a host of specialised research libraries in the western industrialised countries, and also archives in these areas, have stored many important past and present newspapers, which are of foreign origin or come from formerly dependent regions. It is an international duty of those responsible for preserving and transmitting cultural documents that these items, giving evidence of the publishing activity of foreign countries in foreign tongues, should also be saved and user copies supplied to the libraries of the countries of origin when necessary.

Parallel to filming and the exchange of films, information about filming which has been done is also of importance. Since the bodies carrying out filming may be very different institutions and may range from state and private archives and libraries to publishers and service filming companies, there is a need here for considerable efforts at national level. In the Federal Republic of Germany efforts are being made to supplement the list of filmed newspapers given in the contents list of the Microfilm Archive of the German-speaking Press [5] with the filming which has been undertaken by libraries or archives on commission which do not belong to the Microfilm Archive. It is intended in the not too distant future to bring together all the records for newspaper microfilming in the periodicals data base at the German Library Institute, Berlin, which already represents the most comprehensive current bibliography with location information for periodicals and also newspapers [6]. It may be possible later to print a separate newspaper catalogue from the periodicals data base. In the international field the completion and regular updating of the microform index [7] is to be supported. In its next edition this index will contain the complete holdings of the Microform Archive of the German-language Press.

For the preservation and use of newspapers it is important that the international exchange format for newspaper filming remains unambiguously defined and that the techniques of filming/conserving should correspond more or less to the financial and technical resources of libraries and archives. This is the case for the industrialised countries, where libraries and archives do not generally have large financial means at their disposal, and it is even more the case for the developing countries whose available financial means are far less. From this perspective the introduction of new technology like the electronic storage disc must also be viewed with scepticism. This would require technology for use which would demand a corresponding infrastructure which is not even available in all industrialised countries, although it could possibly be built up in the not too distant future.

REFERENCES

1   The possibilities for preserving paper by means of chemical treatment can only be mentioned here, they cannot be described or weighed up individually. Information on this to date points to the fact that all these procedures demand a considerable outlay for equipment which, because of its cost, can scarcely be afforded by the industrialised countries. Consequently microfilming remains the obvious procedure for preserving newspapers long term and keeping them usable.

2   Whether the techniques of electronic storage discs open up new dimensions in colour storage and reproduction is a matter for debate. The problems of photographing and reproduction would seem to be solved with storage discs. But difficulties will clearly arise in the copying of storage discs onto paper. This is particularly the case for colour originals. It remains hard to estimate the cost of this new technique.

3   The degree to which the filming of newspapers has advanced in different countries is of course very variable. While for example in Denmark and Sweden current filming (the continuous filming of newspapers as they appear) is as advanced as could be desired, and considerable progress has

been made in retrospective filming, in the Federal Republic of Germany and France on the other hand considerable efforts have been made to film newspapers but because of the enormity of the task, no large scale results have yet been achieved. While in Italy and Spain, according to the information that we have, interest has been expressed but hardly any filming has actually been started upon. Austria is going in in a big way for deacidification of newspaper paper and has as a result relatively neglected microfilming. The United States developed the microfilming of newspapers first of all and large parts of the historic and current stock of newspapers have been encompassed. Canada too is well provided with newspaper films.

4   In South America and most developing countries the provision of microfilms of newspapers has only been slightly developed. In Argentina for example the filming of newspapers has begun, although only with silver films, since the diazo technique is not practised in that country. Thus the use of films is problematic.

5   See <u>Mikrofilmarchiv der deutschsprachigen Presse</u>: 6. Bestandsverzeichnis. Dortmund, 1982; 7. Mikrofilmarchiv, in press.

6   The periodicals data base is the central bibliography and location index for a continually growing number of general and specialised research libraries in the Federal Republic. At the moment half-yearly editions of its holdings are published on microfiches (obtainable from Harrasowitz, Wiesbaden). Beginning in 1987 the holdings of the central union catalogue for foreign newspapers and magazines compiled by the Staatsbibliothek Preussischer Kulturbesitz in Berlin will be entered in the data bank. From 1989 it is planned to include filmed newspapers from the microfilm archive of the German speaking press.

7   'Guide to microforms in print'. Westport and London, Meckler. 2 volumes.

MICROFILMING THE WORLD'S NEWSPAPERS

Mary-Jane STARR

Office of the Associate National Librarian, National Library of Canada

INTRODUCTION BY Ms STARR

A few minutes ago I noticed again that the programme says Symposium on Newspaper Preservation <u>and Access</u> and I think I would like to remind myself that our goal ultimately in all this endeavour is to bring the user and the information in the newspaper together, and that there are various components in this process beginning with the publication of the paper, about which I learnt a great deal in one of the workshops, preservation is obviously one activity, together with bibliographic control and physical and intellectual access.

This session focuses on one component, namely preservation, and one means or method of preservation, namely microfilming. In my paper I have outlined some early microfilming projects, specifically in the United States and Great Britain because so much of the focus originally in both the Library of Congress and in the British Library was on filming the foreign press and not just their own domestic imprint. There is no discussion in the paper about the considerable preservation efforts that are being made by newspaper publishers themselves, or by the commercial sector, of which we had ample evidence in the exhibits at the Symposium. So the paper restricts itself to several examples of foreign newspaper coverage, does not include all the work that has been, that has gone on in individual countries that we learned a great deal in earlier papers.

When looking at a co-operative endeavour (and this is not restricted just to newspapers, but any kind of library or archival co-operative endeavour), there are some general principles that present themselves and in fact are applicable in this case. First is the adherence to the common acceptable norms or standards. In this case we are looking at standards for preservation microfilming, because we did hear earlier that there has been some substandard filming done in the past. We have an international standard, the ISO standard, we have a whole series of national standards, and in some cases institutional standards. I would suggest it is folly to think that we will ever have everyone in the world microfilming to one standard, but we can have a number of standards that as a group we consider acceptable for our archival quality.

Another element in an international newspaper co-operative effort would be bibliographic control. And I think this flows out of the concept of universal bibliographic control, UBC, where each country looks after documenting its own domestic imprint and thus in a composite manner we are able to have bibliographic control of all the world's newspapers.

Another element of co-operation that I would like to mention is complementarity of effort: that may be between the public and private sectors, it can be between agencies in one country and it can be between countries. Obviously the converse of complimentarity of effort is duplication and that is surely something that we would prefer to avoid, if possible.

The next element is a little more, not elusive, but perhaps a little more abstract and that is the element of trust. If we are going to have an international co-operative effort then there has to be trust on the part of the participants, that information on microfilming efforts will be available, and indeed that the microfilm itself (we must not forget the access side of this) will be available - the negatives and the information on the negatives - for those of us who wish to purchase titles and as well positive copies for both consultation and interlibrary loan.

The element of co-operation that I have saved till the end is the one that I considered the most important and that is the element of co-ordination. My experience with co-operative projects is that co-ordination is often the element that leads to the success or the absence of co-ordination often leads to the failure. This is a mechanism that would act as a focus, that would be responsible for a gathering of information, disseminating information, that would provide direction and thus leadership to a co-operative effort. I do not have a definitive answer, in fact I do not have any answer on where such a co-ordinated mechanism might lie, how it might be formed. I leave it to you, perhaps in a discussion period to talk about how that might come about, but I do strongly believe that an effective co-ordinating mechanism is quite a basic requirement for an international co-operative effort. If we look at the issue of co-operation worldwide there is one principle that if we could all adhere to, I would not even need to speak this afternoon, and that is if each country does its own domestic imprint as part of its commitment to UAP, UBC and the Preservation and Conservation Programme then in fact we would have the problems solved. We heard earlier about some very real and very determined efforts among countries to do so, but it would seem that in the short term there will still be need for some countries to do some foreign title filming. There is a solid groundwork here, and we can build on that activity to date and that activity itself is built on traditional ties and interests between and among countries and geographic regions.

I suggested in the paper a twinning arrangement for countries that are not in a position to do their own filming at the present time. There would be roles within this arrangement for both the country of production where the newspaper is published and for the country of preservation where the newspaper would be filmed, and I think the Library of Congress has provided a very good example of where this has worked to mutual benefit.

Another area that I was asked to cover is the selection of titles for filming. Optimally we would of course have all newspapers filmed in complete runs to archival standards on an ongoing basis, but, as we have also heard resources are finite, and in some cases very limited, for this endeavour and therefore, it is worthwhile looking at some criteria or guidelines for selecting specific titles for preservation filming. We have also heard from some speakers about what some of these guidelines or criteria might be, and I do not pretend to be exhaustive but have a few that I would like to mention. I also found when I came to look at this that there are some inherent conflicts in the area of selecting specific titles for filming. For example, do you film a title because it is complete and in good condition, or do you choose to film a title because there are only a few extant issues and they are in a very fragile condition? Or do you film a title from a large urban centre because it records the life of that city and thus is the history of a large number of people, or do you instead choose a small weekly, because it may be the only documentary evidence of that community? For making choices, I think you will discover, if you have not already, that there are some inherent difficulties.

But let us look at some criteria. First there is the question of the completeness of the file, its extent and its availability. There is the question of the physical condition of the file, be it good or bad, and there are cases where an argument that could be advanced from either side for filming. Place of publication: do you try and film from representative centres, do you try and film the kinds of newspapers that are not going to be saved anywhere else? I think another criterion is the quality of the newspaper. Is it a newspaper that is recognised in its own community and elsewhere, for its journalistic coverage, for its editorial content? Circulation as well is another indication, perhaps of the quality of the paper. Editorial perspective: we heard from Dr Harris and Dr Black that for their kinds of research and their needs, they would like to see a variety or range of perspectives represented in the papers that are saved, be it mainstream, underground, pro- or anti-government; something to think about when selecting.

It is the question of audience. We have dealt mainly with the mainstream press, with those dailies and weeklies, but what about the special interest newspapers, labour and religious, student, ethnic and what have you. Another concept to be kept in mind is the availability of the paper in another form. Is it in electronic form? Can you get access to it on-line? Is it on CD-ROM? We have an example in Canada: the <u>Globe and Mail</u> has brought out one year of its paper on CD-ROM. They also microfilm it at this point. They are also in electronic form. I think that, when you have that variety of formats and means of accessibility, those are factors which temper your decision as to whether or not to select a title for filming.

Last but not least are the needs of researchers. Whether we are librarians or archivists it is our professional responsibility to meet the needs of our researchers, both now and to try and anticipate those needs in the future. I think this is where we do in fact have to exercise our intellects, our professional expertise and be responsible about the titles which we do select for filming. Having said that these criteria are suggestions only, we have heard others from other speakers and all of them would have to be considered in light of your local and national priorities, and local situation.

In conclusion, I personally have learned a great deal at this Symposium. I have heard of successful microfilming programmes, both past and present, and in both the private and the public sectors. I think there is very strong evidence here of a will and a commitment to enhance our collective international resource of newspapers on microfilm. The elements of co-operation that I enumerated, if we could move towards them and if they could be implemented, I think would move us from the stage of commitment to one of accomplishment, that we would begin to realise some of the immediate goals of international co-operation for worldwide coverage and ultimately bring us closer to that final goal of bringing the user and the information in newspapers together.

* * * * * * * * * * * * * * * * *

1.   INTRODUCTION

Microfilming all the world's newspapers is a formidable preservation challenge given the number of newspapers published worldwide, the ever-increasing demand by researchers, the rapid deterioration of newsprint, and the declining economic resources available to support microfilming. Fortunately, some decades ago, the potential of an emerging technology, microphotography, as an appropriate preservation medium for newspapers was recognized and work began on filming newspapers. While the microfilming efforts of the past have been considerable, much remains to be done to ensure that the world's newspapers are preserved and available therefore for present and future generations.

A description of the introduction and development of newspaper microfilming activity worldwide deserves a more thorough examination than is possible in this paper. The information herein was drawn from available secondary sources, and not from consultation with experts in each country. An indicative, rather than exhaustive, approach is taken which seeks to illustrate and highlight a number of different paths that have been followed in several countries. The emphasis throughout is on countries which have undertaken the microfilming of foreign titles. This background information is followed by the identification and description of desirable elements in an international co-operative approach to microfilming the world's newspapers.

2. EARLY MICROFILMING PROJECTS

One of the first reported instances of newspapers on microfilm occurred in the mid-nineteenth century. Micro-copies of pages of the London Evening News were exhibited at the Royal Photographic Society in London in March 1853 [1]. It is not surprising therefore that newspaper microfilming is actively pursued in Great Britain although regular filming programmes were not established until the mid-twentieth century. The British Library's microfilming policy for newspapers has as its objective the development of a national archive of British newspapers on negative microfilm. The British Library seeks to fulfil this objective through the co-operation of other libraries as well as through its own extensive operation at the Newspaper Library [2]. At present, the microfilming workshop has more than thirty cameras, one of the largest operations in the world [3]. Filming there began several decades ago based on the extensive collection of the domestic press acquired on legal deposit and of foreign newspapers where the emphasis is on British Commonwealth countries. Foreign archival microfilming began in 1964 primarily to save space. Barring copyright restrictions all microfilm made by the BL is available for purchase. A recent sales catalogue included newspaper titles from almost one hundred countries.

In 1982, the British Library established NEWSPLAN, a programme to assist other British libraries, on a regional basis, in the co-ordinated preservation of microfilm of United Kingdom provincial newspapers from 1700 to the present day. In NEWSPLAN a series of responsibilities are prescribed for the British Library and for local libraries in order to ensure the preservation and retention of British newspapers [4]. The primary emphasis is on retrospective files but current files are also included [5].

In India, the National Library implemented a microfilming programme in 1935 recognizing the fugitive nature of modern printing and the value of preserving documents from alteration, loss and destruction [6]. Preservation microfilming was assisted there as elsewhere in the late 1950's by the UNESCO Microfilm Unit, a mobile set-up that trained technicians and encouraged authorities to microfilm newspapers and other documents. Beginning in 1956, UNESCO sent its Mobile Microform Units from one member state to another to film irreplaceable material of sufficient value to justify the expense of microfilming. The master negative remained in the country of filming and the positive or UNESCO copy was deposited in one of four regional depots (Latin America, Arab States, Africa or Asia) [7]. Discontinued in 1970, the UNESCO project nonetheless made an early and significant contribution to preservation of the world's newspapers.

In the United States, the first automatic microfilming machine for commercial use was marketed in 1928. Although the technology had been developed somewhat earlier, it was not until 1933 that Recordak, a division of Eastman Kodak, tested the equipment at the New York Public Library [8]. Several years later, microfilming of that collection began, followed by the introduction of a microfilming program at the Library of Congress (LC) in 1938. In 1939, three American newspapers were filmed at LC on 35 mm roll microfilm. The program was extended in 1962 to the filming of American newspaper volumes dating back to 1870 when sulfide paper was first used for newsprint. The Library of Congress early newspaper microfilming programmes were driven by both the need for storage space and the concern and commitment to long-term preservation [9].

The Harvard University Project began in the same year as the LC programme. Securing financial support from the Rockefeller Foundation, the Harvard University Library began to film current foreign newspapers on an ongoing basis. During the life of the project (1938-1955), sixty-two titles were filmed. The entire back file of master negatives and the remaining funds from the Rockefeller Foundation were transferred to the Association of Research Libraries in 1956 [10].

About a decade earlier, the Association of Research Libraries (ARL) had established a Committee on Microfilming Co-operation, on the principle that by working together duplication could be avoided and limited resources used to greater mutual effect. Newspaper microfilming in the United States was not contained within the research library community as more and more local and state libraries took responsibility for filming the newspapers of their jurisdictions. This followed on the decision of the American Library Association Committee on Co-operative Microfilm Projects to give first priority to the preservation of American newspapers. Therefore, the ARL Committee recommended 'a co-ordinated national effort to ensure efficient and comprehensive coverage of foreign newspapers among research libraries.' [11]. By 1956, with the transfer of the Harvard archive, the ARL Foreign Newspaper Microfilm Project was created and situated at the MidWest Interlibrary Centre (now the Center for Research Libraries) in Chicago. By paying an annual subscription fee, ARL participating institutions could borrow positive microfilm of any title held by the project, which would film some titles and purchase others from outside sources [12]. By 1970, some 70,000 domestic and foreign titles had been filmed in the United States. The Library of Congress's own programme had already filmed hundreds of foreign titles including vernacular titles in Oriental languages, and African and Asian newspapers [13]. In 1972, the Library of Congress assumed responsibility for a national foreign newspaper microfilming programme and established the position of co-ordinator of foreign newspaper microfilming. 'At that time there were half a dozen large scale foreign newspaper microfilming programs sponsored by the research community' [14]. The goal of the national programme was increased sharing of foreign newspapers on microfilm.

3. ELEMENTS OF CO-OPERATION

The keynotes of co-operation in any field of endeavour are complementarity of effort and benefits accruing to all participants. The case of international co-operation for the microfilming of the world's newspapers is no exception. If duplication among separate programmes is to be eliminated and if all participants are to derive some benefit, then there are a number of essential elements. These include: establishment of a co-ordinating mechanism; agreement on standards for filming; filing, systematic distribution of responsibility for microfilming among countries; and criteria for selection of titles.

3.1. A co-ordinating mechanism for international co-operation

Co-operative efforts on any level benefit from co-ordination. There is no reason to suspect that a co-operative newspaper preservation programme would differ in this respect. The major benefits of co-ordination are the provision of a single focus or reference point, and a means of avoiding duplication and making individual filming programmes collectively more effective. One of the vital roles played by the co-ordinator is that of a clearinghouse for information on filming projects worldwide. The clearinghouse function includes gathering and disseminating timely and accurate information on newspapers that have been microfilmed, on ongoing filming activities, and on future plans. Bibliographic and holdings information and registers of microform masters are obvious and necessary sources of information. The promulgation of standards for microfilming is another important role. Drawing up and maintaining lists of contacts in various institutions in each country are yet other functions. A co-ordinator may also be given responsibility for liaising with others in the fields of preservation and micropublishing, and, if necessary and appropriate, seeking and securing funds to further the aims of the co-operative effort. Last, and by no means least, is the issue of leadership. Co-operative programmes benefit immeasurably from the sense of direction that a co-ordinator can provide.

There are a number of options for co-ordination. They range from an adequately-funded separate and independent office to the use of an existing volunteer committee such as the IFLA Working Group on Newspapers. Along this spectrum is the possibility of housing a co-operative microfilming endeavour under the aegis of a related programme, such as IFLA's Universal Preservation Programme. As the national libraries of many countries have assumed responsibility for newspaper microfilming programmes, the Conference of Directors of National Libraries might be another possibility. Obviously, there are advantages and difficulties associated with each of these options. However, with co-ordination a vital ingredient in the success of co-operative endeavours, an effective and efficient organizational approach is a fundamental concern.

3.2. Standards for microfilming newspapers

Some of the earliest microfilm of newspapers would not meet today's standards. Among the problems are missing pages and/or issues, inappropriate reduction ratios, incomplete pages when bound volumes were used, insufficient identification of titles and leader information, uneven lighting, lack of clarity, poor resolution, type of film and film deterioration. However, these are issues that, in the main, have been resolved through the development of standards.

The international standard is that of the International Organization for Standardization, no. 4087 "Microfilming of newspapers on 35 mm. unperforated microfilm for archival purposes". The ISO standard covers image placement and reduction ratios, film stock, film thickness, filming procedures, arrangement of the file, film targets, processing the exposed film, quality, correcting the processed camera negative, intermediate copies, storage, and container description. Many member bodies of ISO have approved the standard for microfilming and national standards conform to it, e.g. the British Standard BS 5847, "Specification for 35 mm microfilming of newspapers for archival purposes". Industry standards that are used by some commercial micropublishers and service bureaux may be somewhat less exacting and, while serving the short-term needs of today's consumers, they may not be adequate for archival purposes and long-term preservation requirements. While it may be impossible to reach unanimity on a single standard, adherence to recognized and acceptable contemporary standards is surely a requirement of any international cooperative effort.

3.3. The distribution of responsibility for microfilming

In his research guide on the European press, Iben contends that, generally speaking, the 'resources in foreign newspapers are considerably more rare and much less extensive in any country' than are resources of the country's own print journalism [15]. Given this situation, the basic principle on which responsibility for newspaper microfilming rests is that each country assumes responsibility for its domestic press. If each country were to microfilm its own national imprint, then there would be exhaustive preservation coverage. However, experience to the present has shown that this model is highly unobtainable and it is unlikely the situation wil change radically in the future. Thus, other models for the distribution of responsibility may be put forward.

The distribution of responsibility for foreign newspapers could take advantage of existing microfilming programs. Presumably these programs reflect the political interests and research needs of a particular country. Although such interests and needs shift over time, they provide the basis for the allocation of microfilming responsibility. It is perhaps best to make such allocations on a regional basis where possible and, where not, on a country basis.

Another model related to the first is a twinning arrangement, wherein two countries work together. The country of production (where the newspaper is published) assumes responsibility for collecting a complete set or file in the best possible condition and for supplying a bibliographic description of the title. Creating a complete set at source might be more effective than attempting to acquire, at a distance, items as ephemeral as separate issues of newspapers. The country of preservation assumes the responsibility for microfilming the title. This might be done on site with the use of mobile or local equipment or bureaux, or through the transportation of the files to a preservation filming centre. In any arrangement, adherence to standards must be assured. The disposition of master negatives and positive copies could be worked out to mutual agreement. Because of the special responsibility of national libraries to gather, preserve and make known their country's literary heritage, the twinning approach might best be worked though the medium of national libraries and might be based on historical ties and current interests born of poitical, economic and cultural factors.

For microfilming foreign newspapers, the allocation of responsibility should take into account the work to date of various countries in microfilming foreign newspapers, and the current programs and policies of institutions and countries in microfilming. If a twinning approach were taken, the co-ordinator could assist in the process of matching countries, in addition to documenting and making known all such arrangements.

3.4. Criteria for the selection of titles

Ideally, all the world's newspapers would be filmed in complete runs in optimal condition, to archival standards, and on an ongoing basis. As the realities of economics and resources intrude, this exhaustive 'ideal' fades and the selection of specific titles becomes necessary. In North America, there is evidence of both exhaustive and selective approaches. The United States

Newspaper Program is based on selective microfilming with only certain papers chosen for preservation. The National Library of Canada's Decentralized Program for Canadian Newspapers, on the other hand, adopts the opposite viewpoint and aims for comprehensive microfilming coverage. The difference owes much to the great variation in the number of titles published in the respective countries and therefore the resources necessary for microfilming.

Even with better overall coverage through improved international co-operation, decisions on specific titles for filming will still have to be taken. The criteria for selection are not straightforward and exhibit some inherent conflicts. In the course of applying them, other local factors may be taken into account.

The proposed criteria for the selection of specific newspaper titles include:
* the completeness of the file and its extent and availability;
* the physical condition of the file;
* the place of publication - a national or regional capital, a major trading centre or an isolated community;
* the quality of the newspaper - journalistic coverage and excellence, editorial content, circulation, and importance within the community and elsewhere;
* the editorial perspective - mainstream, underground, or dissident;
* the audience or special interest of the paper - ethnic, student, labour, religions, etc;
* the availability of the paper in microform from other sources; and
* the needs of researchers, both currently and in the future.

4. CONCLUSION

This paper does not propose a single solution or model to international co-operation and worldwide coverage. Rather, it seeks to suggest possible approaches to a co-operative effort that would build on the accomplishments and enthusiasm of the present in informing the way of the future. To reach the goal of microfilming the world's newspapers, there is a need for effective co-ordination, agreement on standards, allocation and assumption of responsibility for both the domestic and the foreign press and a consistent application of selection criteria.

REFERENCES

1   Majumdar, Gopal Kumar, 'The history of microfilming and its use', in: 'Newspaper microfilming: a plea for newsprint documentation'. Calcutta, Firma K L Mukhopadhyay, 1974. p.1.

2   'Access to newspapers', Library Association Record, Vol.84, February 1982, p.60.

3   British Library. National Preservation Advisory Committee, November 27, 1986. [Minutes], p.2.

4   'Two proposals for national co-operation', British Library Newspaper Library Newsletter, No.3, Autumn 1981, pp.1-2.

5   'Conservation microfilming of newspaper', Library Conservation News, No.

3, February 1984.

6   Majumdar, 'The history of microfilming', pp.6-7.

7   Majumdar, 'UNESCO's mobile units', pp.29-30.

8   'The Foreign newspaper microfilm project, 1938-1955', in: <u>Harvard Library Bulletin</u>, No.10, 1956, p.275.

9   La Hood, Charles G, Jr, 'Microfilm for the Library of Congress', in: <u>College and Research Libraries</u>, Vol.34, July 1973, pp.291-2.

10 'The Foreign newspaper microfilm project, 1938-1955', p.280.

11 Cole, John Y, 'Developing a national foreign newspaper microfilming program', in: <u>Library Resources & Technical Services</u>, Vol.18, Winter 1974, p.6.

12 Ibid, p.8.

13 Ibid, p.9.

14 Ibid, p.11.

15 Iben, Icko, 'Introduction', in: 'The Germanic press of Europe: an aid to research. Munster, Verlag C J Fahle, 1965, p.9.

THE INTERNATIONAL EXCHANGE OF INFORMATION

Hana KOMOROUS

Senior Serials Librarian, University of Victoria
British Columbia, Canada

1. INTRODUCTION

In the past three days we have covered all major areas of newspaper management, preservation and access and learned about the latest developments from around the world. It is only fitting that we devote the last session to the possibilities of worldwide co-operation. My task is to talk about the possibilities of the international exchange of information. I will do so concentrating on three major areas: bibliographic and location information on newspapers, information on policies, programmes and standards concerning newspapers, and the role of the IFLA Working Group on Newspapers. For the purpose of my presentation I am defining the newspaper broadly, including weekly community and special interest newspapers. Furthermore, I will examine the issues from the point of view of a hypothetical international user.

2. BIBLIOGRAPHIC AND LOCATION INFORMATION ON NEWSPAPERS

Those of us who have had to provide guidance to library patrons wanting to use newspapers as a resource for their research know that it is not an easy task. The information on local and national newspapers is, as a rule, available. Seeking information on more obscure titles and on newspapers beyond national boundaries can, however, be a difficult and cumbersome task. In the same way as the local user, the international user needs information that will **identify** the newspaper, **describe** and **locate** it. Let us examine the sources.

2.1. Information on currently published newspapers

Identifying current popular daily newspapers is a relatively easy task. Numerous national and international press directories provide information on the press throughout the world. These reference sources usually include data on location, population, circulation, advertising rates, names of executives and editors and publication dates. The major international press directories with a long history include, among others: "Benn's Press Directory" (formerly Newspaper Press Directory) published since 1846 and "Willing's Press Guide" published since 1874 [1]. For the user seeking orientation in the world press, there are also sources offering a selection, evaluation and description of the world's great dailies [2].

Smaller dailies and weeklies may also be included in press directories but the limited circulation and small revenue newspapers are not.

When **bibliographic description** of current newspaper titles is sought, the sources become scarcer. Newspapers have not been traditionally included in national bibliographies and when they have been, the delay between their initial publication and their subsequent appearance in the national bibliography makes the source impractical to use. The Soviet, West German and Austrian national bibliographies can be cited as examples [3]. Newspapers have also not been traditionally fully catalogued by libraries. This practice has, however, changed substantially in the past decade. It is, therefore, necessary to identify the national library or other national information organization or institution which can provide the international user with bibliographic and location information on currently published newspapers in that country. This may not always be a simple task.

2.2. Information on retrospective newspapers [4]

The growing body of professional literature on newspapers describes the lack of bibliographic records for newspapers in a variety of ways. The statement that "newspapers have fallen through the bibliographic net" is perhaps the most accurate one. Identifying and locating retrospective newspapers has always been a laborious process at both the national and international levels. Bibliographic and locating sources for newspapers include specialized **newspaper bibliographies, printed catalogues** of large newspaper collections and union lists. A search through fifteen years of the Library of Congress Subject Catalog reveals a number of newspaper bibliographies from almost every country in the world. The purpose, scope and coverage of these bibliographies vary substantially from listings of local and regional newspapers, listings of special type or language newspapers, or newspapers of one country held by libraries in another country to major bibliographies of the national press. It is unlikely that all these sources would be found in one reference collection, but even if they were, using such a collection to search for the newspaper titles would be extremely cumbersome to say the least.

While these bibliographies are extemely useful as "local" reference sources as well as sources for policy making decisions [5], they are not always readily accessible to the international user. Having made this assumption, I would like to point out that some major newspaper bibliographies have become standard research and reference sources, are included in all major reference collections and are widely used. Two major standard newspaper bibliographies can be cited as examples: the Clarence Brigham and Winifred Gregory bibliographies of United States newspapers [6].

It should also be kept in mind, that in addition to specialized newspaper bibliographies, newspapers have been included in many periodical bibliographies and directories. I have not included those in my research. It is obvious that the compilation of an international list of newspaper bibliographies and locating tools is desirable. However, a set of internationally agreed-upon criteria should be defined and applied in this task. In order to make the initial step, I prepared a very selective list in Appendix 1 to this paper. The selection is partially based on the "Guide to Reference Books" published by the American Library Association [7].

In addition to standard newspaper bibliographies, printed catalogues of major newspaper collections from around the world represent an invaluable source for identification and location of newspaper titles. The largest and best known is, of course, the British Library Newspaper Library printed catalogue which is, as a rule, available in reference collections of all major libraries [8]. According to the 1982/83 survey of national newspaper collections [9], the following libraries published either catalogues of their newspaper collections or union catalogues including holdings of several libraries: Austrian National Library, Bibliothèque Nationale (Paris), Bibliothèque Nationale du Québec, Central Library (Belfast), Central National Library of the SR of Montenegro, Helsinki University Library, Jewish National and University Library (Jerusalem), Library of Congress, Natal Society Library (Pietermaritzburg), National and University Library (Ljubljana), National Diet Library (Tokyo), National Library (Lima), National Library (Singapore), National Library (Teheran), National Library (Warsaw), National Library of China (Beijing), National Library of Scotland, National Library of Serbia, National Szechenyi Library (Budapest), Royal Library (The Hague), South African Library (Cape Town), State Library (Pretoria), State Library of the Latvian SSR, Trinity College Library (Dublin), University of Oslo Library, Viet-Nam National Library. Printed newspaper catalogues have also been published in Nigeria, Rwanda, Tanzania and Mauritius [10].

Two recently published Soviet catalogues should be added to the list: the listing of holdings of foreign language newspapers of the State Library, Moscow and the listing of newspaper collections of large academic libraries in the USSR [11].

While the printed catalogues of major newspaper collections are indeed invaluable research sources, it is the union lists of newspapers which are the most important tools for locating current and retrospective newspaper titles. As is the case with newspaper bibliographies, a search of reference sources shows numerous union lists of newspapers published worldwide. The major ones are listed in Appendix 1.

2.3. Information on newspapers in microform

Information on newspaper titles reproduced in microform is the most important resource for the international user, as it is this format that provides him/her with access to the otherwise inaccessible originals. This is, in my opinion, the most important field where international co-operation and exchange of information are desirable. Issues related to newspapers in microform have already been discussed by previous speakers and the symposium exhibitors provided the most current information on available titles. I will, therefore, focus on the areas in need of more accurate and more comprehensive information.

In addition to the bibliographic and location information, verification of newspapers in microform requires the following data:
* information on the micropublishing organization which publishes and sells the required newspaper(s);
* information on the price and availability of the microform;
* information on the existence and location of the microform masters and service copies.

Furthermore, it should be kept in mind that newspapers have been widely microfilmed by both the commercial and non-commercial microproducers.

The obvious sources of information on newspapers reproduced in microform are the micropublishers' catalogues. On the national level these catalogues are, as a rule, available to the interested user be it an individual or an institution. On the international level, the absence of a single source of information on newspapers in microform produced worldwide makes the identification and selection process difficult. Micropublishers of newspapers can be identified in the "Microform Market Place" [12], an international directory of micropublishing. The 1986/87 edition lists eighty three newspaper micropublishers from around the world. The list (see Appendix 2) is not complete and does not include institutions which do not offer microfilmed newspapers for sale. It is, nevertheless, a helpful source. The individual catalogues can be requested directly from the publisher. Some are included in the "Micropublishers Trade List Annual" (MTLA) which either offers a complete cat-

alogue in its COM list, or includes information on how to obtain it [13].
However, seventeen out of eighty-three newspaper micropublishers listed in the
"Microform Market Place" are not included in MTLA.

The most comprehensive single international listing of newspapers in microform
available for sale appears in the "Subject Guide to Microform in Print" [14].
Newspaper entries in categories 70 - US newspapers and 75 - Non-US newspapers
are generated from entries in the "Guide to Microforms in Print" [15].
Entries include: Title, City, State (or Country), Dates, Price, Publisher
Code, Type of Microform Code. Approximately three thousand United States
titles and the same number of non-US newspapers are included. Despite its
limitation in listing only microfilm available for sale, this source deserves
more support from libraries and institutions producing newspaper microfilms
than it has received to date. In order to achieve a more comprehensive single
listing, the non-commercial producers who make their newspaper microfilms
available for sale should be encouraged to send their data to "Guide to Microforms in Print".

The most comprehensive single tool to bibliographically verify and locate
newspapers reduced to microform is the Library of Congress publication "Newspapers in Microform" (NIM). The 1948-1983 cumulative volumes list 34,289 US
and 8,620 non-US titles with some 1200 worldwide locations [16]. Both the
masters and service copies housed in libraries as well as in vaults of commercial microproducers are also included. "Newspapers in Microform" is *de facto*
an international union catalogue of newspapers reduced to microform and reported to the Library of Congress. Many of the non-US newspapers included in NIM
are not listed in any other bibliography. Most importantly, newspapers in
microform produced by non-commercial producers are included. NIM is not a
complete source and its primary purpose is to provide information for the
United States user but in spite of that it remains an unparalleled international finding tool for newspapers.

In addition to general listings of newspapers in microforms, there is an
urgent need for information on the existence and location of microform
masters. This information is needed for:
* avoidance of useless reprographic duplication;
* indication of availability of further copies;
* clarification of copyright;
* assurance of the preservation of a newspaper by the existence of a
  properly stored preservation master.

Information on microform masters is included in some of the sources which I
mentioned but in order to attain the objectives outlined above, a separate
listing is desirable. The scope of such a listing should be at the national
level. The preparation of national registers of newspaper microform masters
is included as part of the ongoing national newspaper programmes. When compiled, national registers of newspaper microform masters will collectively
form the world register.

2.4. Machine readable records for newspapers

The majority of the bibliographic sources which I described are based on
manual bibliographic and holdings records for newspapers and are available
only in hard copy. However, in the past decade newspaper records have been
gradually included in the database utilities. Machine readable records for
newspapers are now available either as part of a larger database, or as a
separate specialized file. The best example of a large newspaper database is
the file of the United States Newspaper Program on the OCLC Online Computer
Library Center. In Canada, the National Library is in the process of creating

an on-line national union catalogue of newspapers. MARC records for newspapers are also input in the "Australian National Bibliography" and UKMARC.

Technical details about the creation of machine readable records and the standards for them were already discussed at the symposium's earlier session on bibliographic aspects. I would, therefore, like to summarize the broader issues and stress the importance of the exchange of information in this field. It is, in my opinion, imperative that machine readable newspaper bibliographic data are created according to the accepted national standards and are either reported to or created by the national cataloguing agencies. This way the compatibility of newspaper records at the national level and, through the conversion of these records to the UNIMARC format, at the international level is assured. Ultimately, through the exchange of tapes or by direct on-line searching, newspaper records could become accessible worldwide.

Having analyzed problems concerning the bilbliographic and location information on newspapers, I would like to propose the following recommendations for the exchange of information in this area:
* To establish a network of national libraries or other national information agencies which can serve as clearing houses for information on newspaper collections in their country in general, and on newspaper titles of their national imprint in particular.
* To compile and disseminate a list of the most comprehensive newspaper bibliographies and union lists of newspapers for each country.
* To compile and disseminate an international list of printed catalogues of newspaper collections.
* To encourage the creation of a single international tool for information on newspapers in microform. Two existing tools should be considered and supported:
  - "Microforms in Print", and
  - "Newspapers in Microform, Foreign Countries".
* To encourage the compilation of national registers of newspaper microform masters which will collectively form the world register of newspaper microform masters.
* To encourage the exchange of machine readable newspaper bibliographic records between the national cataloguing agencies.

3. INFORMATION ON NATIONAL POLICIES, PROGRAMMES AND STANDARDS CONCERNING NEWSPAPERS

The symposium programme provided detailed insight into national programmes for newspaper management and preservation. My task is to stress the importance of continuous exchange of information on policies, standards and experience between interested countries. While national differences require specific approach and solution of problems, regular exchange of information can help to:

* avoid duplication of efforts in formulating policies and standards;
* avoid repetition of mistakes and improve the methodology used in newspaper related projects;
* reduce costs of both the planning and implementation stages of newspaper programmes;
* speed up the progress of these programmes.

Let me introduce some examples. The IFLA Working Group on Newspapers prepared a draft policy statement for the retention or disposal of newspapers after microfilming. The draft proposal is now being circulated for comments and will be put forward to IFLA as a basis for a statement of official IFLA policy. Concurrently the Australian newspaper experts are addressing the same task. In Canada, a special task force of the Decentralized Program for Canadian Newspapers is formulating a Canadian policy. Clearly, an exchange of information on all three approaches to the same task would be beneficial. Another example I would like to use is the proposed policy for the acquisition and retention of "free" newspapers which is being discussed by the British Library's Consultative Group on Newspapers. Once formulated, it will become a welcome guide to other institutions. The exchange should include information on ongoing microfilming projects, interlending policies, project methodologies, standards for the storage of originals, etc. The list may continue, touching on all aspects of newspaper management and preservation.

Finally, there is a large area which should not be overlooked in planning the international exchange of information: the use of new technology in the production of newspapers. The second edition of the "Directory of Periodicals Online" [17] lists some two hundred and sixty newspapers accessible on-line. The emergence of the electronic newspaper is bringing revolutionary changes to access, storage and preservation of newspapers. What is the role of libraries in this field in the future? What are our responsibilities? The new technology is hardware and software dependent. Does the responsibility for preservation lie with the vendor? Should we co-operate more closely with our colleagues in the libraries of newspaper offices who are already using the new technology? Let me sum up this topic by quoting Eve Johansson, Head of the British Library Newspaper Library:

'... it is possible that in the near future a selection at least of electronically-produced newspapers will be read at terminals in the Newspaper Library, with the facility to call up previous references, browse among the subject headings, and print out pages of text. Research and development will demand very significant resources but it is clear that newspaper publishing is going through a period of great change and that the Newspaper Library ought not to miss the opportunity to capture it.' [18]

In summary, continuous exchange of information on the latest national and international developments in the area of policies, standards, programs and new technological advances concerning newspapers is crucial. Reflection of these developments in professional literature is important but speedier information on current developments is needed. National Libraries should cover newspaper issues more frequently in their publications. The latest issue of British Library Newspaper Library Newsletter announced that it will regularly feature articles on microfilming and preservation of other countries' newspapers, a decision for which the Newsletter should be commended [19].

The following recommendation should improve the exchange of information in this area:
* To encourage exchange of information on national developments in the field of newspapers through:
    - better coverage of these issues in publications of national libraries
    - better coverage in professional literature,
    - direct exchange of information between individual national programmes,
    - presentations on newspaper topics at annual conferences of library associations.

4. ROLE OF THE IFLA WORKING GROUP ON NEWSPAPERS IN THE INTERNATIONAL EXCHANGE OF INFORMATION ON NEWSPAPERS

Since its inception in May 1980, the Working Group on Newspapers has considered and discussed all aspects of newspaper preservation, storage and handling in a truly international manner. The Group's intention in presenting this symposium was to provide a broadly-based international forum to exchange experience and to maximize the benefits and results of its activities through exposure to a worldwide audience. The symposium programme and discussions of the past three days achieved these goals. Furthermore, new topics and ideas, the information on latest national developments, the recommendations and proposals presented by the speakers and participants will influence the Working Group's future agenda. The Group should help carry out the recommendations whenever possible and continue its role as IFLA's expert body in the field of newspapers thus serving as a clearing house for newspaper issues worldwide.

5. CONCLUSION

There are, in my opinion, two major reasons why we ought to exchange information at the international level:
* Newspapers are, relatively speaking, a newly discovered research resource and we are, and will continue to be, asked to provide better access to this source;
* The urgent need for preservation of newspapers has been recognized and has become a task of international scope. We should, therefore, strengthen existing communications in this field and develop the international exchange of information where it does not exist. This gathering has greatly contributed to the achievement of these goals.

APPENDIX 1

SELECTIVE LIST OF NEWSPAPER BIBLIOGRAPHIES AND UNION LISTS

International
'Newspapers in microform. Foreign countries, 1948-1983'. Washington, DC, Library of Congress, Catalog Management and Publication Division, 1984.

Webber, Rosemary, 'World list of national newspapers: a union list of national newspapers in libraries in the British Isles'. London, Butterworths, (1976).

Africa
'African newspapers in selected American libraries'. 1956- . Washington, DC, Library of Congress, Serial Division, 1956- .

Australia
'Newspapers in Australian libraries: a union list'. 4th ed., Canberra, National Library of Australia, 1984-85. 2 Volumes. Contents: pt. 1, Overseas newspapers; pt. 2, Australian newspapers.

Belgium
Bertelson, Lionel, 'La presse d'information: tableau chronologique des journaux belges'. (Bruxelles, 1974).

Canada
'Union list of Canadian newspapers held by Canadian libraries'. (Liste collectiv des journaux canadiens disponibles dans les bibliothèques canadiennes.) Ottawa, National Library of Canada, 1977.

China Coast
King, Frank H H and Clark, Prescott, 'A research guide to China-Coast newspapers, 1822-1911'. (Cambridge), East Asian Research Center, Harvard University, 1965.

Czechoslovakia
Potemra, Michal, 'Bibliografia slovenskych novin a casopisov do roku 1918'. Martin, Matica Slovenska, 1958.

Denmark
'Avismikrofilm i Statsbibliotek'. (Aarhus), Staatsbibliotek, 1980.

Finland
Kaarna, Vaino, and Winter, Kaarina, 'Suomen sanomalehdiston bibliografia, 1771-1963'. (Bibliography of the Finnish newspapers, 1771-1963). Helsinki, Helsingin Ylipisto Kirjasto, 1965.

France
'Bibliographie de la presse française politique et d'information générale, 1865-1944'. Paris, Bibliothèque Nationale, 1964- (in progress).

'Repertoire collectif des quotidiens et hebdomadaires publiés dans les departments de la France métropolitaine de 1944 á 1956 et conservés dans les archives et bibliothèques de France'. Paris, Université de Paris, Institut Français de Presse, 1958.

'Catalogue collectif des journaux quotidiens d'information générale publiés en France métropolitaine de 1957 á 1961'. Paris, Université de Paris, Institut Français de Presse, 1962.

Germany
Hagelweide, Gert, 'Deutsche Zeitungsbestände in Bibliotheken und Archiven'. Düsseldorf, Droste Verlag, (1974).

Israel
Newspapers and periodicals appearing in Israel. 1966- ,(Tel-Aviv?), Government Press Office, 1966- .

Italy
'Catalogo dei microfilms di giornali e periodici posseduti dalle biblioteche statali'. Roma, Istituto centrale per il catalogo unico delle biblioteche italiane e per le informazioni bibliografiche, 1983.

Japan
Japanese press. 1949- . (Tokyo), Japan Newspaper Publishers' and Editors' Association, 1949- .

'Shimbun mokuroku'. Tokyo, Kokuritsu Kokkai Toshokan, 1981. (Lists titles and holdings of all newspapers available at the National Diet Library).

Latin America
Charno, Steven M, 'Latin American newspapers in United States libraries'. Austin, University of Texas Press, (1969).

Near and Middle East
'Arab-world newspapers in the Library of Congress'. Washington, Library of Congress, 1980.

Auchterlonie, James Paul Crawford, and Safadi, Yasin H, 'Union catalogue of Arabic serials and newspapers in British libraries'. London, Mansell, 1977.

Pourhadi, Ibrahim Vaqfi, 'Persian and Afgan newspapers in the Library of Congress, 1871-1978'. Washington, DC, Library of Congress, 1979.

Netherlands
Handboek van de Nederlandse pers en publiciteit. Sept 1974 - .

New Zealand
'A checklist of newspapers in New Zealand libraries 1938-1959: a provisional supplement to the Union catalogue of New Zealand newspapers, 1938'. Wellington, 1959.

Harvey, D R, 'Union list of New Zealand newspapers published before 1940 preserved in libraries, newspaper offices, local authority offices and museums in New Zealand'. Wellington, National Library, 1984.

'A union catalogue of New Zealand newspapers preserved in public libraries, newspaper offices, etc.'. Wellington, E.V. Paul, Government Printer, 1938.

Norway
'Norske aviser, 1973-1969'. Oslo, Universitetsbibliotek, 1973-74.

Pakistan
'General list of newspapers and periodicals published in Pakistan'. Karachi, Government of Pakistan Press, 1956- .

Phillippines
Saito, Shiro, and Mak, Alice W, 'Phillippine newspapers: an international union list'. Honolulu, University of Hawaii, 1984.

Poland
'Materiały do bibliografii dzennikarstwa i prasy w Polsce w latach 1944-1954: wybór'. Warszawa, Państwowe Wydawnictwo Naukowe, 1957.

South Africa
'A list of South African newspapers, 1800-1982, with library holdings'. Pretoria, State Library, 1983.

'South African newspapers available on microfilm'. Pretoria, State Library, 1975.

Switzer, Les, and Switzer, Donna. 'The black press in South Africa and Lesotho'. Boston, G K Hall, (1979).

Switzerland
Blaser, Fritz, 'Bibliographie der schweizer Presse, mit Einschluss der Fürstentums Liechtenstein'. Basel, Birkhäuser Verlag, 1956-58.

Southeast Asia
'A checklist of Southeast Asian newspapers and other research materials in microform held by the Center for Research Libraries'. 7th ed., Madison, Wis,

Center for Southeast Asian Studies, University of Wisconsin - Madison, 1984.

USSR
'Gazety SSSR 1917-1960: Bibliograficheskii spravochnik'. Moskva, Kniga, 1970.

Kuznetsov, Ivan Vasil'evich, and Fingerit, Efim Markovich, 'Gazetnyi mir Sovetskogo Soiuza, 1917-1970 gg'. Moskva, Izd. Mosk. Un-ta, 1972-76.

Letopis' periodicheskikh izdanii SSSR. Chast' 2, Gazety. 1961/65- , Moskva, Kniga, 1967- .

'Newspapers of the Soviet Union in the Library of Congress (Slavic 1954-1960; non-Slavic, 1917-1960)'. Washington, DC, Library of Congress, 1962.

'Periodychni vydannia URSR, 1917-1960: hazety'. Kharkiv, Redaktsiino-vydavnychyi viddil Knyzhkovoi palaty URSR, 1965.

Publichnaia biblioteka (Leningrad). Gazetnyi otdel, 'Alfavitnyi sluzhebnyi katalog russkikh dorevoliutsionnykh gazet, 1703-1916'. Leningrad, Biblioteka, 1958.

'Russian Ukrainian, and Belorussian newspapers, 1917-1953: a union list'. Washington, DC, Library of Congress, 1953.

United Kingdom
British Library. Newspaper Library, 'Catalogue of the Newspaper Library, Colindale'. London, British Museum Publications Ltd for the British Library Board, 1975.

Hewitt, Arthur Reginald, 'Union list of Commonwealth newspapers in London, Oxford and Cambridge'. (London), Athlone Press, University of London for the Inst. of Commonwealth Studies, 1960.

Times (London), 'Tercentenary handlist of English & Welsh newspapers, magazines & reviews'. London, Times, 1920.

Ireland
Munther, Robert LaVerne, 'A handlist of Irish newspapers, 1685-1750'. London, Bowes & Bowes, 1960.

Scotland
Ferguson, Joan P, 'Directory of Scottish Newspapers'. Edinburgh, National Library of Scotland, 1984.

United States
Brigham, Clarence S, 'History and bibliography of American newspapers, 1690-1820'. Repr. Westport, Conn., Greenwood Press, 1976.

Campbell, Georgetta Merritt, 'Extant collections of early black newspapers: a research guide to the black press, 1880-1915'. Troy, NY, Whitston, 1981.

Gregory, Winifred, (editor) 'American newspapers, 1821-1936: a union list of files available in the United States and Canada'. Repr. New York, Kraus, 1967.

'Jewish newspapers and periodicals on microfilm, available at the American Jewish Periodical Center'. Cincinnati, The Center, 1957.

- - Supplement 1. Cincinnati, 1960.

Lathem, Edward Connery, (compiler) 'Chronological tables of American newspapers, 1690-1820'. Barre, Mass, American Antiquarian Society and Barre Pub., (1972).

'Newspapers in microform. United States, 1948-1983'. Washington, DC, Library of Congress, Catalog Management and Publication Division, 1984.

'Newspapers received currently in the Library of Congress'. 9th ed., Washington, DC, Library of Congress, 1984.

'United States Newspaper Program national union list'. Dublin, Oh., OCLC, 1985.

APPENDIX 2

LIST OF NEWSPAPER MICROPUBLISHERS

African Imprint Library Services
Alpha Com
American Baptist Historical Society
American Jewish Periodical Center
Archives of Ontario
Asia Library Services
Association pour la Conservation et la Réproduction Photographique de la Presse
Biblioteca Nacional
Biblioteca Santa Ana
Bibliothèque Nationale du Québec
Bloch and Company
British Library Newspaper Library
Brookhaven Press
Buffalo and Erie County Historical Society
Canadian Library Association
Canadian Microfilming Co Ltd/Société Canadienne du Microfilm
Center for Archival Collections
Center for Chinese Research Materials
Center for Research Libraries
China National Microforms Import and Export Corp.
Clearwater Publishing Co.
Colorado Historical Society
Commonwealth Microfilm Library
Current Digest of the Soviet Press
Datacorp
Datamics
EIC/Intelligence, Inc.
Erasmus Press
Fairchild Microfilm
Gay Community News
General Microfilm Company
Harvester Press Microform Publications Ltd.
Historical Society of Pennsylvania
Hoover Institution Press
Immigration History Research Center
Information Access Company

Institute for Advanced Studies of World Religions
Institute of Early American History and Culture
Institute of Texan Cultures
Inter-documentation Company AG
Irish Microforms Ltd.
Irish Times Ltd.
JA Micropublishing Inc.
Kansas State Historical Society
Kraus Microform
Kungliga Biblioteket
Lawrence Newspapers, Inc.
Library Microfilms
Library of Congress, Photoduplication Service
Library of Florida History
Manchester Public Libraries
Maryland State Archives
Massachusetts Historical Society
Matco Micrographics, Inc.
McLaren Micropublishing Ltd.
Microfile Pty Limited
Microfilm Corporation of Pennsylvania
Microform Academic Publishers
Mikrofilmarchiv der Deutschsprachigen Presse E.V.
Mikropress GMBH
Minerva Mikrofilm A/S
National Archives of South Africa
New China Services
New York Public Library
Newsbank, Inc.
Ohio Historical Society
George Olms Verlag AG
Oregon Historical Society Library
Pascoe (W & F) Pty Limited
Readex Microprint Corp.
Research Publications, Inc.
Scholarly Resources, Inc.
Southern Baptist Convention Historical Commission
Transmission Books & Microforms Co, Ltd.
University Microfilms International
University Music Editions
University of Notre Dame Archives
University Publications of America, Inc.
Western Reserve Historical Society
Women's History Research Center
World Microfilms Publications Ltd.
Yushodo Film Publications Ltd.

The list is based on Ellen S Wasserman, (editor) 'Microform Market Place, 1986-1987'. Westport, Conn.: Meckler, 1986.

APPENDIX 3

SUMMARY OF RECOMMENDATIONS

* To establish a network of national libraries or other national information agencies which can serve as clearing houses for information on newspaper collections in their country in general, and on newspaper titles of their national imprint in particular.

* To compile and disseminate a list of the most comprehensive newspaper bibliographies and union lists of newspapers for each country.

* To compile and disseminate an international list of printed catalogues of newspaper collections.

* To encourage the creation of a single international tool for information on newspapers in microform. Two existing tools should be considered and supported:
  - "Microforms in Print", and
  - "Newspapers in Microform, Foreign Countries".

* To encourage the compilation of national registers of newspaper microform masters which will collectively form the world register of newspaper microform masters.

* To encourage the exchange of machine readable newspaper bibliographic records between the national cataloguing agencies.

* To encourage exchange of information on national developments in the field of newspapers through:
  - better coverage of these issues in publications of national libraries,
  - better coverage in professional literature,
  - direct exchange of information between individual national programmes,
  - presentations on newspaper topics at annual conferences of library associations.

REFERENCES

1 Benn's Press directory, 1978- , Tonbridge, Eng., Benn's Publications Ltd., 1978- .

   Willing's Press Guide, 1874- , London, British Media Publications, 1874- .

2 John C Merril, and Harold A Fisher, 'The World's Great Dailies', New York, NY, Communication Arts Books, 1980.

3 Letopis' Periodicheskikh Izdanii SSSR. Chast' 2, Gazety, 1961/1965- Moskva, Kniga, 1967- .

   Österreichische Bibliographie, 1945- , Wien, Verein der Österr. Buch-, Kunst-, Musikalien-, Zeitungs- und Zeitschriftenhändler, 1945- .

Deutsche Bibliographie, 1951- , Frankfurt am M., Buchhändler-Vereinigung, 1951- .

4   For the purpose of this paper, a retrospective newspaper is defined as a newspaper title which ceased publication, or a currently published newspaper with a long publication history.

5   A list of newspaper bibliographies from the South-West region of England compiled by Rosemary Wells for the Newsplan is an example of the use of existing newspaper bibliographies for a major project.

Rosemary Wells, 'Newsplan: Report of the Pilot Project in the South-West,' London, The British Library, 1986.

6   Brigham, Clarence S, 'History and Bibliography of American Newspapers, 1690-1820', (Reprint) Westport, Conn., Greenwood Press, 1976.

Gregory, Winifred, (editor) 'American Newspapers, 1821-1936': A Union List of Files Available in the United States and Canada, Repr. New York, Kraus, 1967.

7   Sheehy, Eugene Paul, 'Guide to Reference Books', 10th ed., Chicago, American Library Association, 1986.

8   British Library. Newspaper Library, 'Catalogue of the Newspaper Library, Colindale', London, British Museum Publications Ltd for the British Library Board, 1975.

9   A survey of national newspaper collections was conducted by Dr Hofig and Mr Mannerheim for the IFLA Working Group on Newspapers in 1982/83. Results of the survey are published as Appendix 2 in this volume.

10 The list is based on: Willi Höfig, 'Zeitungssammlungen weltweit', in: Publizistik, Vol.29 no.3/4, Juli-Dezember 1984, pp581-587. English trans lations of names of libraries are based on the 1986 edition of the 'World of Learning'.

11 Gosundarstvennaia biblioteka SSSR imeni V.I. Lenina. Otdel gazet. 'Gazety na Innostrannykh Evropeiskikh Iazykakh v Fondakh Gosudarstvennoi Biblioteki SSSR Imeni V.I. Lenina', Moskva, Gos. biblioteka SSSR im. V.I. Lenina, 1985.

Bessonova, N N, 'Krupneishie Gazetnye Fondy Nauchnykh Bibliotek Strany', Moskva, Gos. biblioteka SSSR im. V.I. Lenina, Otdel gazet, 1984.

12 Wasserman, Ellen S, (editor) 'Microform Market Place, 1986-1987', Westport, Conn., Meckler, 1986.

13 'The Micropublishers' Trade List Annual, 1986-1987'. (Alexandria, Chadwyck-Healey, 1986).

14 'Subject Guide to Microforms in Print', 1961- , Westport, Conn., Meckler, 1961- .

15 'Guide to Microforms in Print', 1961- , Westport, Conn., Meckler, 1961- .

16 'Newspapers in Microform. United States, 1948-1983', Washington, DC, Library of Congress, Catalog Management and Publication Division, 1984.

   'Newspapers in Microform. Foreign Countries. 1948-1983', Washington, DC, Library of Congress, Catalog Management and Publication Division, 1984.

17 <u>Directory of Periodicals Online</u>. Vol. 1, News, Law & Business, 1985- , Washington, DC, Federal Document Retrieval, Inc., 1985- .

18 Johansson, Eve, 'The British Library Newspaper Library: Looking Ahead', in: <u>Journal of Newspaper and Periodical History</u>, Vol.2 no.3, Summer 1986, p.37.

19 'The British Library Newspaper Library Newsletter', Vol.7, April 1987, p.7.

THE NEEDS OF DEVELOPING COUNTRIES

Subhas C BISWAS

Director, Central Secretariat Library, India

Let me express my regret for two reasons: first, I am afraid, I am not the competent person to really cover such a vast area - the third world - as I have not seen much of their professional activities. Secondly, I have not prepared a formal paper on the topic, which would have been the ideal for a fruitful discussion. What I intend to do is more like thinking aloud my views based on these three day's discussions, some published literature and informal talks with some of the delegates present here.

'Third World' covers the largest global area - over three continents - countries that are economically undeveloped in Asia, Africa and Latin America. Even by taking economic conditions as the parameter, it is difficult to put all the countries within one bracket. There are several major and minor differences, such as language, education, culture, political system, etc., which would affect each to adopt different attitudes and approaches. I shall try to make an overview of the scene, as I see it, having kept in mind these limitations.

Over the last two days, we have been mostly discussing the papers reflecting the experience of the developed countries, including the situation as it is in such large national libraries, like, the Library of Congress, British Library and major libraries of West Germany and Sweden where a representative collection of newspapers published in the developing countries are also received and preserved. The total number of newspapers published in the Third World countries would be likely to be double the figure known for the developed countries. Secondly, these countries have more problems and different conditions. Question comes into my mind as to why the needs of these countries are kept for discussion at the fag end. I think, this needed more time and should have been discussed more thoroughly.

Conditions that affect these countries in relation to their newspaper publication, circulation and preservation cannot be easily put under some broad groups, for example, country's population, size of area or levels of education and literacy have not always the guiding factors in its growth and development of the newspaper industry. For example, a country under military rule or following not exactly parliamentary system of government, such as Great Britain and the USA do, may have only a dozen newspapers, whereas, a country like India with illiteracy as high as 70% has over 1200 daily newspapers in 83 various languages. One has to take these figures into consideration while discussing their accessibility and preservation problems. None of the developed countries including the libraries, like Library of Congress and British Library, has to face anything near to this.

So far what we have heard over the last two days at the Symposium of newspaper preservation and their accessibility covers very little of the third world countries. Publication of newspapers in some third world countries started in the late 18th century and a large number of countries have started slowly with one or two in the 19th century. This is also the growth pattern of newspapers in the Western World as well. A large number of these third world countries were under colonial rule and gradually became independent after the Second World War. Newspapers, books, etc., published before their Independence are more likely to be available in the libraries of colonialist powers. In most cases, all printed materials were sent to the libraries of the respective countries in power under some statutory provisions. There are a number of instances where such repository copies are the only ones known to exist as primary source material for historians. Volumes of the contemporary period may be available in the countries of their origin but complete back-runs may not be easy to get.

In these countries, the value and influence of newspapers in mass-media have not reached the same level of importance as in the Western World. One reason is that it has yet to reach the real mass who are in the majority but illiterate. It only reflects the views of more powerful social/political groups and in influencing the élites. Its value within the educated mass as a source of historical records which should be worth preserving for future consultation has not been strongly lobbied. Again, there have been some inherent shortcomings in the coverage of information in a large country like India that could be put across through one newspaper with limited number of pages. This is due to shortage of modern sophisticated information and computer technologies in making news reach fast enough from a centralised point.

We have all agreed that Third World countries' climatic conditions are very harmful for preservation of newspapers as compared to that of the developing countries. It has been the practice of western experts to advise that newspapers should be preserved whether in their original form or in any other form, in an air-conditioned or humidity-controlled environment. The capital investment as well as maintenance costs are very high in making the building fully air-conditioned round the clock for an economically poor country. Secondly, the power supply condition may not also be all that reliable in some cases round the year. The library may not get the priority over others when supply of energy is less than demand.

There is hardly any private collection of newspapers worth mentioning in the Indian sub-continent. Reasons are obvious - bulky, takes up lot of space, rare utility, durability and quality of paper are very low, etc.. But there is another factor which to a small extent deters people in preserving newspapers. Old newspapers are sold in the open market to be used for packaging and may fetch as much as 20% of the cost of the newspaper. It may sound a small amount, but this factor, in combination with the others mentioned above, would have considerable impact in discouraging the preservation of newspapers. In addition, quality of newsprint, ink and printing process may not in some cases be up to the mark. These factors have also some impact in the maintenance process of newspapers published in the third world countries. In one case, a reader wanted a particular issue which was found to have a page so blurred that it was impossible to read.

Access to a history of a particular established newspaper or newspaper publishing house is not very common. Neither is it easy to find special catalogues of newspapers or union-lists for each country or region separately. Indexes of one particular newspaper or a set of newspapers of these countries are a recent phenomenon. There is no retrospective index (e.g. <u>The Times Index</u>) of any established daily - the reason being that a complete set or a long run of the newspaper will not be available easily. Processing and bibliographical control did not get the right weightage or follow any constant pattern.

Again, when we talk in terms of preservation technology, that is readily
available to us, we always tends to be one step behind the latest, i.e., what
you are using. I was quite impressed when our Brazilian colleague showed the
slides of microfilm readers that are in use in her library. If you go to any
library in Great Britain or any developed country, you will find these comparatively out of date or obsolete. Similar kinds of local make microfilm/fiche
readers are also available in India. These are some of the handicaps, but it
makes a lot of difference, because the quality may not be the same. When a
user who is familiar with modern technical equipment goes to use our machines,
he may not feel very comfortable as the result may not be so satisfactory with
bright and sharp images.

These are some of the issues that require thorough investigation. There
cannot be a standard solution universally applicable to all the Third World
countries. Our main problem, in some cases, is to know what are the newspapers and where are they published from and how to get them at a central
repository. In some countries these are quite properly documented, though
they may not be very up to date and regular. In some cases, even the national
libraries or archives do not know how large is the country's newspaper production, where they are published from or how to get them regularly. These
problems are very serious in many countries.

I have already mentioned about acute unfavourable climatic conditions in these
countries whose solutions are not all that easy to identify. The cost of
fighting against this major factor, in relation to creating suitable storage
space, providing well-trained manpower and acquiring advanced technology is in
most cases prohibitive. This unfavourable climatic condition also affects
human beings in a big way in terms of their capacity to work. Cost of living,
standard of living and average _per capita_ income - these economic factors are
not always given much weight while calculating workload and output per head.
They have some psychological effects on the workers. For example, people from
these Third World countries who have migrated to the industrialised countries
are capable of working as hard and efficiently as their local counterparts.
But, it is a fact that their efficiency and output were not so high in their
own countries.

Take the case of National Library of India, where more than 1200 daily newspapers in 83 Indian languages are received every day. To get language experts
in so many languages under one roof is not an easy task. To find out when
these have started, how to get their back issues or when they die or change
their titles frequently, even the script changes, is really a hard job. It
requires qualified staff and adequate financial support. This is one of the
reasons, I think, why my colleague, the Director of the National Library,
identified two scapegoats - shortage of funds and lack of language experts. I
shall not blame him.

We have accepted that microfilming is, perhaps, the easiest (not safest!) way
of preserving newspaper back volumes. There are some small hazards we face
here. Let me take up one such example, that I faced recently: I have a
fairly modern microfiche processing system. The exposure lamp required replacement and it took us 5 weeks to get a new one. During this period, the
camera and the technician were kept idle. This kind of situation you may not
have to face - at least not for such a long period. Again, raw materials
cannot be kept stored for a long period. This also may take a long time to
get delivered, which would affect the production, output and disturb the time
schedule.

These problems link up with shortage of trained man-power, which I cannot remember being mentioned so far. Everybody knows that operating microfilming equipment is so simple and does not require much rigorous specialised training. But in a country where only half a dozen or so equipments are in operation, to get people interested in learning these types of jobs may not be very easy. Moreover, when you have an expert technician on your team, it may be a difficult job to retain him for a long period and also to get trained the next generation of technicians under his supervision, as their pay scales, etc., may not be comparatively very attractive.

This problem, I personally feel, could be given serious consideration by IFLA and the Working Group. They may produce some a.v. training packages which could be made available to the polytechnics and other training institutions by dubbing languages of their choice. It may not be always possible to send all the prospective technicians abroad or supply specialists from the developed countries even on a time bound scale. A video or tape-slide programme supplemented by printed literature - guide books, teach yourself series, handbooks or manuals etc., could be of much help to an organisation deciding to go for a microfilm system.

Another way the developed countries could consider of providing support to us is to conduct training courses on a regional basis with IFLA/UNESCO support. There are several such programmes being conducted at bilateral as well as multilateral levels in various disciplines at different centres but hardly any so far on reprography. A few specialists from developed countries could be put on secondment attached to a few training institutions in the Third World countries having adequate infra-structural facilities with IFLA/UNESCO support. Government of the country where such training programme is arranged may be asked to bear 50% of the total cost. Some financial support may also be obtained through regional inter-governmental organisations such as OAU, Arab League, SAARC, ASEAN, etc. Local/regional factors should be given adequate coverage in the curriculum designed for these training programmes. I know, in the whole of South Asia, there is no full-time comprehensive training programme run by any polytechnic though a few short term courses are occasionally being arranged in some countries.

We have been stressing the need of joint efforts for the nations to preserve newspapers by making microfilm copies. Again, coming back to my Indian experience, I find that a few main national dailies are microfilmed by several libraries. This sad state of affairs must be avoided through a conscious drive to avoid harmful duplications. I would like to point out one such matter where some co-ordinated move between the Library of Congress and the local national library could help both by avoiding duplication of efforts in a big way. Library of Congress through its local Book Procurement Centre carries out a large newspaper microfilming operation. If any library wants copies of these microfilms, they may be obtained from Washington by paying hard currency. I wonder why there cannot be a co-operative approach in such cases. The Indian National Library and a few major local libraries might draw up a joint newspaper microfilming programme with the Library of Congress's Local Book Procurement Centre. Microfilm copies made by one could be made available to the other in exchange. This kind of joint venture could be given serious consideration by this Symposium. IFLA's forum of Directors of National Libraries might draw out a programme of action and prepare model guidelines on newspaper microfilm exchange programme between the countries.

Secondly, we do get microfilm/fiche copies from several commercial sources based in Europe and North America. Is there any way to take safeguards on their quality? Our experience in some cases are not very pleasant. Thirdly, I would like the Symposium participants and IFLA to consider if it would be possible to standardise the cost of microfilm and microfiche prints as costs of raw materials and processing would not differ much from country to country.

I would like to consider exchange of microfilms of newspapers between the national libraries and to work out a programme of action in sharing the bulk of newspaper microfilming as the two most important issues which IFLA Working Group could consider adopting as the recommendations of the Symposium. Until and unless we decide to share between the major national libraries the microfilming load of significant national dailies of the world, and bibliographical records of newspaper (in microform) holdings are made available to the larger users groups, then the whole purpose of arranging this international symposium would sound to me at least a bit half-hearted.

I have been told by some of the delegates in informal discussions that one is to go slow in this processs for the third world. I consider it would be more appropriate for the third world countries to move fast so that the gap is narrowed. Someone has suggested that if a country wants to start fresh the preservation of its newspaper it may by-pass reprographic process and move straight onto CD-ROM or optical disc. It may sound very exciting but the costs of adopting these processes are rather high and anticipated life span is thought to be around 20 years at most, whereas microfilm copy may easily be copied and frequently handled with a life span of possibly up to 100 years. Secondly, our goal of establishing exchange of newspapers (preserved in microform) may take a long time to materialise as no library in the world has this technology for this purpose.

We believe co-operation can only be effectively practised amongst equal partners. This is why the third world countries must move fast to bring their house in order. It is they who must realise the value of newspapers as a primary source of records of a nation's socio-economic and cultural history and take steps to preserve them. Extra copies may then be used in developing a co-operative exchange system at the international level.

SUMMARY AND CONCLUSION

Ian P GIBB

British Library, (Retired)

Newspapers are in many ways the problem children of libraries, bulky, fast growing and ultimately self-destructive. But we love them even if some of our colleagues and administrators do not. The main problem in trying to summarise in 30 minutes the proceedings of a Symposium such as this, with nearly thirty papers and workshop sessions, is that I cannot possibly do justice to all the speakers. May I say first of all how grateful I am to all of them for the care they have taken in their presentations and for the considerable interest of what they have had to say. I hope they will forgive me if I do not always refer specifically to their papers but particularly since the participants have copies of most of them I see my task as being primarily to identify some of the themes and issues which have arisen.

This gathering has brought together the most welcome combination of newspaper producers, professional users, librarians and those concerned with the technical processes of preservation, whether of originals or by microfilming. We all, I think, have much to learn from one another. However IFLA is of course primarily a body of librarians and therefore the questions which librarians need to address and have addressed in relation to newspapers are naturally paramount in our discussions. I said that the combination of participants from different backgrounds is very welcome, because the task of librarians is to serve users by building collections, preserving them and by providing the right sort of access to them, in order to encourage the spread of knowledge and help to extend the frontiers of knowledge.

It seemed in the late 1970's at the genesis of the IFLA Working Group on Newspapers that, while quite a lot of activity was going on in various places, it was unco-ordinated. Priorities differed and many were only becoming aware that they had a problem, often because of the continually increasing use of newspapers which speeded their deterioration. The intention of the IFLA Working Group was to try to inform those concerned in this area and to some extent to relieve the anxieties of those recognising the problem without really knowing what to do. So there were those at that time who had large microfilming programmes, but very little in the way of bibliographic programmes. The tendency there was to look almost entirely at techniques. There were those who were anxious about newspaper bibliography but who had tackled little of the preservation problem. There were those who were tackling the preservation of originals and again would be primarily concerned with technical issues, and those whose prime interests were with the present users and were less concerned about the future. Finally, those unaware almost totally, since research use in some places is comparatively new or at least the quantity as I have said was rapidly increasing. So I think it is very gratifying to find these streams coming together a decade later.

One of the frequent characteristics of librarians is the wish to be precise. This is an admirable quality for much library work but it cannot be allowed normally to lead to perfectionism. Most of us cannot afford this, or to put it in another way, the resources which we use to perfect one programme will mean no resources for some other programme. There is an English saying which is: the best is the enemy of the good. We all want to do all we can with our newspapers, or most of us do, though we have to assess our own priorities within the resources available. This is not intended in any way to be critical of all that has been said to show how we can do things properly. In allocating resources we must always be aware of the effects of not fully achieving some part of a programme, and we can only do this properly by measuring it against the best standards and ensuring that nothing essential is left undone. As Hana Komorous said in her workshop report the concensus for location information was in favour of having information about as many titles as possible rather than the perfect census for fewer titles, and that is really the point I am trying to get at. Do not be too depressed if you cannot do everything perfectly immediately.

After these introductory remarks I would like briefly to try to run through the course of the symposium to mention what have seemed to me to be the most significant themes and issues raised, although I am aware there will be many that I cannot cover, and at the end I shall try to summarize these as a series of questions.

First of all the keynote address. Traditionally one does not comment on this, but I do not think that I can let the occasion pass without saying how grateful we all were for the very wise words of Sir Denis Hamilton, who showed such an understanding of our problems, from his experience both as a newspaperman and as a member of the British Library Board.

The sessions on the history and the bibliography of the press and on uses of the press helped to set the professional and technical sessions which followed in perspective. Dr Bohrmann pointed to some of the needs for a bibliographical basis for communications research and to the problems which have arisen in Germany in satisfying these. Despite these problems I am sure that there were many of us who were envious of the extent of the work in Germany which he revealed.

Dr Harris, Dr Black, Mr Griffiths and Dr Porter all spoke and wrote very elequently about their use of newspapers in historical research, and to some extent for teaching purposes. Some of the issues raised, to some of which we often returned from different directions later, were:

- first, the status of newspapers, which were said often, truly, I think, to have been regarded as low level material, but perhaps less so nowadays. (We can all laugh now at the idea of the British Museum Trustess wanting to throw the newspapers away in the 1890's, though with a slight shiver down our spine as we laugh).

- second, originals versus microforms, the one big bone of contention, especially since originals may well be required for some forms of research as well as being, for some people at least, more comfortable to use. But we need to face the fact that continued use of originals accelerates their destruction, perhaps to a point where satisfactory microfilm can no longer be made from them.

- third, the scope of acquisitions, or if you like collection development policies in current jargon. Especially in developed countries, the national heritage may often be well covered, but the provision of foreign papers and local provision of any papers may be inadequate.

— fourth, the accuracy of newspapers and the selective way in which they are
used as a source, which I think may give some food for thought.

My feeling following those papers was that there needs to be a much closer
discussion between librarians, historians and other users. We have made quite
a lot of progress in the last decade on library technical problems, ranging
from cataloguing to microfilming, though much still needs to be done. But I
feel that we are only really at the beginning of trying to define users' needs
and how librarians can plan to meet these within the context of their limited
resources. One of the problems in looking at users' needs, is that users' may
say 'I want everything'. We cannot provide everything so we need a dialogue
to show why we cannot produce some things, and how we can best meet some of
the needs we can meet.

The papers by Dr Höfig and Mr Bergmann helped to start to look at these questions from the librarian's position. Dr Höfig's findings for Germany were
interesting and not at all always predictable. However, in this context and
in relation to the need for greater dialogue with users it seems to me that
national differences may be quite significant. I would suggest therefore,
that the IFLA Working Group, however constituted, would very much want to look
at the developments but is not itself the body to undertake them.

The next two papers by Else Delauney on the general management of newspaper
collection and Johan Mannerheim on the planning of newspaper microfilming
together with that of Hana Komorous on the international exchange of information were, in my view, with no disrespect to all the other papers, the core
of the Symposium. We have all learnt very much from them. You have Mr Mannerheim's and Mrs Komorous's papers and you will have Madame Delauney's. I can
only say read them and then read them again and make sure that all who need to
see them do so. The one point which I think must be made again is that if, as
is likely, microfilm is seen as at least a partial solution to our problems of
preservation, then we must ensure that satisfactory technical standards are
maintained, otherwise we may be wasting our resources.

The next sessions were the workshops. These were very valuable in two ways.
Firstly, we, or at least some of us, were able to follow up some of the papers
in greater detail than time allowed in the general sessions. This applies
particularly to those on bibliographical aspects, users' viewpoints, microfilming, preservation strategies and conserving the original. Secondly, we
were able to cover some topics which were squeezed out of the plenary
sessions, such as indexing, press cuttings and data bases and new developments, including the applications of computer technology. For the first category, that is those for which we had substantive papers, discussion centred
quite properly in most cases on detail, and as such cannot be covered in this
summary. (Summaries from the rapporteurs of those groups are printed
earlier).

The group on indexing etc., led by Mr Dunn, who works with the new technology
on the Today newspaper, stimulated a good discussion and will have provided
much thought for the future. It is certainly a topic which will need to be
returned to, as is the case of new technology such as on-line access. The
interesting point was that, when we talk about the new technology of optical
discs and so on, the consensus seemed to be 'wait and see'. It is often rash
to abandon proven technology, such as microfilming for a new technology until
it is quite clear that this new technology has established a reasonably permanent place in everyday use, and can offer advantages over the old. Now this
is not intended in any way to discourage development which may indeed be cruc-

ial to our activities in 10 or 20 years' time. Quite the contrary: we need
to participate fully in such developments to try to ensure that they can meet
our needs. We are, however, somewhat reassured by the view that was expressed
that microfilm input can be a medium to new storage technology.

The session on national approaches was extremely valuable as information for
us and will, I hope, act as help to us to develop our own programmes. As I
said this morning co-ordination is the key activity. Each country will pursue
what works best for them, but international co-ordination can be considerably
helped, or perhaps one should put it more strongly, can hardly exist unless we
use agreed standards. I am sure that the exchange of experience will be most
helpful to us all, especially I hope to persuade those who finance us. I
think this point was made once or twice but one of the values of a Symposium
such as this, is that it adds impetus to your own arguments.

Finally, we heard papers on internationl co-operation by Mary Jane Starr, Hans
Bohrmann and Hana Komorous. They have all produced stimulating papers which
will contribute most usefully to the further debate of this topic in IFLA.
Clearly there is a need for some form of international co-ordination, without
in any way attempting to dictate patterns, which can, we hope, be achieved
through IFLA because that is our international body. The paper by Hana
Komorous was of central importance, especially on the bibliographical aspects,
in which I also include things like location tools and catalogues of microform
masters. It is very gratifying to hear of the acceptance of the Guidelines on
newspaper cataloguing which she prepared for the Working Group, which will be
of great benefit to the development of international co-operation in newspaper
bibliography, and there are many points raised in that paper which will aid
future discussion of bibliographical and organisational questions. We are
also most grateful to Mr Biswas for giving us a lead on the needs of developing coutries and their particular problems. I think he is quite right to
say that we in developed countries do not realise some of the problems, some
of which are so minor to us, but can be so enormous there, and some of which
we tend not to comprehend.

I said I would finally sum up by trying to identify a number of major themes
and issues, which I shall put in the form of questions. I have 14 of them.

1. Do you microfilm or preserve the original or attempt both?

2. If you microfilm, do you tackle first old papers, at least post-1860,
because of the bad quality of the newsprint, or current papers to avoid future
problems? If you do the latter, will some of the old papers have deteriorated
too far while you tackle the current problem? So do you try to do both and
can you get the resources?

3. How can we seek to ensure that microfilming, whether by libraries, commercial organisations or other agencies reaches the required archival standard?
How can we improve our own equipment for the production and use of microforms?

4. Do we retain originals after microfilming or dispose of them? There
seemed to be two opposing camps here.

5. How can we best improve our management of our newspaper collections?
Does it help or hinder if these collections are separated from the general
collections? One can instance the Newspaper Library at Colindale which was
put out in the green fields in the 1900's to get it out of the way, and the
more recent developments in the Bibliothèque Nationale, with the devolution
from Paris of much of this material.

6. How can we improve our collection development policies?

7. What should be the lending policies, both for originals and for microfilms? Very few will lend originals. How much demand can be satisfied by paper copies of items from newspapers? Will we have easy and cheap methods of copying, say from microfilm reels to microfiche which might meet loan demand better, since even if we lend reels they are unwieldly for much use. This might meet the demands better at a lower cost and with less potential damage to valuable reels.

8. What more do we need to do about indexing newspapers and in what form?

9. How can we improve our public services? Rather little attention was given to this. In the broad sense, we talked about access but we did not really talk about, for instance, training our staff in guiding users in the use of newspapers. It is not the same sort of thing as working in other parts of our libraries. And how can we improve the mutual understanding of users and librarians?

10. How fast can we make progress on the compilation of bibliographical and location tools, which can help librarians and users identify what they need and where they can find this more rapidly? Do we have to rely totally in future on bibliographical data-bases which may be expensive, or impossible for some countries to gain access to? Or is there still a place for printed guides? This has been further developed by Hana Komorous in her paper.

11. How can we meet the need to improve our knowledge of the location of microfilm masters and their availability for purchase to aid our preservation decisions and avoid wasteful duplication of work?

12. How can the industrialized world best help the developing countries? Money is clearly one need but this is not usually the responsibility of the librarians, of governments, who provide money for libraries and who provide money for overseas aid. But technical assistance, written if not personal as Mr Biswas suggested, can obviously be helpful, and we should follow up the points he made.

13. Are there solutions in other countries which have similar problems to yours, and what patterns of international co-ordination would most help? Again this would help to avoid wasteful duplication of effort and repetition of mistakes, or even what we call in English, re-inventing the wheel.

14. How can we improve co-ordination within each of our own countries?

I hope that many of these points will be the topic of future discussion in IFLA, though some may be primarily for national discussion.

In the last 10 years the IFLA Working Group, which started off by consisting of just three members trying as best we could to find out what was happening about newspapers in the rest of the world, has increased in numbers, but it is still a small group. I hope that it will be possible somehow to widen the forum for discussion in future still further. I think that the numbers attending this Symposium, over 100, and the enthusiasm of you all should not have to wait for another Symposium at some perhaps distant date, for following up the discussion of these questions.

Finally, how has the Symposium helped generally? It is a cliche to say that the value of conferences lies not so much in the papers as in the opportunities for meeting people and discussing common problems. I know that discussion has continued, very enthusiastically, outside our formal sessions and I am sure that you have found benefit in both formal and informal discussions. I hope you will be able to use what you have learned here to help with the problems in your own countries and that you will feel now that you know how common these problems very often are, and that you know some more people who can help you with them. There is nothing quite like meeting people and talking at length to them at a gathering like this and then when you go home, you know who to write to, you know their faces and they know you, and it is much easier to correspond with them in future. So I am sure that whatever else we have not benefited from here, we have benefited from that. It has been a successful conference, I think everyone has looked very happy and very enthusiastic, you all worked very hard and thank you all very much.

APPENDICES

APPENDIX 1

THE RETENTION OR DISPOSAL OF NEWSPAPERS AFTER MICROFILMING: DRAFT POLICY STATEMENT

IFLA Working Group on Newspapers

This draft was prepared by the Working Group on Newspapers following its discussions at the meeting in Vienna on 11 and 12 April 1986. It has been circulated for further comment to members of the IFLA Section on Serial Publications with the intention that it should be put forward to IFLA as the basis for a statement of official IFLA policy.

Draft statement of policy

A. Within the country of publication:

Each country should be responsible for preserving the original of newspapers produced within that country.

(i) This responsibility will be met so long as the originals are maintained in viable form, good enough to permit re-microfilming and are used only in exceptional cases.

(ii) It may be divided by agreement between the library or libraries of legal deposit and other special or local libraries as appropriate, but final responsibility rests with the national library.

(iii) Discarding of titles from a library's own country should not be undertaken without consultation with other research libraries and libraries of legal deposit in the country to ensure the survival of one copy of the original.

(iv) National libraries or libraries of legal deposit, in consultation with other libraries in the country, should take responsibility for promoting:

    (a) the observation of the highest technical standards in the microfilming of their country's newspapers

    (b) the preservation of master negatives and duplicate negatives, so that further positive copies can be made to replace film in use

    (c) the conservation of microfilm stocks in satisfactory conditions. This should be interpreted to include filming done by commercial micro publishers and microfilming bureaux as well as by libraries themselves

(v) Libraries, possibly in co-operation, may give priority in the allocation of limited resources to the preservation of their own country's production.

B. Titles published in other countries.

(i) The survival of the originals and ease of access to them in the country of origin should always be taken into account, particularly in cases where originals may have been lost through political events (e.g. war-time clandestine newspapers) or where a reliable base of library service with the necessary preservation resources is lacking. If a title is considered for discarding, efforts should be made to ensure acceptance of the originals in the country of origin. Originals which are the unique surviving copies should not be discarded if acceptance in the country of origin cannot be secured.

(ii) Where titles have been acquired from a former colony under deposit arrangements, a library should consider itself responsible for the survival of the item as if it were a legal deposit item.

(iii) The resources of other libraries in the country should be taken into account and unique titles disposed of only after consultation.

C. General.

(i) Disposal should form one part of a co-ordinated approach to newspaper preservation, as an element in the most effective use of resources. Decisions should be based on sound costings. Policy on disposals should be seen as part of forward planning and should not be made in an _ad hoc_ solution to space problems.

(ii) Disposals should be selective and should not be undertaken without expert examination of individual titles.

(iii) The establishment of policy in individual libraries should take into account:

- legal deposit and other deposit obligations

- accurate information on the costs of retention, including storage, conservation treatment, and making available the originals

- the alternative of cheaper storage

- the adequacy of microfilm surrogates, including the standard of purchased microfilm, the security and preservation of the first master or duplicate negative, and the adequacy of the library's own storage of microfilm positive for users and its facilities for users

- the consequent costs of disposing of originals

- level of use of the originals

- other holdings of the title in the country or in the country of origin

- the complementarity of overseas or home newspaper holdings with other collections of library materials (e.g. books, pamphlets from another country)

- the desirability of disposing of originals to other libraries, particularly in the country of origin of overseas titles

- the possibility of future technical developments (e.g. optical disc) which might permit better reproduction of material in which graphic illustration, photographs or the use of colour are important.

APPENDIX 2

SURVEY ON NATIONAL NEWSPAPER COLLECTIONS OF THE WORLD: Answers to a
IFLA Working Group on Newspapers Questionnaire 1981-83

Johan MANNERHEIM
with the assistance of
Willi HÖFIG

1. INTRODUCTION

One of the first tasks the newly formed IFLA Newspaper Group undertook was the investigation of the world wide situation of the materia the Group was formed around. Therefore a "first" questionnaire was written. The questions needed to be fairly basic and simple to provide for a high percentage of answers. You will find the questionnaire in Annex 1.

2. THE EXTENT OF ANSWERS

We approached 348 institutions in 149 countries with the questionnaire. Answers came eventually from 99 institutions in 61 countries. That means that the survey covers 41% of the countries in the world. This is a much better result than a previous attempt made by a former IFLA Newspaper Group in 1970-72 with two questionnaires, which got answers from 33 and 41 libraries.

	Questioned institutions	countries	Answering institutions	countries	countries %
Africa	84	47	23	15	32
N & C America	64	19	21	7	37
South America	23	12	3	3	25
Asia	62	36	14	13	36
Australasia	9	5	3	3	60
Europe	106	30	35	20	67
Total	348	149	99	61	41

TABLE 1
Responses to the questionnaire

A reasonable hypothesis is that the answering countries in general are those doing more to preserve newspapers and give scholars access to them, and that those countries, which have not answered, in general are doing less and are less aware of the historical value of newspapers.

If that is true, the answers to the following questions do not give a typical picture of the state of newspaper collections in the world, but a rosy one.

There are comparatively more answering countries in Europe and Australasia

than in other parts of the world. Unfortunately there are no answers from
large and important countries like India and Brazil. But in my judgement,
with the exception of South and Central America, there are enough answers to
get a fairly good picture of the overall situation.

Annex 2 contains a complete list of answering countries and institutions.

Looking at the answering institutions I think that in almost all cases we have
reached a body which has both the knowledge and will to give accurate answers.
The amibiguities which do exist in the material are rather due to unclear
questions and undeveloped statistics.

Most of the institutions are national libraries of some kind, as you can see
in the following table:

Countries	NL	NL-R	NL-N	NUL	NA	UL	PL	L	O	Total
Africa (15)	7	1	-	-	6	3	1	4	1	23
N & C America (7)	3	8	-	-	-	3	2	5	-	21
South America (3)	3	-	-	-	-	-	-	-	-	3
Asia (13)	10	-	-	1	1	2	-	-	-	14
Australasia (3)	2	-	-	-	-	1	-	-	-	3
Europe (20)	13	13	2	1	-	2	2	1	1	35
Total (61)	38	22	2	2	7	11	5	10	2	99

NL	National Library		UL	University Library
NL-R	National Library for a region		PL	Public Library
NL-N	National Library for newspapers		L	Library (unspecified)
NUL	National and University Library		O	Other
NA	National Archives			

(As others are listed Office Rwandais d'Information and a special compilation
about Italian libraries made by Angela Vinay).

TABLE 2
Answering institutions according to category

3. COUNTRY (AND REGION) COVERED

Almost all libraries answering are mainly covering their own country or a
region thereof. (Compare the answers to question 4).

There are some exceptions. The National Diet Library of Japan collects newspapers from 'almost all over the world' and the National Library of China is
acquiring newspapers from 110 foreign countries.

More well known are the worldwide, but selective, collections of the British
Library Newspaper Library.

The America Antiquarian Society of Worcester, Massachussetts, covers Canada,
English West Indies and Mexico besides the United States. Unfortunately we
did not get any answer from the Library of Congress with its broad collections.

The South African libraries collect English and Dutch newspapers. They are also covering as completely as possible 'Southern Africa', that is as far up as Angola, Zambia and Malawi. Dar es Salaam University Library of Tanzania is trying to cover East Africa.

4. NUMBER OF CURRENT NEWSPAPERS IN THE COUNTRY

In the identification part of the questionnaire we asked for the approximate number of _current_ newspaper in the country/region.

The numbers given in the answers are not compatible, as (which will be seen in the next section) the definitions of newspapers vary a lot between countries. In some cases we have got completely different asnwers from two institutions in the same country. The answers reflect what is collected as newspapers more that the real number of newspaper titles. Also, some regional libraries have failed to make it clear if the figure concerns the region or the country.

Anyhow, with these limitations in mind, we present the answers given to us in Annex 3.

5. DISTINGUISHING NEWSPAPERS (Question 1)

Most varying principles are used to distinguish newspapers from other periodicals in practise. Dr Höfig has analysed answers given by 52 institutions and extracted 18 criteria used by them in different combinations.

The most common criterion is the frequency of publication. This is used in 36 cases. Six of the libraries regard only dailies as newspapers. Most libraries include periodicals printed as seldom as once a week, while two were so liberal that even monthly publications could be regarded as newspapers.

The size was used as a criterion by no less than 23 institutions. A combination of these two criteria would read something like 'a frequent periodical of large size'. Another criterion, the type of paper, was mentioned in 11 of the answers.

Many libraries looked into the contents of the publications to distinguish newspapers. 13 of them demanded of newspapers that they should contain general information (as opposed to special information) and 10 that they should deal with current events. Additionally six libraries used content as a criterion without specifying anything further. The readership (for instance that newspapers are intended for the general public) was a criterion for four libraries.

Among less frequently used criteria were masthead and columns, absence of cover and sewing, and registration as newspaper by the postal authorities.

It is of course impossible to reach an agreement on the best definition of newspapers by statistical means. The results of the survey might however be interesting as a basis for discussion on the subject.

6. SCOPE OF NATIONAL COLLECTIONS

Only 70% of the answering countries claim that they collect all their newspaper. Probably the percentage is much lower among countries outside the survey.

Q.2. Are the newspapers of your country/region completely collected?

Countries in:	Yes	No
Africa (15)	11	4
N & C America (7)	4	3
South America (3)	1	2
Asia (13)	8	5
Australasia (3)	2	1
Europe (20)	17	3
Total (61)	43	18
	70%	30%

TABLE 3
Libraries collecting all newspapers of the country

Q.2.1-2. Are there different editions of the same paper and are they collected?

Countries in:	Editions exist Yes	No	Editions are collected Yes	No	No answer
Africa (15)	4	11	3	1	-
N & C America (7)	3	4	3	-	-
South America (3)	2	1	2	-	-
Asia (13)	9	4	5	4	-
Australia (3)	1	2	-	1	-
Europe (20)	20	-	19	-	1
Total (61)	39	22	32	6	1
	64%	36%	82%	15%	3%

of countries claiming that editions exist

TABLE 4
Collection of various editions of newspapers

There might be two reasons why a country answers no to the first question. Either there are not any editions in that country, or the answering institution is unaware of their existence. There is a surprising discrepancy between the answers to question 3.3. where for instance nine African countries collect editions, and the answers above.

It is evident from the commentaries that countries, which collect editions, seldom collect all of them.

7. LAWS AND APPLICATION

Q.3. and Q.3.2. Are newspaper collected because of a deposit law or according to copyright regulations?

Countries in:	Law or regulation		If yes: prescribing criteria		
	Yes	No	geographical	language	other
Africa (15)	8	7	8	-	-
N & C America (7)	5	2	5	-	-
South America (3)	3	-	3	-	-
Asia (13)	11	2	11	-	-
Australasia (3)	3	-	3	-	-
Europe (20)	18	2	18	-	-
Total (61)	48	13	48	-	-

TABLE 5
Regulations governing collection of newspapers

This shows that newspapers are collected by deposit law or copyright regulations in 79% of the countries of the survey. In this case there are large differences. Only 53% of the African countries rely on law, while 87% of the other countries do it.

There are no criteria other than geographical in the prescriptions.

Q.3.3. What is demanded in practice and really collected?

	Editions					Supplements		Others e.g. newsbills	
	Both geogr & chron	Geogr only	Chron only	with own title	No	All	Some	Yes	No
Countries in:									
Africa (15)	5	3	1	3	6	7	2	3	6
N & C America (7)	4	1	-	3	2	4	2	1	2
South America (3)	-	-	2	-	1	2	-	1	1
Asia (13)	7	1	-	4	5	8	2	3	7
Australasia (3)	-	1	-	-	2	1	-	-	1
Europe (20)	14	5	-	15	-	15	3	9	7
Total (61)	30	11	3	25	16	37	9	17	24
	49%	18%	5%	41%	26%	61%	15%	28%	39%

TABLE 6
Actual editions collected

The answers show a certain confusion about the editions. Whereas only 32 countries answered that they collect editions to the direct question 2.2. here altogether 45 countries say that they collect editions of at least some sort. Perhaps it is reflecting the fact stated by some that they have chosen to collect just a few of the editions published. The same is mostly the case for newsbills, Sweden being an exception collecting all.

8. NEWSPAPERS FROM ABROAD

Q.4 Do you collect newspapers from abroad?

Countries in:	No	Yes	As national heritage	Other criteria	From 3rd world Yes	No
Africa (15)	2	10	6	8	7	7
N & C America (7)	2	5	3	3	3	4
South America (3)	1	2	2	–	1	1
Asia (13)	1	11	7	5	9	4
Australasia (3)	–	3	1	–	1	2
Europe (20)	–	19	13	12	9	9
Total (61)	6	50	32	28	30	27
	10%	82%	52%	46%	49%	44%

TABLE 7
Collection of newspapers from other countries

9. CATALOGUES

Q.5 Are there newspaper catalogues or lists in your country?

Countries in:	Yes	Union catalogues	Printed catalogues	No
Africa (15)	6	3	5	8
N & C America (7)	5	4	2	2
South America (3)	2	–	1	1
Asia (13)	10	4	8	2
Australasia (3)	2	2	1	1
Europe (20)	17	9	14	2
Total (61)	42	22	31	16
	69%	36%	51%	26%

TABLE 8
Existence of newspaper lists and catalogues

10. NEWSPAPER MICROFILMS

Q.6.1. Which share do microfilms have in your newspaper collections?

In the following table all those countries which have reported any share of microfilms at all are registered.

Countries in:	domestic	foreign	3rd world
Africa (15)	5	2	-
N & C America (7)	5	2	2
South America (3)	2	1	-
Asia (13)	11	6	1
Australasia (3)	2	2	-
Europe (20)	16	11	-
Total (61)	41	24	3
	67%	39%	5%

TABLE 9
Types of newspaper microfilms held

This question was dubious. Were we asking for volumes or titles? It was also misunderstood. Some institutions have apparently answered another question: Which share of your newspapers have been microfilmed? They tend to give high figures, like 90%, also when they keep the newspaper originals after microfilming. Other institutions have answered a third question: Which share of your microfilms are domestic, foreign and from the third world?

Anyhow, there are libraries with large shares of microfilms in their domestic newspaper collections. The Dar-es-Salaam University Library in Tanzania and the National Diet Library in Tokyo, Japan, have 30% in microfilm form. The national libraries of China and Canada have 20%. The Central National Library of Rome has 17%, The Royal Library in Stockholm, Sweden, 30% and The State Newspaper Collection in Aarhus, Denmark, has as much as 40%.

Other national libraries do have small domestic newspaper microfilm collections, like The Royal Library of Netherlands with 4%, the Austrian National Library with less than 5% and the National Library of Philippines with 385 rolls of microfilm.

The share is higher in some foreign collections. British Library Newspaper Library state that about 80% of their foreign newspapers are microfilms, the library of the Chinese University of Hong Kong 68% and the National Diet Library 50%. Many libraries buy more and more current foreign newspapers in microform. Helsinki University Library, Finland, say they receive 70% as microfilms.

Even so the older collections of originals are still usually dominant. In the National Library of Canada and the Royal Library of Sweden microfilms are 10% of the foreign newspaper collections and in the Bibliothèque Nationale in Paris they only reach 1%.

Q.6.2. In your country, are there any projects of current microfilming?

Countries in:	Domestic titles								Foreign titles	Third world titles
	Yes	Editions included		Supplements		Other material		No		
		all	some	all	some	all	some			
Africa (15)	3	1	-	1	-	-	-	10	1	1
N & C America (7)	3	1	2	1	2	-	2	4	-	-
South America (3)	1	-	1	-	1	-	-	2	1	-
Asia (13)	8	2	1	4	1	1	2	3	2	2
Australasia (3)	1	-	-	-	-	-	-	2	-	-
Europe (20)	17	2	9	4	5	2	-	2	3	-
Total (61)	33	6	13	10	9	3	4	23	7	3
	54%	10%	21%	16%	15%	5%	7%	38%	11%	5%

TABLE 10
Coverage of current microfilming projects

Only 54% of the answering countries are currently microfilming some of their own newspapers.

Full current microfilming programmes are reported from Singapore, Bermuda, Denmark and Sweden, while the British Library Newspaper Library says it will microfilm '100% eventually', something that has not become true yet, to my knowledge.

Israel and Norway are filming 90% of their current newspapers, Finland 60%, Peru and Australia 50%, Malaysia 40%, Canada 35%, Japan, Belgium and France 30%, Ireland 25%, Namibia 20%, South Africa and Netherlands 15% and Thailand 10%.

It is evident that many countries, which microfilm, concentrate on retrospective microfilming of older newspapers.

Q.6.3. Are there any projects of retrospective microfilming?

Countries in:	Domestic titles		Foreign titles	Third world titles
	Yes	No		
Africa (15)	6	7	1	1
N & C America (7)	5	2	1	1
South America (3)	2	1	-	-
Asia (13)	11	-	1	1
Australasia (3)	1	2	-	-
Europe (20)	18	1	2	1
Total (61)	43	13	5	4
	70%	21%	8%	7%

TABLE 11
Retrospective microfilming projects

Q.6.4. Are there any gap filling projects?

This question was unfortunately ambiguous. It was interpreted as using originals from several collections to make the newspaper film as complete as possible (State Library, Pretoria), as complementing incomplete runs of originals by microfilm copies (British Library Newspaper Library) and as filming gaps in older newspaper microfilms. Gap filling projects of domestic titles were reported in 36 countries, of foreign titles in 12 countries and of third world countries in 4 countries.

Q.6.5. Are there lists and catalogues of newspaper microfilms in your country?

Countries in:	Yes	Union catalogues	Printed catalogues	No
Africa (15)	4	1	2	10
N & C America (7)	5	3	2	2
South America (3)	2	–	1	1
Asia (13)	9	4	5	4
Australasia (3)	2	–	2	1
Europe (20)	13	4	10	7
Total (61)	35	12	22	25
	57%	20%	36%	41%

TABLE 12
Existence of newspaper microfilm lists and catalogues

The lack of union catalogues is noteworthy as it hampers interlibrary landing, something microfilm copies are most suitable for.

Q.6.6. Are there any copyright restrictions?

Countries in:	Filming		Sale of copies to libraries at home and abroad	
	Yes	No	Yes	No
Africa (15)	6	9	6	7
N & C America (7)	3	4	3	3
South America (3)	1	2	1	2
Asia (13)	4	6	6	4
Australasia (3)	2	1	2	1
Europe (20)	7	11	14	5
Total (61)	23	33	32	22
	38%	54%	52%	36%

TABLE 13
Types of copyright restrictions

Q.6.7. In which form do you film newspapers?

Countries in:	No answer	35 mm unperf. negative film	Other	whereof 16 mm	microfiche	micro-opaque
Africa (15)	10	5	-	-	-	-
N & C America (7)	2	5	1	-	-	1
South America (3)	2	1	-	-	-	-
Asia (13)	5	8	1	1	-	-
Australasia (3)	1	2	-	-	-	-
Europe (20)	2	18	4	1	3	-
Total (61)	22	39	6	2	3	1

TABLE 14
Format of newspaper microfilms

Three countries (Japan, Malaysia, Ireland) have written 'positive 35mm' but that must be a misunderstanding not distinguishing between camera film and user copies.

The six institutions, which use other microforms, use 35mm unperforated roll-film as well.

Q.6.8. Do you send microfilms of newspapers on inter-library lending?

Countries in:	Yes	Only within the country	Both domestic and abroad	No
Africa (15)	4	1	3	9
N & C America (7)	4	1	2	3
South America (3)	-	-	-	3
Asia (13)	5	2	3	8
Australasia (3)	2	1	1	1
Europe (20)	16	1	14	3
Total (61)	31 / 51%	6 / 10%	23 / 38%	27 / 44%

TABLE 15
Inter library lending

Sometimes institutions in the same country give different answers. United Kingdom, for instance, has been included because the National Library of Scotland lends microfilms abroad. But the British Library Newspaper Library does not lend microfilms to other libraries at all.

11. FINALLY

The IFLA Newspaper Group hopes that the presentation of the survey can be useful for reference. If you refer to it you should be aware that it is based on answers from 61 out of 149 countries. It is my judgement that the picture it gives therefore is a bit better than reality.

Summing up the results of the survey I think it is fair to say that newspaper collection and newspaper microfilming is most unevenly developed over the world. There seems not yet to be a consensus about the importance of newspapers as part of the national heritage and source for historical research strong enough to give national and other libraries the resources needed to preserve all newspapers and give proper access to them.

It would be interesting to make a new survey in 1991 to get a picture not only of the state then but also of the development of newspaper collecting in the libraries of the world.

REFERENCE

Höfig, Willi, 'Zeitungssammlungen weltweit. Erste Ergebnisse einer Umfrage 1982/83', in: <u>Publizistik</u>, Vol.29, 1984, pp.3-4.

ANNEX 1

The original questionnaire is reproduced on the following pages.

International Federation
of Library Associations and Institutions
Fédération Internationale des
Associations de Bibliothécaires et des Bibliothèques
Internationaler Verband
der bibliothekarischen Vereine und Institutionen
Международная Федерация
Библиотечных Ассоциаций и Учреждений

Section on Serial Publications
Newspaper Working Group
c/o Kungliga biblioteket
att. Johan Mannerheim
Box 5039
S-102 41 Stockholm
Sweden

IFLA Newspaper Group Questionnaire 1981:
SURVEY ON NATIONAL NEWSPAPER COLLECTIONS
==

Name of your library/institution: _____

Address: _____

Your name and position: _____

Country (and region) you are covering: _____

Approximate number of current newspapers in your country/region: _____

−=o=−

1. DISTINGUISHING NEWSPAPERS
   Please specify how you would distinguish newspapers from other periodicals in practice: _____

2. SCOPE OF NATIONAL COLLECTIONS
   Are the newspapers of your country/region completely collected? Yes __ No __
   Commentaries: _____

   (For the next two questions, see explanations in Annex)
   2.1. Are there different editions of the same paper?   Yes __ No __
   2.2. Are they collected?   Yes __ No __
   Commentaries: _____

3. LAWS AND APPLICATION
   Are newspapers collected because of a deposit law or according to copyright regulations?   Yes __ No __
   (If the answer is no, go to question 3.3.)
   3.1. If yes, which are these? _____

3.2. Which extent of collections does the law/regulations prescribe?
- geographic scope: _____
- by language: _____
- other criteria: _____

3.3. What is demanded in practice and really collected?
1. - editions: Yes __ geographical __ chronological __
   with title of its own __ with subtitle of its own __ No
   (For explanations, see Annex)
   Commentaries: _____

2. - supplements: Yes, all __ Yes, to some extent __ No
   Commentaries: _____

3. - other material, e.g. newsbills (placards): Yes __ No
   Commentaries: _____

4. NEWSPAPERS FROM ABROAD
   Do you collect newspapers from abroad? Yes __ No
4.1. - as a part of the national heritage: Yes __ No
   Commentaries: _____

4.2. - according to other criteria: Yes __ No
   Commentaries: _____

4.3. - newspapers from the Third World: Yes __ No
   Commentaries: _____

5. CATALOGUES
   Are there newspaper catalogues or lists, including union catalogues of newspapers, in your country? Yes __ Union __ No
5.1. Are these catalogues printed? Yes __ No
   Titles/commentaries: _____

6. NEWSPAPER MICROFILMS
6.1 Which share do microfilms have in your newspaper collections?
   1. - among domestic papers: around ____ %
   2. - among foreign papers: around ____ %
   3. - among papers of the Third World: around ____ %
   Commentaries: _____

6.2. In your country/region, are there any projects of current microfilming?
    1. - domestic titles: Yes __ , covering ____ %   No __
    1.1. Are editions filmed?   All __   Some __   No __
    1.2. Supplements   All __   Some __   No __
    1.3. Other material, e.g. newsbills   All __   Some __   No __
    Commentaries: _____

    2. - foreign titles: Yes __   No __
    3. - titles of the Third World: Yes __   No __
    Commentaries: _____

6.3. Are there any projects of retrospective microfilming?
    1. - domestic titles: Yes __   No __
    2. - foreign titles: Yes __   No __
    3. - titles of the Third World: Yes __   No __
    Commentaries: _____

6.4. Are there any gap filling projects?
    1. - domestic titles: Yes __   No __
    2. - foreign titles: Yes __   No __
    3. - titles of the Third World: Yes __   No __
    Commentaries: _____

6.5. Are there lists and catalogues of newspaper microfilms, including union catalogues, in your country?   Yes __   Union __   No __
    1. Are these catalogues printed?   Yes __   No __
    Titles/commentaries: _____

6.6. Are there any copyright restrictions?
    1. - concerning the filming itself: Yes __   No __
    2. - concerning sale of copies to libraries at home and abroad: Yes __   No __
    Commentaries: _____

6.7. In which form do you film newspapers?

        35 mm unperforated negative film ___

        other: _____

6.8. Do you send microfilms of newspapers on inter library lending?

        Yes __ within your country ___ abroad ___   No

-=o=-

THANK YOU FOR YOUR COOPERATION!

Please, return the completed questionnaire to:

KUNGLIGA BIBLIOTEKET (Royal Library)
att. Johan Mannerheim
Box 5039
S-102 41 STOCKHOLM
Sweden

ANNEX 2

ANSWERING INSTITUTIONS

Country	Place	Name
Africa		
Algeria	Alger	Bibliothèque Nationale d'Algerie
Botswana	Gaborone	Botswana National Library
	Gaborone	Botswana National Archives
Lesotho	Lesotho	National University of Lesotho Library
	Lesotho	Lesotho National Library Services
Libya	Benghazi	National Library of Lybia
Malawi	Lilongwe	National Library Service
Mali	Bamako	Bibliothèque Nationale du Mali
Mauritius	Coromandel	Mauritius Archives Department
Namibia	Windhoek	Government Archives
(=SW Africa)	Windhoek	Cultural Promotion, Administration Library
Nigeria	Ibadan	National Archives Departmental Library
	Owerri	State Central Library, Imo State
Rwanda	Butare	Bibliothèque, Université Nationale du Rwanda
	Kigali	Office Rwandais d'Information
Seychelles	Maho	Archives & Museum Research Library
Sierra Leone	Freetown	Fourah Bay College Library
South Africa	Pretoria	The State Library
	Cape Town	South African Library
	Pietermaritzburg	Natal Society Library
Tanzania	Dar-es-Salaam	National Archives
	Dar-es-Salaam	Dar-es-Salaam University Library
Zimbabwe	Causeway	National Archives
North and Central America		
Barbados	Bridgetown	Library, University of the West Indies
	Bridgetown	Public Library
Belize	Belize City	National Library Service
Bermuda	Hamilton	The Bermuda Library
Canada	Ottawa	National Library of Canada
	Montreal	Bibliothèque Nationale de Québec
Cuba	Habana	Biblioteca Nacional Joso Marti
Netherland Antilles	Willemstad	Library, University of the Netherlands Antilles
	Philipsburg	Philipsburg Jubilee Library
USA		
Hawaii	Honolulu	Hawaii State Library
	Honolulu	Library, University of Hawaii at Manoa
Massachusetss	Boston	Boston Public Library
	Worcester	American Antiquarian Society
New Hampshire	Concord	New Hampshire State Library
New Jersey	Trenton	New Jersey State Library
New York	Albany	New York State Library
Ohio	Columbus	Ohio Historical Society
Pennsylvania	Harrisburg	State Library of Pennsylvania
Virginia	Richmond	Virginia State Library
	Williamsburg	Earl Gregg Swem Library
Washington	Olympia	Washington State Library

South America
Chile	Santiago	Biblioteca Nacional de Chile
Guyana	Georgetown	National Library, Guyana
Peru	Lima	Biblioteca Nacional

Asia
Bangladesh	Dacca	National Library of Bangladesh
China, PR	Beijing	National Library of China
China, Hongkong	Hongkong	Library, The Chinese University of Hongkong
Indonesia	Jakarta	National Library of Indonesia
Iran	Teheran	Iran National Library
Israel	Jerusalem	Jewish National & University Library
Japan	Tokyo	National Diet Library
Malaysia	Kuala Lumpur	National Library of Malaysia
Philippines	Manila	The National Library
	Manila	Anteneo de Manila Libraries
Singapore	Singapore	National Library
Sri Lanka	Colombo	Department of National Archives
Thailand	Bangkok	National Library of Thailand
Vietnam	Hanoi	National Library of Vietnam

Australasia
Australia	Canberra	National Library of Australia
Fiji	Suva	Library, University of the South Pacific
Solomon Islands	Honiara	Solomon Islands National Library Service

Europe
Austria	Vienna	Oesterreichische Nationalbiblioteket
Belgium	Brussels	Bibliothèque Royale Albert ler
Czechoslovakia	Prague	State Library of the CSR
Denmark	Copenhagen	The Royal Library
	Aarhus	State Newspaper Collection
	Torshavn	National Library of Faroe Islands
Finland	Helsinki	Helsinki University Library
France	Paris	Bibliothèque Nationale
Germany, DR	Berlin	Deutsche Staatsbibliothek
	Leipzig	Deutsche Bücherei
Germany, FR	Frankfurt	Deutsche Bibliothek
Hungary	Budapest	National Szechenyi Library
Ireland	Dublin	National Library of Ireland
	Dublin	Trinity College Dublin
	Dublin	Dublin Public Libraries
Italy	Compilation by Angela Vinay, Rome	
	Rome	Central National Library of Rome
	Florence	Central National Library of Florence
	Turin	National Library of Turin
Netherlands	The Hague	The Royal Library
Norway	Oslo	University Library in Oslo
Poland	Warsaw	Biblioteka Narodowa
Portugal	Lisbon	Biblioteca Nacional
Soviet Union	Leningrad	Saltikov-Schedrin State Library
	Riga	Vilis Lacis State Library of the Latvian SSR
Sweden	Stockholm	The Royal Library
Switzerland	Bern	Schweizerische Landesbibliothek
United Kingdon	London	British Library Newspaper Library
	Belfast	Central Library
	Edinburgh	National Library of Scotland
	Aberystwyth	National Library of Wales

Yugoslavia	Belgrade	National Library of Serbia
	Ljubljana	National & University Library (Slovenia)
	Cetinje	Central National Library (Montenegro)
	Sarajevo	National & University Library of Bosnia and Hercegovina

ANNEX 3

APPROXIMATE NUMBER OF CURRENT NEWSPAPERS IN DIFFERENT COUNTRIES

(less probable answers in brackets)

Africa

Algeria	8	Mali	10	Sierra Leone	7
Botwana	1	Namibia	10	South Africa	246(190)
Lesotho	4	Nigeria	55(19)	Tanzania	20(2500?)
Libya	14	Rwandan	4(1)	Zimbabwe	30
Malawi	4	Seychelles	3		

North and Central America

Barbados	8(3)	Canada	760(750)	Netherlands	
Belize	6	Cuba	18	Antilles	5(4)
Bermuda	5			USA	843?

South America

Chile	104	Guayana	6	Peru	115

Asia

Bangladesh	148	Iran	100	Singapore	12
China, PR	2620	Israel	?	Sri Lanka	135
China, Hongkong	?	Japan	1566	Thailand	201
Indonesia	118	Malaysia	82	Vietnam	60
		Philippines	111		

Australasia

Australia	600	Fiji	13	Solomon Isl.	2

Europe

Austria	700	Germany, FR	950	Portugal	?
Belgium	26	Hungary	200	Soviet Union	8000
Czechoslovakia	?	Ireland, Republic of	80	Sweden	172
Denmark	53(398)	Italy	110(101)	Switzerland	395
Finland	292	Netherlands	1075	United Kingdom	2500
France	1000	Norway	212	Yugoslavia	1000(3000)
Germany, DR	?	Poland	64		

APPENDIX 3

FINAL LIST OF PARTICIPANTS

As one of the objectives of the Symposium was to provide for continuing contact between those concerned with newspaper collections, the lists of participants and exhibitors are printed to facilitate this. They will also allow those unable to be present at the Symposium to make appropriate contacts. The details below are given as they appeared on the Participant's Booking Form or on the Speakers list.

Name   Position, Institution, Country

1. Amos, Mrs Amelia   Agent, Instituto Autonoma Biblioteca Nacional
                              Caracas, Venezuela

2. Aspey, Miss Melanie   Deputy Archivist, News International PLC, UK

3. Baker, Mr John P   Associate Director, Preservation
                              New York Public Library, USA

4. Balague-Mola, Miss Nuria   Responsible Librarian, Hemerotecas
                              Universitat Autonoma de Barcelona, Spain

5. Banik, Dr Gerhard   Director, Institut für Restaurierung,
                              Österreichischer Nationalbibliothek

6. Belfrage, Dr Esbjorn   Librarian, Lund University Library, Sweden

7. Bergmann, Mr Helmuth   Periodicals Department, Universitätsbibliothek,
                              Wien

8. Bertoletti, Dr Esther   Coordenadora, Biblioteca Nacional, Rio de Janeiro

9. Biswas, Mr Subhas Chandra Director, Central Secretariat Library, India

10. Black, Dr Jeremy   Lecturer, Department of History,
                              University of Durham

11. Bohrmann, Dr H   Director, Institut für Zeitungsforschung,
                              Dortmund

12. Botha, Mrs M A   State Library, Pretoria, South Africa

13. Bourke, Mr Thomas A   Chief Microforms Division
                              New York Public Library, USA

14.	Boyde, Miss Susan J	Press Librarian Royal Institute of International Affairs, UK
15.	Button, Mr E P	Assistant Local Studies Librarian Suffolk Record Office, UK
16.	Cabral, Mrs Maria Luisa	Deputy Director Biblioteca Nacional, Lisbon, Portugal
17.	Carrion, Mr Manuel	Director, Hemeroteca Nacional, Madrid, Spain
18.	Carroll, Mr Frank J	Head, Newspaper Section, Serial Division Library of Congress, USA
19.	Casaca, Mrs Maria F	Head of Periodicals Dept., Biblioteca Nacional Lisbon, Portugal
20.	Christopoulos, Panayotis	Head of Microform Unit Library of Parliament, Athens, Greece
21.	Cranfield, Mr Graham	Head, Public Services British Library Newspaper Library, UK
22.	Das Gupta, Dr Ashin	Director, National Library of India
23.	Delaunay, Mme Else	Conservateur au Département des Périodiques, Chef de Service du Catalogue Générale des périodiques, Bibliothèque Nationale, Paris
24.	Dixon, Ms Diana	Lecturer, Department of Library & Information Studies Loughborough University of Technology, UK
25.	Downing, Miss Alice C	Assistant Librarian, James Hardiman Library, University College, Galway, Ireland
26.	Dunn, Mr Frank	Librarian, *Today*
27.	Dyas, Mr Eamon	Information Officer, British Library Newspaper Library, UK
28.	Elola-Olaso, Miss Maria	Documentalista, El Pais, Spain
29.	Englert, Mrs Marianne	Zentralarchiv, Frankfurter Allgemeine Zeitung Frankfurt am Main, West Germany
30.	Fathallah, Mrs Asma	Head of Cataloging American University of Beirut, Lebanon
31.	Field, Mr Jeffrey	Assistant Preservation Officer, Office of Preservation, National Endowment for the Humanities, USA
32.	Gao, Mr Guangang	Assistant Professor, Journalism Department, Fudan University, Shanghai, People's Republic of China
33.	Garcia Fernandez, Miss Aurora	Hemeroteca Nacional, Madrid, Spain

34. Garroni, Dr Maria Luisa — Ispettore, Ministero Beni Culturali Ambientali Italy

35. Gazvoda, Mrs Jelka — Head, Newspaper Department National and University Library, Yugoslavia

36. Gibb, Mr I P — Director for Public Services, British Library (Humanities and Social Sciences) (Retired)

37. Gibson, Mr K — Head of Public Services, British Library, UK

38. Giron, Mrs Alicia — Biblioteca Nacional, Madrid, Spain

39. Griffith, Ms Penny — Deputy Director, Alexander Turnbull Library, National Library of New Zealand

40. Griffiths, Mr Dennis — Former Director of Development, Express Newspapers, London

41. Hallerby, Mr Mats — Chief Archivist, Pressens Bild AB, Sweden

42. Hamilton, Sir Denis — Formerly Editor in Chief of The Times, London, Trustee of the British Museum and Member of the British Library Board

43. Harmer, Mrs Deborah A — Manager, Newspaper P R and Indexing University Microfilms International, USA

44. Harper, Miss Judith — Chief Librarian, Birmingham Post and Mail Ltd, UK

45. Harriman, Mr Robert B — Technical Co-ordinator, US National Newspaper Project, Library of Congress. Chairman, IFLA Working Group on Newspapers

46. Harris, Dr Michael — Lecturer, Department of Extra-Mural Studies, University of London

47. Hashim, Miss Elinor M — Program Director, OCLC Inc, USA

48. Höfig, Dr Willi — Newspaper Librarian, Staatsbibliothek Preussischer Kulturbesitz, Berlin(West)

49. Holm-Olsen, Miss Anne G — Head, Norwegian Dept, Royal University Library Oslo, Norway

50. Hutton, Mr B G — Secretary and Deputy Librarian National Library of Soctland, Edinburgh, UK

51. Ilbury, Mr T J — Reprographic Operations Manager British Library, UK

52. Ithell, Kelvin — Reprographics Manager, British Library, UK

53. Johansson, Miss Eve — Head, British Library Newspaper Library, Secretary IFLA Working Group on Newspapers

54.	Johnson, Mr George	Reference Library Manager Mail Newspapers PLC, UK
55.	Jones, Mrs Beti	Assistant Librarian National Library of Wales, UK
56.	Jorgensen, Claus Ingemann	Research Librarian Aalborg University Library, Denmark
57.	Kampmann, Mrs Dorrit	Librarian, Newspaper 'Information', Denmark
58.	Karim, Dr Khondkar M	Director Directorate of Archives and Libraries, Bangladesh
59.	Kastaly, Mrs Beatrice	Head of Newspaper Section National Széchényi Library, Budapest, Hungary
60.	Kefallineou, Mrs Eugenia	National Library of Greece, Athens, Greece
61.	Komorous, Mrs Hana	Senior Serials Librarian, University of Victoria, British Columbia, Canada
62.	Kranzler, Dr David	Director, US National Holocaust Microfilm Archives, New York, USA
63.	Larsen, Mr Svend,	Deputy Librarian, State and University Library (National Newspaper Collection) Denmark
64.	Levi, Mrs Silvia	Assessorato Cultura Regione Piemonte Torino, Italy
65.	Lim, Miss Kek-Hua	Librarian, National Library, Singapore
66.	McGreevy, Dr Jim	Archivist, DOE (NI), Northern Ireland
67.	McNaughton, Ms Susan	Senior Editor, Gower Publishing Company Aldershot, UK
68.	Malmquist, Mr Jan-Eric	Bibliotekstjanst AB, Sweden
69.	Mannerheim, Mr Johan	Head, Newspaper Section and National Microfilming Programme, Kungliga Biblioteket, Stockholm
70.	Marshall, Mr Alan	Head, Acquisitions British Library Newspaper Library, UK
71.	Martin, Miss Felicity A	Conservator, Australian Archives, Victorian Regional Office, Australia
72.	Matheson, Dr Ann	Keeper of Printed Books National Library of Scotland, UK
73.	Medina, Mrs Mirna	Biblioteca Nacional, Caracas, Venezuela
74.	Menassa, Mr Samuel	Manager, Lebanese Center for Documentation and Research, Beirut, Lebanon

75. Moon, Ms Myra Jo — Preservation Librarian, Colorado State University Libraries, CO, USA

76. Oakley, Miss Glenda — Librarian, Newspapers State Library Service of Western Australia

77. Olivier, Mrs Marie-Hélène — Conservateur, Bibliothèque Nationale, Annexe de Versailles, France

78. Olney, Ms Dawn — Cataloguer British Library Newspaper Library, UK

79. O'Luanaigh, Donal — Keeper, National Library of Ireland Dublin, Eire

80. Ortiz de Solorzano, Miss Isabela — Documentalista, El Pais, Spain

81. Perraud, Mlle Françoise — Conservateur au Département des Périodiques, Chef de Service des dons, acquisitions et microfilm des périodiques, Bibliothèque Nationale, Paris

82. Petitou, Mrs Françoise — Conservateur, Bibliothèque Nationale, France

83. Phillips, Mr A B — Director of Public Services British Library, UK

84. Picard, Dr Bertold — Bibliotheksdirektor, Deutsche Bibliothek German Federal Republic

85. Porter, Dr Roy — Fellow, Wellcome Institute for the History of Medicine, London

86. Prakoso, Miss Hardjo — Director, National Library of Indonesia Jakarta, Indonesia

87. Primmer, Mrs Madeleine — Librarian, Kungliga Biblioteket, Stockholm, Sweden

88. Prochazka, Dr Frantisek — Deputy Director, International Organisations of Journalists, Czechoslovakia

89. Regner, Mr Filip — Librarian, University Library, 1 DPT Copenhagen, Denmark

90. Russell, Mr Roy — Manager, British Library Binderies, UK

91. Scott, Ms Marianne — National Librarian, National Library of Canada

92. Sećić, Mrs D — Chief, Information Centre, National and University Library, Zagreb, Yugoslavia

93. Sirl, Mr Miroslav — Director, International Organization of Journalists, Czechoslovakia

94.	Smith, Merrily A	Director IFLA/PAC, Library of Congress, USA
95.	Starr, Ms Mary Jane	Office of the Associate National Librarian, National Library of Canada
96.	Swartzburg, Mrs Susan G	Preservation Specialist Rutgers University, New Jersey, USA
97.	Thulin, Mrs Irja	Librarian, Kungliga Biblioteket, Stockholm, Sweden
98.	Tillman, Mr Kenneth A	V P, Newspapers University Microfilms International, USA
99.	Tracey, Miss Joyce A	Curator of Newpapers and Serials American Antiquarian Society, USA
100.	Ubbens, Dr W	Official responsible for Communication, theatre literature, newspapers, Staats- und Universitatsbibliothek Bremen, Chairman, Zeitungskommission des Deutschen Bibliotheksinstituts
101.	Veuve, J P	Directeur, Association pour la Conservation et Reproduction Photographique de la Presse, France
102.	Watthews, Miss Elizabeth	Senior Local Studies Librarian Suffolk Record Office, UK
103.	Western, Mr M	Manager, Conservation and Binding British Library, UK
104.	Westra, Mr Pieter E	Director, South African Library
105.	Whiffin, Miss Jean I	Head, Serials Division University of Victoria Library, Canada
106.	Williams, Mr B J S	Director, Centre for Information Media and Technology (Cimtech), Hatfield Polytechnic, UK
107.	Wilmott, Miss Deirdre	Newspaper Librarian State Library of Victoria, Australia
108.	Yasue, Mr Akio	Librarian, National Diet Library, Japan

APPENDIX 4

LIST OF EXHIBITORS

ARCHIVAL AIDS LTD.   P.O. Box 5, Spondon, Derby, UK
                            Tel: 0332 666400
                            Telex 377769 PPCHEM

ATLANTIS PAPER COMPANY LTD. Gulliver's Wharf, 105 Wapping Lane,
                            London E1 9RW, UK
                            Tel: 01-481 3784
                            Telex: 916058 ATPAP G
                            Fax: 01-488 3570

                            ATLANTIS FRANCE
                            26 Rue des Petits Champs,
                            75002, Paris, France
                            Tel: (1) 4296 5385

BELL & HOWELL LTD.   Micromedia Division,
                            Telford Road, Bicester,
                            Oxon. OX6 OUP, UK
                            Tel: 0869 245711

BRITISH NEWSPAPER LIBRARY   Colindale Avenue, London NW9 5HE, UK
                            Tel: 01-200 5515

CHINA NATIONAL MICROFORMS IMPORT AND EXPORT CORPORATION
                            21 Chegongzhuang Xilu, Beijing, China.

                            Represented in the UK by:

                            Cypress Book Co. (UK) Ltd.,
                            10 Swinton Street, London WC1 9NX, UK
                            Tel: 01-833 0220

INTER DOCUMENTATION COMPANY B.V. Industriestrasse 7, 6300 ZUG, Switzerland
                            Tel: 42-214974

MICROFORMAT SYSTEMS B.V.   Heereweg 331a, Postbus 287,
                            2180 AG Lisse, Netherlands
                            Tel: 02521 17250
                            Telex: 41430

MICROPHAX LTD.   36 Nuffield Way, Abingdon,
                            Oxon OX14 1TF, UK
                            Tel: 0235 25695
                            Telex: 837991
                            Fax: 0235 24570

W & F PASCOE PTY LTD.	7 Hayes Street, Balgowlah, New South Wales, 2093, Australia Tel: (02) 949 1133
PROFILE MARKETING (Kent) LTD.	Image House, 344 High Street Rochester, Kent ME1 1JU, UK Tel: 0634 813751
RESEARCH PUBLICATIONS LTD.	77 Milford Road, Reading, Berks. RG1 8HF, UK Tel: 0734 583247 And in the USA: 12 Lunar Drive, Woodbridge, Conn. 06525, USA Tel: (203) 397 2600
SECOL LTD.	Kelvin Place, Thetford, Norfolk IP24 3RR, UK Tel: 0842 2341
UNIVERSITY MICROFILMS INTERNATIONAL	300 North Zeeb Road, Ann Arbor, Michigan 48106, USA Tel: (313) 7614700 And in the UK: White Swan House, 60 High Street, Godstone, Surrey RH9 8LW, UK Tel: 0883 844123

INTERNATIONAL FEDERATION
OF LIBRARY ASSOCIATIONS
AND INSTITUTIONS
Series IFLA Publications
Edited by Willem R.H. Koops

28 **Library Work for Children and Young Adults in the Developing Countries.**
Edited by Geneviève Patte and Sigrún Klara Hannesdóttir.
1984. 283 p. Bd. DM 68.00,
IFLA members DM 51.00
ISBN 3-598-20389-6

29 **Guide to the Availability of Theses.**
II Non University-Institutions.
Edited by G.G. Allen and K. Deubert. Compiled for the Section of University Libraries and other General Research Libraries.
1984. VI, 124 p. Bd. DM 42.00,
IFLA members DM 33.60
ISBN 3-598-20394-2

30 **A guide to Developing Braille and Talking Book Services.**
Edited by L. L. Clark.
1984. 108 p. Bd. DM 42.00,
IFLA members DM 33.60
ISBN 3-598-20395-0

31 **World Directory of Map Collections.**
Edited by J. A. Wolter, R. E. Grimm and D. Carrington.
2nd ed. 1985. 350 p. Bd. DM 88.00,
IFLA members DM 66.00
ISBN 3-598-20374-8

32 **International Guide to Library and Information Science Education.**
Edited by J. Riss Fang and P. Nauta.
1985. 537 p. Bd. DM 120.00,
IFLA members DM 90.00
ISBN 3-598-20396-9

33 **University Libraries in Developing Countries.**
Proceedings of the IFLA/Unesco pre-session Seminar, Munich, 1983. Edited by A. J. Loveday and G. Gattermann
1985. 183 p. Bd. DM 48.00,
IFLA members DM 36.00
ISBN 3-598-20397-7

K·G·Saur München·London·New York·Paris
K·G·Saur Verlag · Postfach 71 10 09 · 8000 München 71 · Tel. (0 89) 7 91 04-0

INTERNATIONAL FEDERATION
OF LIBRARY ASSOCIATIONS
AND INSTITUTIONS
Series IFLA Publications
Edited by Willem R.H. Koops

34 A Reader in Art Librarianship.
Edited by Philip Pacey.
1985. 190 p. Bd. DM 48.00
IFLA members DM 36.00
ISBN 3-598-20398-5

35 Inventaire général des bibliographies nationales rétrospectives/Retrospective National Bibliographies: an International Survey.
Edited by Marcelle Beaudiquez.
1986. 189 p. Bd. DM 64.00,
IFLA members DM 48.00
ISBN 3-598-20399-3

36 Guidelines for Public Libraries.
Prepared for the IFLA Section of Public Libraries.
3rd enlarged and revised edition.
1986. 90 p. Bd. DM 28.00,
IFLA members DM 21.00
ISBN 3-598-21766-8

37 Paula A. Baxter: International Bibliography of Art Librarianship. An annotated compilation.
1987. V, 94 p. Bd. DM 40.00,
IFLA members DM 32.00.
ISBN 3-598-21767-6

38 Automated Systems for Access to Multilingual and Multiscript Library Materials. Problems and Solutions. Papers from the Pre-Conference Seminar, Tokyo, 1986
Edited by C. Bossmeyer and S. W. Massil
1987. 225 p. Bd. DM 68.00,
IFLA members DM 51.00
ISBN 3-598-21768-4

39 Adaptation of Buildings to Library Use. Proceedings of the Seminar held in Budapest, 1984
Edited by Michael Dewe.
1987. 254 p. Bd. DM 58.00,
IFLA members DM 43.50
ISBN 3-598-21769-2

K·G·Saur München·London·New York·Paris
K·G·Saur Verlag · Postfach 71 10 09 · 8000 München 71 · Tel. (0 89) 7 91 04-0

INTERNATIONAL FEDERATION
OF LIBRARY ASSOCIATIONS
AND INSTITUTIONS
Series IFLA Publications
Edited by Willem R.H. Koops

40/41 **Preservation of Library Materials.** Proceedings of the CDNL/IFLA/Unesco Conference, Vienna, 1986. Edited by Merrily A. Smith. 2 volumes. 1987. IX, 159 p. and VI, 155 p. Bd. Per volume DM 68.00, ISBN 3-598-21770-0 (Vol.1) ISBN 3-598-21771-4 (Vol.2)

42 **World Directory of Biological and Medical Sciences Libraries.** Edited by Ursula H. Poland. 1988. XII, 203 p. Bd. DM 48.00, IFLA members DM 36.00 ISBN 3-598-21772-2

43 **Education and Research in Library and Information Science in the Information Age: Means of Modern Technology and Management.** Proceedings of the IFLA/China Society of Library Science Seminar, Beijing, 1986. Edited by Miriam H. Tees. 1988. 202 p. Bd. DM 68.00, IFLA members DM 51.00 ISBN 3-598-21773-0

44 **Open Systems Interconnection: The Communications Technology of the 1990's.** Papers from the Pre-Conference Seminar held in London, 1987. Edited by Christine H. Smith. 1988. 254 p. Bd. DM 68.00, IFLA members DM 51.00 ISBN 3-598-21774-9

45/46 **Newspaper Preservation and Access.** Proceedings of the Symposium held in London, 1987. Edited by Ian P. Gibb. 2 volumes. 1988. Together, 449 p. Bd. Per volume DM 68.00, IFLA members DM 51.00 ISBN 3-598-21775-7 (Vol.1); ISBN 3-598-21776-5 (Vol.2)

In preparation

47 **A l'écoute de l'oeil.** Les collections iconographiques et les bibliothèques. Edités par Huguette Rouit et Jean-Pierre Dubouloz.

K·G·Saur München·London·New York·Paris
K·G·Saur Verlag · Postfach 71 10 09 · 8000 München 71 · Tel. (0 89) 7 91 04-0

Z 692 .N4 .N39 1988 v.2

	DATE DUE		